CUDA Application Design
and Development

CUDA Application Design and Development

Rob Farber

AMSTERDAM • BOSTON • HEIDELBERG • LONDON
NEW YORK • OXFORD • PARIS • SAN DIEGO
SAN FRANCISCO • SINGAPORE • SYDNEY • TOKYO

Morgan Kaufmann is an imprint of Elsevier

Acquiring Editor: Todd Green
Development Editor: Robyn Day
Project Manager: Danielle S. Miller
Designer: Dennis Schaeffer

Morgan Kaufmann is an imprint of Elsevier
225 Wyman Street, Waltham, MA 02451, USA

Notices
Knowledge and best practice in this field are constantly changing. As new research and experience broaden our understanding, changes in research methods or professional practices, may become necessary. Practitioners and researchers must always rely on their own experience and knowledge in evaluating and using any information or methods described herein. In using such information or methods they should be mindful of their own safety and the safety of others, including parties for whom they have a professional responsibility.

To the fullest extent of the law, neither the Publisher nor the authors, contributors, or editors, assume any liability for any injury and/or damage to persons or property as a matter of products liability, negligence or otherwise, or from any use or operation of any methods, products, instructions, or ideas contained in the material herein.

Library of Congress Cataloging-in-Publication Data
Application submitted.

British Library Cataloguing-in-Publication Data
A catalogue record for this book is available from the British Library.

ISBN: 978-0-12-388426-8

For information on all MK publications visit our
website at *www.mkp.com*

Typeset by: diacriTech, Chennai, India

Printed in the United States of America
12 13 14 15   10 9 8 7 6 5 4 3 2

Dedication

This book is dedicated to my wife Margy and son Ryan, who could not help but be deeply involved as I wrote it. In particular to my son Ryan, who is proof that I am the older model – thank you for the time I had to spend away from your childhood.

To my many friends who reviewed this book and especially those who caught errors, I cannot thank you enough for your time and help. In particular, I'd like to thank everyone at ICHEC (the Irish Center for High-End Computing) who adopted me as I finished the book's birthing process and completed this manuscript. Finally, thank you to my colleagues and friends at NIVDIA, who made the whole CUDA revolution possible.

Contents

Foreword

GPUs have recently burst onto the scientific computing scene as an innovative technology that has demonstrated substantial performance and energy efficiency improvements for the numerous scientific applications. These initial applications were often pioneered by early adopters, who went to great effort to make use of GPUs. More recently, the critical question facing this technology is whether it can become pervasive across the multiple, diverse algorithms in scientific computing, and useful to a broad range of users, not only the early adopters. A key barrier to this wider adoption is software development: writing and optimizing massively parallel CUDA code, using new performance and correctness tools, leveraging libraries, and understanding the GPU architecture.

Part of this challenge will be solved by experts sharing their knowledge and methodology with other users through books, tutorials, and collaboration. *CUDA Application Design and Development* is one such book. In this book, the author provides clear, detailed explanations of implementing important algorithms, such as algorithms in quantum chemistry, machine learning, and computer vision methods, on GPUs. Not only does the book describe the methodologies that underpin GPU programming, but it describes how to recast algorithms to maximize the benefit of GPU architectures. In addition, the book provides many case studies, which are used to explain and reinforce important GPU concepts like CUDA threads, the GPU memory hierarchy, and scalability across multiple GPUs including an MPI example demonstrated near-linear scaling to 500 GPUs.

Lastly, no programming language stands alone. Arguably, for any language to be successful, it must be surrounded by an ecosystem of powerful compilers, performance and correctness tools, and optimized libraries. These pragmatic aspects of software development are often the most important factor to developing applications quickly. *CUDA Application Design and Development* does not disappoint in this area, as it devotes multiple chapters to describing how to use CUDA compilers, debuggers, performance profilers, libraries, and interoperability with other languages.

I have enjoyed learning from this book, and I am certain you will also.

Jeffrey S. Vetter
20 September 2011
Distinguished Research Staff Member,
Oak Ridge National Laboratory;
Professor, Georgia Institute of Technology.

Preface

Timing is so very important in technology, as well as in our academic and professional careers. We are an extraordinarily lucky generation of programmers who have the initial opportunity to capitalize on inexpensive, generally available, massively parallel computing hardware. The impact of GPGPU (General-Purpose Graphics Processing Units) technology spans all aspects of computation, from the smallest cell phones to the largest supercomputers in the world. They are changing the commercial application landscape, scientific computing, cloud computing, computer visualization, games, and robotics and are even redefining how computer programming is taught. Teraflop (trillion floating-point operations per second) computing is now within the economic reach of most people around the world. Teenagers, students, parents, teachers, professionals, small research organizations, and large corporations can easily afford GPGPU hardware and the software development kits (SDKs) are free. NVIDIA estimates that more than 300 million of their programmable GPGPU devices have already been sold.

Programmed in CUDA (Compute Unified Device Architecture), those third of a billion NVIDIA GPUs present a tremendous market opportunity for commercial applications, and they provide a hardware base with which to redefine what is possible for scientific computing. Most importantly, CUDA and massively parallel GPGPU hardware is changing how we think about computation. No longer limited to performing one or a few operations at a time, CUDA programmers write programs that perform many tens of thousands of operations simultaneously!

This book will teach you how to think in CUDA and harness those tens of thousands of threads of execution to achieve orders-of-magnitude increased performance for your applications, be they commercial, academic, or scientific. Further, this book will explain how to utilize one or more GPGPUs within a single application, whether on a single machine or across a cluster of machines.

In addition, this book will show you how to use CUDA to develop applications that can run on multicore processors, making CUDA a viable choice for *all* application development. No GPU required!

Not concerned with just syntax and API calls, the material in this book covers the thought behind the design of CUDA, plus the architectural reasons why GPGPU hardware can perform so spectacularly. Various guidelines and caveats will be covered so that you can write concise, readable, and maintainable code. The focus is on the latest CUDA 4.x release.

Working code is provided that can be compiled and modified because playing with and adapting code is an essential part of the learning process. The examples demonstrate how to get high-performance from the Fermi architecture (NVIDIA 20-series) of GPGPUS because the intention is not just to get code working but also to show you how to write efficient code. Those with older GPGPUs will benefit from this book, as the examples will compile and run on all CUDA-enabled GPGPUs. Where appropriate, this book will reference text from my extensive *Doctor Dobb's Journal* series of CUDA tutorials to highlight improvements over previous versions of CUDA and to provide insight on how to achieve good performance across multiple generations of GPGPU architectures.

Teaching materials, additional examples, and reader comments are available on the http://gpucomputing.net wiki. Any of the following URLs will access the wiki:

- My name: http://gpucomputing.net/RobFarber.
- The title of this book as one word: http://gpucomputing.net/CUDAapplicationdesignanddevelopment.
- The name of my series: http://gpucomputing.net/supercomputingforthemasses.

Those who purchase the book can download the source code for the examples at http://booksite.mkp.com/9780123884268.

To accomplish these goals, the book is organized as follows:

Chapter 1. Introduces basic CUDA concepts and the tools needed to build and debug CUDA applications. Simple examples are provided that demonstrates both the thrust C++ and C runtime APIs. Three simple rules for high-performance GPU programming are introduced.
Chapter 2. Using only techniques introduced in Chapter 1, this chapter provides a complete, general-purpose machine-learning and optimization framework that can run 341 times faster than a single core of a conventional processor. Core concepts in machine learning

and numerical optimization are also covered, which will be of interest to those who desire the domain knowledge as well as the ability to program GPUs.

Chapter 3. Profiling is the focus of this chapter, as it is an essential skill in high-performance programming. The CUDA profiling tools are introduced and applied to the real-world example from Chapter 2. Some surprising bottlenecks in the Thrust API are uncovered. Introductory data-mining techniques are discussed and data-mining functors for both Principle Components Analysis and Nonlinear Principle Components Analysis are provided, so this chapter should be of interest to users as well as programmers.

Chapter 4. The CUDA execution model is the topic of this chapter. Anyone who wishes to get peak performance from a GPU must understand the concepts covered in this chapter. Examples and profiling output are provided to help understand both what the GPU is doing and how to use the existing tools to see what is happening.

Chapter 5. CUDA provides several types of memory on the GPU. Each type of memory is discussed, along with the advantages and disadvantages.

Chapter 6. With over three orders-of-magnitude in performance difference between the fastest and slowest GPU memory, efficiently using memory on the GPU is the *only* path to high performance. This chapter discusses techniques and provides profiler output to help you understand and monitor how efficiently your applications use memory. A general functor-based example is provided to teach how to write your own generic methods like the Thrust API.

Chapter 7. GPUs provide multiple forms of parallelism, including multiple GPUs, asynchronous kernel execution, and a Unified Virtual Address (UVA) space. This chapter provides examples and profiler output to understand and utilize all forms of GPU parallelism.

Chapter 8. CUDA has matured to become a viable platform for *all* application development for both GPU and multicore processors. Pathways to multiple CUDA backends are discussed, and examples and profiler output to effectively run in heterogeneous multi-GPU environments are provided. CUDA libraries and how to interface CUDA and GPU computing with other high-level languages like Python, Java, R, and FORTRAN are covered.

Chapter 9. With the focus on the use of CUDA to accelerate computational tasks, it is easy to forget that GPU technology is also a splendid platform for visualization. This chapter discusses primitive restart and how it can dramatically accelerate visualization and gaming applications. A complete working example is provided that allows the reader to create and fly around in a 3D world. Profiler output is used to demonstrate why primitive restart is so fast. The teaching framework from this chapter is extended to work with live video streams in Chapter 12.

Chapter 10. To teach scalability, as well as performance, the example from Chapter 3 is extended to use MPI (Message Passing Interface). A variant of this example code has demonstrated near-linear scalability to 500 GPGPUs (with a peak of over 500,000 single-precision gigaflops) and delivered over one-third petaflop (10^{15} floating-point operations per second) using 60,000 x86 processing cores.

Chapter 11. No book can cover all aspects of the CUDA tidal wave. This is a survey chapter that points the way to other projects that provide free working source code for a variety of techniques, including Support Vector Machines (SVM), Multi-Dimensional Scaling (MDS), mutual information, force-directed graph layout, molecular modeling, and others. Knowledge of these projects—and how to interface with other high-level languages, as discussed in Chapter 8—will help you mature as a CUDA developer.

Chapter 12. A working real-time video streaming example for vision recognition based on the visualization framework in Chapter 9 is provided. All that is needed is an inexpensive webcam or a video file so that you too can work with real-time vision recognition. This example was designed for teaching, so it is easy to modify. Robotics, augmented reality games, and data fusion for heads-up displays are obvious extensions to the working example and technology discussion in this chapter.

Learning to think about and program in CUDA (and GPGPUs) is a wonderful way to have fun and open new opportunities. However, performance is the ultimate reason for using GPGPU technology, and as one of my university professors used to say, "The proof of the pudding is in the tasting." Figure 1 illustrates the performance of the top 100 applications as reported on the NVIDIA CUDA Showcase[1] as of July 12, 2011. They demonstrate the wide variety of applications that GPGPU technology can accelerate by two or more orders of magnitude (100-times) over multi-core processors, as reported in the peer-reviewed scientific literature and by commercial entities. It is worth taking time to look over these showcased applications, as many of them provide freely downloadable source code and libraries.

GPGPU technology is a disruptive technology that has redefined how computation occurs. As NVIDIA notes, "from super phones to supercomputers." This technology has arrived during a perfect storm of opportunities, as traditional multicore processors can no longer achieve significant speedups

---

[1] http://developer.nvidia.com/cuda-action-research-apps.

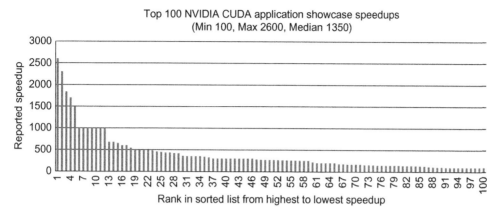

FIGURE 1

Top 100 NVIDIA application showcase speedups.

through increases in clock rate. The only way manufacturers of traditional processors can entice customers to upgrade to a new computer is to deliver speedups two to four times faster through the parallelism of dual- and quad-core processors. Multicore parallelism is disruptive, as it requires that existing software be rewritten to make use of these extra cores. Come join the cutting edge of software application development and research as the computer and research industries retool to exploit parallel hardware! Learn CUDA and join in this wonderful opportunity.

First Programs and How to Think in CUDA

The purpose of this chapter is to introduce the reader to CUDA (the parallel computing architecture developed by NVIDIA) and differentiate CUDA from programming conventional single and multicore processors. Example programs and instructions will show the reader how to compile and run programs as well as how to adapt them to their own purposes. The CUDA Thrust and runtime APIs (Application Programming Interface) will be used and discussed. Three rules of GPGPU programming will be introduced as well as Amdahl's law, Big-O notation, and the distinction between data-parallel and task-parallel programming. Some basic GPU debugging tools will be introduced, but for the most part NVIDIA has made debugging CUDA code identical to debugging any other C or C++ application. Where appropriate, references to introductory materials will be provided to help novice readers. At the end of this chapter, the reader will be able to write and debug massively parallel programs that concurrently utilize both a GPGPU and the host processor(s) within a single application that can handle a million threads of execution.

At the end of the chapter, the reader will have a basic understanding of:

- How to create, build, and run CUDA applications.
- Criteria to decide which CUDA API to use.
- Amdahl's law and how it relates to GPU computing.
- Three rules of high-performance GPU computing.
- Big-O notation and the impact of data transfers.
- The difference between task-parallel and data-parallel programming.
- Some GPU-specific capabilities of the Linux, Mac, and Windows CUDA debuggers.
- The CUDA memory checker and how it can find out-of-bounds and misaligned memory errors.

SOURCE CODE AND WIKI

Source code for all the examples in this book can be downloaded from http://booksite.mkp.com/9780123884268. A wiki (a website collaboratively developed by a community of users) is available to share information, make comments, and find teaching material; it can be reached at any of the following aliases on gpucomputing.net:

- My name: http://gpucomputing.net/RobFarber.
- The title of this book as one word: http://gpucomputing.net/ CUDAapplicationdesignanddevelopment.
- The name of my series: http://gpucomputing.net/ supercomputingforthemasses.

DISTINGUISHING CUDA FROM CONVENTIONAL PROGRAMMING WITH A SIMPLE EXAMPLE

Programming a sequential processor requires writing a program that specifies each of the tasks needed to compute some result. See Example 1.1, "seqSerial.cpp, a sequential C++ program":

Example 1.1

```
//seqSerial.cpp
#include <iostream>
#include <vector>
using namespace std;

int main()
{
  const int N=50000;

  // task 1: create the array
  vector<int> a(N);

  // task 2: fill the array
  for(int i=0; i < N; i++) a[i]=i;

  // task 3: calculate the sum of the array
  int sumA=0;
  for(int i=0; i < N; i++) sumA += a[i];

  // task 4: calculate the sum of 0 .. N-1
  int sumCheck=0;
  for(int i=0; i < N; i++) sumCheck += i;

  // task 5: check the results agree
  if(sumA == sumCheck) cout << "Test Succeeded!" << endl;
```

```
    else {cerr << "Test FAILED!" << endl; return(1);}

    return(0);
}
```

Example 1.1 performs five tasks:

1. It creates an integer array.
2. A **for** loop fills the array **a** with integers from 0 to N−1.
3. The sum of the integers in the array is computed.
4. A separate **for** loop computes the sum of the integers by an alternate method.
5. A comparison checks that the sequential and parallel results are the same and reports the success of the test.

Notice that the processor runs each task consecutively one after the other. Inside of tasks 2–4, the processor iterates through the loop starting with the first index. Once all the tasks have finished, the program exits. This is an example of a *single thread of execution*, which is illustrated in Figure 1.1 for task 2 as a single thread fills the first three elements of array *a*.

This program can be compiled and executed with the following commands:

- Linux and Cygwin users (Example 1.2, "Compiling with g++"):

Example 1.2
```
g++ seqSerial.cpp -o seqSerial
./seqSerial
```

- Utilizing the command-line interface for Microsoft Visual Studio users (Example 1.3, "Compiling with the Visual Studio Command-Line Interface"):

Example 1.3
```
cl.exe seqSerial.cpp -o seqSerial.exe
seqSerial.exe
```

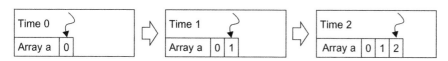

FIGURE 1.1
A single thread of execution.

- Of course, all CUDA users (Linux, Windows, MacOS, Cygwin) can utilize the NVIDIA **nvcc** compiler regardless of platform (Example 1.4, "Compiling with nvcc"):

Example 1.4

```
nvcc seqSerial.cpp -o seqSerial
./seqSerial
```

In all cases, the program will print "Test succeeded!"

For comparison, let's create and run our first CUDA program seqCuda.*cu*, in C++. (Note: CUDA supports both C and C++ programs. For simplicity, the following example was written in C++ using the Thrust data-parallel API as will be discussed in greater depth in this chapter.) CUDA programs utilize the *file extension* suffix ".*cu*" to indicate CUDA source code. See Example 1.5, "A Massively Parallel CUDA Code Using the Thrust API":

Example 1.5

```cpp
//seqCuda.cu
#include <iostream>
using namespace std;

#include <thrust/reduce.h>
#include <thrust/sequence.h>
#include <thrust/host_vector.h>
#include <thrust/device_vector.h>

int main()
{
  const int N=50000;

  // task 1: create the array
  thrust::device_vector<int> a(N);

  // task 2: fill the array
  thrust::sequence(a.begin(), a.end(), 0);

  // task 3: calculate the sum of the array
  int sumA= thrust::reduce(a.begin(),a.end(), 0);

  // task 4: calculate the sum of 0 .. N−1
  int sumCheck=0;
  for(int i=0; i < N; i++) sumCheck += i;

  // task 5: check the results agree
  if(sumA == sumCheck) cout << "Test Succeeded!" << endl;
  else { cerr << "Test FAILED!" << endl; return(1);}

  return(0);
}
```

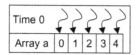

FIGURE 1.2
Parallel threads of execution.

Example 1.5 is compiled with the NVIDIA **nvcc** compiler under Windows, Linux, and MacOS. If **nvcc** is not available on your system, download and install the free CUDA tools, driver, and SDK (Software Development Kit) from the NVIDIA CUDA Zone (http://developer.nvidia.com). See Example 1.6, "Compiling and Running the Example":

Example 1.6

```
nvcc seqCuda.cu -o seqCuda
./seqCuda
```

Again, running the program will print "Test succeeded!"

Congratulations: you just created a CUDA application that uses 50,000 software threads of execution and ran it on a GPU! (The actual number of threads that run concurrently on the hardware depends on the capabilities of the GPGPU in your system.)

Aside from a few calls to the CUDA Thrust API (prefaced by **thrust::** in this example), the CUDA code looks almost identical to the sequential C++ code. The highlighted lines in the example perform parallel operations.

Unlike the single-threaded execution illustrated in Figure 1.1, the code in Example 1.5 utilizes many threads to perform a large number of concurrent operations as is illustrated in Figure 1.2 for task 2 when filling array **a**.

CHOOSING A CUDA API

CUDA offers several APIs to use when programming. They are from highest to lowest level:

1. The data-parallel C++ Thrust API
2. The runtime API, which can be used in either C or C++
3. The driver API, which can be used with either C or C++

Regardless of the API or mix of APIs used in an application, CUDA can be called from other high-level languages such as Python, Java, FORTRAN, and many others. The calling conventions and details necessary to correctly link vary with each language.

Which API to use depends on the amount of control the developer wishes to exert over the GPU. Higher-level APIs like the C++ Thrust API are convenient, as they do more for the programmer, but they also make some decisions on behalf of the programmer. In general, Thrust has been shown to deliver high computational performance, generality, and convenience. It also makes code development quicker and can produce easier to read source code that many will argue is more maintainable. Without modification, programs written in Thrust will most certainly maintain or show improved performance as Thrust matures in future releases. Many Thrust methods like reduction perform significant work, which gives the Thrust API developers much freedom to incorporate features in the latest hardware that can improve performance. Thrust is an example of a well-designed API that is simple yet general and that has the ability to be adapted to improve performance as the technology evolves.

A disadvantage of a high-level API like Thrust is that it can isolate the developer from the hardware and expose only a subset of the hardware capabilities. In some circumstances, the C++ interface can become too cumbersome or verbose. Scientific programmers in particular may feel that the clarity of simple loop structures can get lost in the C++ syntax.

Use a high-level interface first and choose to drop down to a lower-level API when you think the additional programming effort will deliver greater performance or to make use of some lower-level capability needed to better support your application. The CUDA runtime in particular was designed to give the developer access to all the programmable features of the GPGPU with a few simple yet elegant and powerful syntactic additions to the C-language. As a result, CUDA runtime code can sometimes be the cleanest and easiest API to read; plus, it can be extremely efficient. An important aspect of the lowest-level driver interface is that it can provide very precise control over both queuing and data transfers.

Expect code size to increase when using the lower-level interfaces, as the developer must make more API calls and/or specify more parameters for each call. In addition, the developer needs to check for runtime errors and version incompatibilities. In many cases when using low-level APIs, it is not unusual for more lines of the application code to be focused on the details of the API interface than on the actual work of the task.

Happily, modern CUDA developers are not restricted to use just a single API in an application, which was not the case prior to the CUDA 3.2 release in 2010. Modern versions of CUDA allow developers to use any of the three APIs in their applications whenever they choose. Thus, an initial code can be written in a high-level API such as Thrust and then refactored to use some special characteristic of the runtime or driver API.

Let's use this ability to mix various levels of API calls to highlight and make more explicit the parallel nature of the sequential fill task (task 2) from our previous examples. Example 1.7, "Using the CUDA Runtime to Fill an Array with Sequential Integers," also gives us a chance to introduce the CUDA runtime API:

Example 1.7

```
//seqRuntime.cu
#include <iostream>
using namespace std;
#include <thrust/reduce.h>
#include <thrust/sequence.h>
#include <thrust/host_vector.h>
#include <thrust/device_vector.h>

__global__ void fillKernel(int *a, int n)
{
  int tid = blockIdx.x*blockDim.x + threadIdx.x;
  if (tid < n) a[tid] = tid;
}

void fill(int* d_a, int n)
{
  int nThreadsPerBlock= 512;
  int nBlocks= n/nThreadsPerBlock + ((n%nThreadsPerBlock)?1:0);

  fillKernel <<< nBlocks, nThreadsPerBlock >>> (d_a, n);
}

int main()
{
  const int N=50000;

  // task 1: create the array
  thrust::device_vector<int> a(N);

  // task 2: fill the array using the runtime
  fill(thrust::raw_pointer_cast(&a[0]),N);

  // task 3: calculate the sum of the array
  int sumA= thrust::reduce(a.begin(),a.end(), 0);

  // task 4: calculate the sum of 0 .. N-1
  int sumCheck=0;
  for(int i=0; i < N; i++) sumCheck += i;

  // task 5: check the results agree
  if(sumA == sumCheck) cout << "Test Succeeded!" << endl;
  else { cerr << "Test FAILED!" << endl; return(1);}

  return(0);
}
```

The modified sections of the code are in bold. To minimize changes to the structure of **main()**, the call to **thrust::sequence()** is replaced by a call to a routine **fill()**, which is written using the runtime API. Because array **a** was allocated with **thrust::device_vector<>()**, a call to **thrust::raw_pointer_cast()** is required to get the actual location of the data on the GPU. The **fill()** subroutine uses a C-language calling convention (e.g., passing an int* and the length of the vector) to emphasize that CUDA is accessible using both C and C++. Astute readers will note that a better C++ programming practice would be to pass a reference to the Thrust device vector for a number of reasons, including: better type checking, as **fill()** could mistakenly be passed a pointer to an array in host memory; the number of elements in the vector **a** can be safely determined with **a.size()** to prevent the parameter **n** from being incorrectly specified; and a number of other reasons.

SOME BASIC CUDA CONCEPTS

Before discussing the runtime version of the **fill()** subroutine, it is important to understand some basic CUDA concepts:

- **CUDA-enabled GPUs are separate devices that are installed in a host computer.** In most cases, GPGPUs connect to a host system via a high-speed interface like the PCIe (Peripheral Component Interconnect Express) bus.
  Two to four GPGPUs can be added to most workstations or cluster nodes. How many depends on the host system capabilities such as the number of PCIe slots plus the available space, power, and cooling within the box. Each GPGPU is a separate device that runs asynchronously to the host processor(s), which means that the host processor and all the GPGPUs can be busily performing calculations at the same time. The PCIe bus is used to transfer both data and commands between the devices. CUDA provides various data transfer mechanisms that include:
  - Explicit data transfers with **cudaMemcpy()** (the most common runtime data transfer method). Those who use Thrust can perform an assignment to move data among vectors (see Example 1.8, "Code Snippet Illustrating How to Move Data with Thrust"):

Example 1.8

```
//Use thrust to move data from host to device
d_a = h_a;

//or from device to host
h_a = d_a;
```

- Implicit transfers with mapped, pinned memory. This interface keeps a region of host memory synchronized with a region of GPU memory and does not require programmer intervention. For example, an application can load a data set on the host, map the memory to the GPU, and then use the data on the GPU as if it had been explicitly initialized with a copy operation. The use of mapped, pinned memory can increase the efficiency of a program because the transfers are asynchronous. Some low-power GPGPUs utilize host memory to save cost and power. On these devices, using mapped, pinned memory results in a *zero-copy* operation, as the GPU will access the data without any copy operation.

  At the very lowest level, the host and GPGPU hardware interact through a software component called a *device driver*. The device driver manages the hardware interface so the GPU and host system can interact to communicate, calculate, and display information. It also supports many operations, including mapped memory, buffering, queuing, and synchronization. The components of the CUDA software stack are illustrated in Figure 1.3.
- **GPGPUs run in a memory space separate from the host processor.** Except for a few low-end devices, all GPGPUs have their own physical memory (e.g., RAM) that have been designed to deliver significantly higher memory bandwidth than traditional host memory. Many current

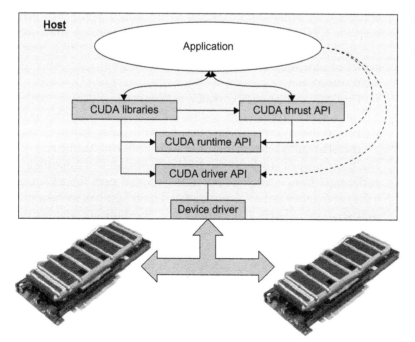

FIGURE 1.3
Components of the software stack.

GPGPU memory systems deliver approximately 160–200 GB/s (gigabytes or billions of bytes per second) as compared to traditional host memory systems that can deliver 8–20 GB/s. Although CUDA 4.0 provides Unified Virtual Addressing (UVA), which joins the host and GPGPU memory into a single unified address space, do not forget that accessing memory on another device will require some transfer across the bus—even between GPGPUs. However, UVA is important because it provides software running on any device the ability to access the data on another device using just a pointer.

- **CUDA programs utilize** *kernels*, **which are subroutines callable from the host that execute on the CUDA device.** It is important to note that kernels are not functions, as they cannot return a value. Most applications that perform well on GPGPUs spend most of their time in one or a few computational routines. Turning these routines into CUDA kernels is a wonderful way to accelerate the application and utilize the computational power of a GPGPU. A kernel is defined with the __**global**__ declaration specifier, which tells the compiler that the kernel is callable by the host processor.

- **Kernel calls are** *asynchronous*, **meaning that the host queues a kernel for execution only on the GPGPU and does not wait for it to finish but rather continues on to perform some other work**. At some later time, the kernel actually runs on the GPU. Due to this asynchronous calling mechanism, CUDA kernels cannot return a function value. For efficiency, a *pipeline* can be created by queuing a number of kernels to keep the GPGPU busy for as long as possible. Further, some form of synchronization is required so that the host can determine when the kernel or pipeline has completed. Two commonly used synchronization mechanisms are:
    - Explicitly calling **cudaThreadSynchronize()**, which acts as a *barrier* causing the host to stop and wait for all queued kernels to complete.
    - Performing a blocking data transfer with **cudaMemcpy()** as **cudaThreadSynchronize()** is called inside **cudaMemcpy()**.

- **The basic unit of work on the GPU is a** *thread.* It is important to understand from a software point of view that each thread is separate from every other thread. Every thread acts as if it has its own processor with separate registers and identity (e.g., location in a computational grid) that happens to run in a shared memory environment. The hardware defines the number of threads that are able to run concurrently. The onboard GPU hardware thread scheduler decides when a group of threads can run and has the ability to switch between threads so quickly that from a software point of view, thread switching and scheduling happen for free. Some simple yet elegant additions to the C language allow threads to communicate through the CUDA shared memory spaces and via atomic memory operations.

A kernel should utilize many threads to perform the work defined in the kernel source code. This utilization is called *thread-level parallelism*, which is different than *instruction-level parallelism*, where parallelization occurs over processor instructions. Figure 1.2 illustrates the use of many threads in a parallel fill as opposed to the single-threaded fill operation illustrated in Figure 1.1.

An *execution configuration* defines both the number of threads that will run the kernel plus their arrangement in a 1D, 2D, or 3D computational grid. An execution configuration encloses the configuration information between triple angle brackets "<<<" and ">>>" that follow after the name of the kernel and before the parameter list enclosed between the parentheses. Aside from the execution configuration, queuing a kernel looks very similar to a subroutine call. Example 1.7 demonstrates this syntax with the call to **fillKernel()** in subroutine **fill()**.

- **The largest shared region of memory on the GPU is called *global memory*.** Measured in gigabytes of RAM, most application data resides in global memory. Global memory is subject to *coalescing* rules that combine multiple memory transactions into single large load or store operations that can attain the highest transfer rate to and from memory. In general, best performance occurs when memory accesses can be coalesced into 128 consecutive byte chunks. Other forms of onboard GPU programmer-accessible memory include *constant*, *cache*, *shared*, *local*, *texture*, and *register memory*, as discussed in Chapter 5.

The latency in accessing global memory can be high, up to 600 times slower than accessing a register variable. CUDA programmers should note that although the bandwidth of global memory seems high, around 160–200 GB/s, it is slow compared to the teraflop performance capability that a GPU can deliver. For this reason, data reuse within the GPU is essential to achieving high performance.

UNDERSTANDING OUR FIRST RUNTIME KERNEL

You now have the basic concepts needed to understand our first kernel.

From the programmer's point of view, execution starts on the host processor in **main()** of Example 1.7. The constant integer **N** is initialized and the Thrust method **device_vector<int>** is used to allocate **N** integers on the GPGPU device. Execution then proceeds sequentially to the **fill()** subroutine.

A simple calculation is performed to define the number of blocks, **nBlocks**, based on the 512 threads per block defined by **nThreadsPerBlock**. The idea is to provide enough threads at a granularity of **nThreadsPerBlock** to dedicate one thread to each location in the integer array **d_a**. By convention, device variables are frequently noted by a preceding "**d_**" before the variable name and host variables are denoted with an "**h_**" before the variable name.

The CUDA kernel, **fillKernel()**, is then queued for execution on the GPGPU using the **nBlocks** and **nThreadsPerBlock** execution configuration. Both **d_a** and **n** are passed as parameters to the kernel. Host execution then proceeds to the return from the **fill()** subroutine. Note that **fillKernel()** must be preceded by the **__global__** declaration specifier or a compilation error will occur.

At this point, two things are now happening:

1. The CUDA driver is informed that there is work for the device in a queue. Within a few microseconds (μsec or millionths of a second), the driver loads the executable on the GPGPU, defines the execution grid, passes the parameters, and—because the GPGPU does not have any other work to do—starts the kernel.
2. Meanwhile, the host processor continues its sequential execution to call **thrust::reduce()** to perform task 3. The host performs the work defined by the Thrust templates and queues the GPU operations. Because **reduce()** is a blocking operation, the host has to wait for a result from the GPGPU before it can proceed.

Once **fillKernel()** starts running on the GPU, each thread first calculates its particular thread ID (called **tid** in the code) based on the grid defined by the programmer. This example uses a simple 1D grid, so **tid** is calculated using three constant variables that are specific to each kernel and defined by the programmer via the execution configuration:

- **blockIdx.x**: This is the index of the block that the thread happens to be part of in the grid specified by the programmer. Because this is a 1D grid, only the x component is used; the y and z components are ignored.
- **blockDim.x**: The dimension or number of threads in each block.
- **threadIdx.x**: The index within the block where this thread happens to be located.

The value of **tid** is then checked to see if it is less than **n**, as there might be more threads than elements in the **a** array. If **tid** contains a valid index into the **a** array, then the element at index **tid** is set to the value of **tid**. If not, the thread waits at the end of the kernel until all the threads complete. This example was chosen to make it easy to see how the grid locations are converted into array indices.

After all the threads finish, **fillKernel()** completes and returns control to the device driver so that it can start the next queued task. In this example, the GPU computes the reduction (the code of which is surprisingly complicated, as discussed in Chapter 6), and the sum is returned to the host so that the application can finish sequentially processing tasks 4 and 5.

From the preceding discussion, we can see that a CUDA kernel can be thought of in simple terms as a parallel form of the code snippet in Example 1.9, "A Sequential Illustration of a Parallel CUDA Call":

Example 1.9

```
// setup blockIdx, blockDim, and threadIdx based on the execution
// configuration
for(int i=0; i < (nBlocks * nThreadsPerBlock); i++)
    fillKernel(d_a, n);
```

Though Thrust relies on the runtime API, careful use of C++ templates allows a C++ *functor* (or *function object*, which is a C++ object that can be called as if it were a function) to be translated into a runtime kernel. It also defines the execution configuration and creates a kernel call for the programmer. This explains why Example 1.5, which was written entirely in Thrust, does not require specification of an execution configuration or any of the other details required by the runtime API.

THREE RULES OF GPGPU PROGRAMMING

Observation has shown that there are three general rules to creating high-performance GPGPU programs:

1. Get the data on the GPGPU and keep it there.
2. Give the GPGPU enough work to do.
3. Focus on data reuse within the GPGPU to avoid memory bandwidth limitations.

These rules make sense, given the bandwidth and latency limitations of the PCIe bus and GPGPU memory system as discussed in the following subsections.

Rule 1: Get the Data on the GPU and Keep It There

GPGPUs are separate devices that are plugged into the PCI Express bus of the host computer. The PCIe bus is very slow compared to GPGPU memory system as can be seen by the 20-times difference highlighted in Table 1.1.

Table 1.1 PCIe vs. GPU Global Memory Bandwidth		
	Bandwidth (GB/s)	**Speedup over PCIe Bus**
PCIe x16 v2.0 bus (one-way)	8	1
GPU global memory	160 to 200	20x to 28x

Rule 2: Give the GPGPU Enough Work to Do

The adage "watch what you ask for because you might get it" applies to GPGPU performance. Because CUDA-enabled GPUs can deliver teraflop performance, they are fast enough to complete small problems faster than the host processor can start kernels. To get a sense of the numbers, let's assume this overhead is 4 μsec for a 1 teraflop GPU that takes 4 cycles to perform a floating-point operation. To keep this GPGPU busy, each kernel must perform roughly 1 million floating-point operations to avoid wasting cycles due to the kernel startup latency. If the kernel takes only 2 μsec to complete, then 50 percent of the GPU cycles will be wasted. One caveat is that Fermi GPUs can run multiple small kernels at the same time on a single GPU.

Rule 3: Focus on Data Reuse within the GPGPU to Avoid Memory Bandwidth Limitations

All high-performance CUDA applications exploit internal resources on the GPU (such as registers, shared memory, and so on, discussed in Chapter 5) to bypass global memory bottlenecks. For example, multiplying a vector by a scale factor in global memory and assigning the result to a second vector also in global memory will be slow, as shown in Example 1.10, "A Simple Vector Example":

Example 1.10
```
for(i=0; i < N; i++) c[i] = a * b[i];
```

Assuming the vectors require 4 bytes to store a single-precision 32-bit floating-point value in each element, then the memory subsystem of a teraflop capable computer would need to provide at least 8 terabytes per second of memory bandwidth to run at peak performance—assuming the constant scale factor gets loaded into the GPGPU cache. Roughly speaking, such bandwidth is 40 to 50 times the capability of current GPU memory subsystems and around 400 times the bandwidth of a 20-GB/s commodity processor. Double-precision vectors that require 8 bytes of storage per vector element will double the bandwidth requirement. This example should make it clear that CUDA programmers must reuse as much data as possible to achieve high performance. Please note that data reuse is also important to attaining high performance on conventional processors as well.

BIG-O CONSIDERATIONS AND DATA TRANSFERS

Big-O notation is a convenient way to describe how the size of the problem affects the consumption by an algorithm of some resource such as processor time or memory as a function of its input. In this way, computer scientists can describe the worst case (or, when specified, the average case behavior) as a function to compare algorithms regardless of architecture or clock rate. Some common growth rates are:

- $O(1)$: These are constant time (or space) algorithms that always consume the same resources regardless of the size of the input set. Indexing a single element in a Thrust host vector does not vary in time with the size of the data set and thus exhibits $O(1)$ runtime growth.
- $O(N)$: Resource consumption with these algorithms grow linearly with the size of the input. This is a common runtime for algorithms that loop over a data set. However, the work inside the loop must require constant time.
- $O(N^2)$: Performance is directly proportional to the square of the size of the input data set. Algorithms that use nested loops over an input data set exhibit $O(N^2)$ runtime. Deeper nested iterations commonly show greater runtime (e.g., three nested loops result in $O(N^3)$, $O(N^4)$ when four loops are nested, and so on.

There are many excellent texts on algorithm analysis that provide a more precise and comprehensive description of big-O notation. One popular text is *Introduction to Algorithms* (by Cormen, Leiserson, Rivest, and Stein; The MIT Press, 2009). There are also numerous resources on the Internet that discuss and teach big-O notation and algorithm analysis.

Most computationally oriented scientists and programmers are familiar with the BLAS (the Basic Linear Algebra Subprograms) library. BLAS is the *de facto* programming interface for basic linear algebra. NVIDIA provides a GPGPU version of BLAS with their CUBLAS library. In fact, GPGPU computing is creating a resurgence of interest in new high-performance math libraries, such as the MAGMA project at the University of Tennessee Innovative Computing Laboratory (http://icl.cs.utk.edu/magma/). MAGMA in particular utilizes both the host and a GPU device to attain high performance on matrix operations. It is available for free download.

BLAS is structured according to three different levels with increasing data and runtime requirements:

- Level-1: Vector-vector operations that require $O(N)$ data and $O(N)$ work. Examples include taking the inner product of two vectors or scaling a vector by a constant multiplier.
- Level-2: Matrix-vector operations that require $O(N^2)$ data and $O(N^2)$ work. Examples include matrix-vector multiplication or a single right-hand-side triangular solve.
- Level-3 Matrix-vector operations that require $O(N^2)$ data and $O(N^3)$ work. Examples include dense matrix-matrix multiplication.

Table 1.2 illustrates the amount of work that is performed by each BLAS level, assuming that N floating-point values are transferred from the host to the GPU. It does not take into account the time required to transfer the data back to the GPU.

Table 1.2 tells us that level-3 BLAS operations should run efficiently on graphics processors because they perform $O(N)$ work for every floating-point value transferred to the GPU. The same work-per-datum analysis applies to non-BLAS-related computational problems as well.

To illustrate the cost of a level-1 BLAS operation, consider the overhead involved in moving data across the PCIe bus to calculate **cublasScal()** on the GPU and then return the vector to the host. The BLAS **Sscal()** method scales a vector by a constant value. CUBLAS includes a *thunking* interface for FORTRAN compatibility. It works by transferring data from the host to the GPU, performing the calculation, and then transferring the data back to the host from the GPU. Thunking is inefficient, as it requires moving $4N$ bytes of data (where N is the number of floats in the vector) twice across the PCIe bus to perform N multiplications, as shown in Example 1.10. The best possible performance would be the transfer bandwidth divided by 8 (to account for two transfers of $4N$ bytes of data each way), as the time to perform the multiplication would be tiny compared to the data transfers. Such an application might achieve 1 Gflop (1 billion floating-point operations per second) floating-point performance assuming an 8-GB/s transfer rate

Table 1.2 Work per Datum by BLAS Level

BLAS Level	Data	Work	Work per Datum
1	$O(N)$	$O(N)$	$O(1)$
2	$O(N^2)$	$O(N^2)$	$O(1)$
3	$O(N^2)$	$O(N^3)$	$O(N)$

between the host and GPU.[1] Modest laptop processors and even some cell phones can exceed this calculation rate.

This analysis applies to all programs, not just level-1 and level-2 BLAS calculations. Getting good performance requires keeping as much data as possible on the GPU. After that, attaining high performance requires performing as many calculations per datum like the level-3 BLAS operations. Creating a pipeline of many lower arithmetic density computations can help, but this will only increase performance when each operation can keep the GPU busy long enough to overcome the kernel startup latency. Alternatively, it is possible to increase performance—sometime significantly—by combining multiple low-density operations like BLAS level-2 and level-2 operation into a single functor or kernel.

CUDA AND AMDAHL'S LAW

Amdahl's law is named after computer architect Gene Amdahl. It is not really a law but rather an approximation that models the ideal speedup that can happen when serial programs are modified to run in parallel. For this approximation to be valid, it is necessary for the problem size to remain the same when parallelized. In other words, assume that a serial program is modified to run in parallel. Further, assume that the amount of work performed by the program does not change significantly in the parallel version of the code, which is not always true. Obviously, those portions of the application that do not parallelize will not run any faster, and the parallel sections can run much, much faster depending on the hardware capabilities. Thus, the expected speedup of the parallel code over the serial code when using n processors is dictated by the proportion of a program that can be made parallel, P, and the portion of that cannot be parallelized, $(1 - P)$. This relationship is shown in Equation 1.1, "Amdahl's law".

$$S(n) = \frac{1}{(1 - P) + P/n} \tag{1.1}$$

Amdahl's law tells us that inventive CUDA developers have two concerns in parallelizing an application:

1. Express the parallel sections of code so that they run as fast as possible. Ideally, they should run N times faster when using N processors.
2. Utilize whatever techniques or inventiveness they have to minimize the $(1 - P)$ serial time.

---

[1] Asynchronous data transfers can improve performance because the PCIe bus is full duplex, meaning that data can be transferred both to and from the host at the same time. At best, full-duplex asynchronous PCIe transfers would double the performance to two Gflop.

Part of the beauty of CUDA lies in the natural way it encapsulates the parallelism of a program inside computational kernels. Applications that run well on GPGPU hardware tend to have a few computationally intensive sections of the code (e.g., hotspots) that consume most of the runtime. According to Amdahl's law, these are programs with kernels that can deliver good parallel speedups $(P \gg 1 - P)$.

Observation has also shown that refactoring an application to use CUDA also tends to speed up performance on moderately parallel hardware such as multicore processors because CUDA allows developers to better see parallelism so that they can restructure the code to reduce the time spent in the serial $(1 - P)$ sections. Of course, this assumes observation that the overhead consumed in transferring data to and from the GPGPU does not significantly affect application runtime.

DATA AND TASK PARALLELISM

The examples in this chapter have thus far demonstrated *data parallelism* or *loop-level parallelism* that parallelized data operations inside the **for** loops. *Task parallelism* is another form of parallelization that reduces the $(1 - P)$ serial time by having multiple tasks executing concurrently. CUDA naturally supports task parallelism by running concurrent tasks on the host and GPU. As will be discussed in Chapter 7, CUDA provides other ways to exploit task parallelism within a GPU or across multiple GPUs.

Even the simple GPU examples, like Examples 1.5 and 1.7, can be modified to demonstrate task parallelism. These examples performed the following tasks:

1. Create an array.
2. Fill the array.
3. Calculate the sum of the array.
4. Calculate the sum of $0 .. N-1$.
5. Check that the host and device results agree.

The representative timeline in Figure 1.4 shows that the previous examples do not take advantage of the asynchronous kernel execution when task 2 is queued to run on the GPU.

However, there is no reason why task 4 cannot be started after task 2 queues the kernel to run on the GPU. In other words, there is no *dependency* that

FIGURE 1.4

Sequential timeline.

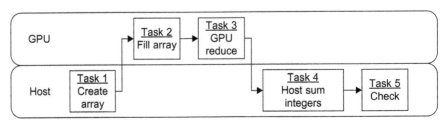

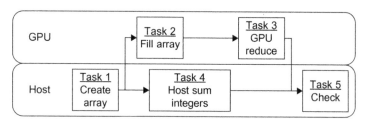

FIGURE 1.5
Asynchronous timeline.

forces task 4 to run after any other task, except that it must run before the check for correctness in task 5. In other words, task 5 depends on the results from task 4. Similarly, task 2 must run sometime after task 1, which allocates the array on the GPU.

Switching tasks 3 and 4 allows both the host and GPU to run in parallel, as shown in Figure 1.5, which demonstrates that it is possible to leverage CUDA asynchronous kernel execution to exploit both task and data parallelism in even this simple example. The benefit is a further reduction in application runtime.

HYBRID EXECUTION: USING BOTH CPU AND GPU RESOURCES

The following example demonstrates a hybrid application that application runs simultaneously on both the CPU and GPU. Modern multicore processors are also parallel hardware that supports both data parallel and task parallel execution. OpenMP (Open Multi-Processing) is an easy way to utilize multithreaded execution on the host processor. The NVIDIA **nvcc** compiler supports OpenMP. Though this book is not about the OpenMP API, CUDA programmers need to know that they can exploit this host processor parallelism as well as the massive parallelism of the GPGPU. After all, the goal is to deliver the fastest application performance. It is also important to be fair when making benchmark comparisons between CPUs and GPUs by optimizing the application to achieve the highest performance on both systems to make the comparison as fair as possible.

Example 1.11, "An Asynchronous CPU/GPU Source Code" is the source code that switches the order of execution between task 3 and 4. The OpenMP parallel for loop pragma was used in task 4 to exploit data parallelism on the host processor:

Example 1.11

```
//seqAsync.cu
#include <iostream>
using namespace std;
```

```
#include <thrust/reduce.h>
#include <thrust/sequence.h>
#include <thrust/host_vector.h>
#include <thrust/device_vector.h>

int main()
{
  const int N=50000;

  // task 1: create the array
  thrust::device_vector<int> a(N);

  // task 2: fill the array
  thrust::sequence(a.begin(), a.end(), 0);

  // task 4: calculate the sum of 0 .. N-1
  int sumCheck=0;
#pragma omp parallel for reduction(+ : sumCheck)
  for(int i=0; i < N; i++) sumCheck += i;

  // task 3: calculate the sum of the array
  int sumA= thrust::reduce(a.begin(),a.end(), 0);

  // task 5: check the results agree
  if(sumA == sumCheck) cout << "Test Succeeded!" << endl;
  else { cerr << "Test FAILED!" << endl; return(1);}

  return(0);
}
```

To compile with OpenMP, add "**-Xcompiler -fopenmp**" to the **nvcc** command-line argument as shown in Example 1.12 to compile Example 1.11. Because we are timing the results, the "**−O3**" optimization flag was also utilized.

Example 1.12

```
nvcc -O3 -Xcompiler -fopenmp seqAsync.cu - seqAsync
```

The output from seqAsync (Example 1.13, "Results Showing a Successful Test") shows that the sum is correctly calculated as it passes the golden test:

Example 1.13

```
$ ./a.out
Test Succeeded!
```

REGRESSION TESTING AND ACCURACY

As always in programming, the most important metric for success is that the application produces the correct output. Regression testing is a critical part of this evaluation process that is unfortunately left out of most computer science books. Regression tests act as sanity checks that allow the programmer to use the computer to detect if some error has been introduced into the code. The computer is impartial and does not get tired. For these reasons, small amounts of code should be written and tested to ensure everything is in a known working state. Additional code can then be added along with more regression tests. This greatly simplifies debugging efforts as the errors generally occur in the smaller amounts of new code. The alternative is to write a large amount of code and hope that it will work. If there is an error, it is challenging to trace through many lines of code to find one or more problems. Sometimes you can get lucky with the latter approach. If you try it, track your time to see if there really was a savings over taking the time to use regression testing and incremental development.

The examples in this chapter use a simple form of regression test, sometimes called a *golden test* or *smoke test*, which utilizes an alternative method to double-check the parallel calculation of the sum of the integers. Such simple tests work well for exact calculations, but become more challenging to interpret when using floating-point arithmetic due to the numerical errors introduced into a calculation when using floating-point. As GPGPU technology can perform several *trillion* floating-point operations per second, numerical errors can build up quickly. Still, using a computer to double-check the results beats staring at endless lines of numbers. For complex programs and algorithms, the regression test suite can take as much time to plan, be as complex to implement, and require more lines of code than the application code itself!

While hard to justify to management, professors or to you (especially when working against a tight deadline), consider the cost of delivering an application that *does not* perform correctly. For example, the second startup I co-founded delivered an artificial learning system that facilitated the search for candidate drug leads using some of the technology discussed later in this book. The most difficult question our startup team had to answer was posed by the research executive committee of a major investor. That question was "how do we know that what you are doing on the computer reflects what really happens in the test tube?" The implied question was, "how do we know that you aren't playing some expensive computer game with our money?" The solution was to perform a double-blind test showing that our technology could predict the chemical activity of relevant compounds in real-world experiments using only on a very small set of measurements and no knowledge of the correct result. In other words, our team utilized a form of sanity checking to demonstrate the efficacy of our model and software. Without such a reality check, it likely that the company would not have received funding.

SILENT ERRORS

A challenge with regression testing is that some errors can still silently pass through the test suite and make it to the application that the end-user sees. For example, Andy Regan at ICHEC (the Irish Center for High-End Computing) pointed out that increasing the value of **N** in the examples in this chapter can cause the sum to become so large that it cannot be contained in an integer. Some systems might catch the error and some systems will miss the error.

Given that GPUs can perform a trillion arithmetic operations per second, it is important that CUDA programmers understand how quickly numerical errors can accumulate or computed values overflow their capacity. A quick introduction to this topic is my *Scientific Computing* article "Numerical Precision: How Much Is Enough?" (Farber, 2009), which is freely available on the Internet.

Thrust provides the ability to perform a reduction where smaller data types are converted into a larger data type, *seqBig.cu*, demonstrates how to use a 64-bit unsigned integer to sum all the 32-bit integers in the vector. The actual values are printed at the end of the test. See Example 1.14, "A Thrust Program that Performs a Dual-Precision Reduction":

Example 1.14

```
//seqBig.cu
#include <iostream>
using namespace std;

#include <thrust/reduce.h>
#include <thrust/sequence.h>
#include <thrust/host_vector.h>
#include <thrust/device_vector.h>

int main()
{
  const int N=1000000;

  // task 1: create the array
  thrust::device_vector<int> a(N);

  // task 2: fill the array
  thrust::sequence(a.begin(), a.end(), 0);

  // task 3: calculate the sum of the array
  unsigned long long sumA= thrust::reduce(a.begin(),a.end(),
      (unsigned long long) 0, thrust::plus<unsigned long long>() );
```

```
// task 4: calculate the sum of 0 .. N-1
unsigned long long sumCheck=0;
for(int i=0; i < N; i++) sumCheck += i;

cerr << "host   " << sumCheck << endl;
cerr << "device " << sumA << endl;

// task 5: check the results agree
if(sumA == sumCheck) cout << "Test Succeeded!" << endl;
else { cerr << "Test FAILED!" << endl; return(1);}

return(0);
}
```

The **nvcc** compiler has the ability to compile and run an application from a single command-line invocation. Example 1.15, "Results Showing a Successful Test" shows the **nvcc** command line and the successful run of the *seqBig.cu* application:

Example 1.15

```
$ nvcc seqBig.cu -run
host    499999500000
device 499999500000
Test Succeeded!
```

Can you find any other silent errors that might occur as the size of **N** increases in these examples? (Hint: what limitations does **tid** have in the runtime example?)

INTRODUCTION TO DEBUGGING

Debugging programs is a fact of life—especially when learning a new language. With a few simple additions, CUDA enables GPGPU computing, but simplicity of expression does not preclude programming errors. As when developing applications for any computer, finding bugs can be complicated.

Following the same economy of change used to adapt C and C++, NVIDIA has extended several popular debugging tools to support GPU computing. These are tools that most Windows and UNIX developers are already proficient and comfortable using such as **gdb**, **ddd**, and Visual Studio. Those familiar with building, debugging, and profiling software under Windows, Mac, and UNIX should find the transition to CUDA straightforward. For the most part, NVIDIA has made debugging CUDA code identical to debugging any other C or C++ application. All CUDA tools are freely available on the NVIDIA website, including the professional edition of Parallel Nsight for Microsoft Visual Studio.

UNIX DEBUGGING

NVIDIA's cuda-gdb Debugger

To use the CUDA debugger, **cuda-gdb**, the source code must be compiled with the **-g -G** flags. The **-g** flag specifies that the host-side code is to be compiled for debugging. The **-G** flag specifies that the GPU side code is to be compiled for debugging (see Example 1.16, "nvcc Command to Compile for cuda-gdb"):

Example 1.16

```
nvcc —g —G seqRuntime.cu —o seqRuntime
```

Following is a list of some common commands, including the single-letter abbreviation and a brief description:

- breakpoint (b): set a breakpoint to stop the program execution at selected locations in the code. The argument can either be a method name or line number.
- run (r): run the application within the debugger.
- next (n): move to the next line of code.
- continue (c): continue to the next breakpoint or until the program completes.
- backtrace (bt): shows contents of the stack including calling methods.
- thread: lists the current CPU thread.
- cuda thread: lists the current active GPU threads (if any).
- cuda kernel: lists the currently active GPU kernels and also allows switching "focus" to a given GPU thread.

Use **cuda-gdb** to start the debugger, as shown in Example 1.17, "cuda-gdb Startup":

Example 1.17

```
$ cuda-gdb seqRuntime
NVIDIA (R) CUDA Debugger
4.0 release
Portions Copyright (C) 2007-2011 NVIDIA Corporation
GNU gdb 6.6
Copyright (C) 2006 Free Software Foundation, Inc.
GDB is free software, covered by the GNU General Public License, and you
are welcome to change it and/or distribute copies of it under certain
conditions.
Type "show copying" to see the conditions.
There is absolutely no warranty for GDB. Type "show warranty" for details.
This GDB was configured as "x86_64-unknown-linux-gnu"…
Using host libthread_db library "/lib/libthread_db.so.1".
```

Use the "l" command to show the source for **fill**, as shown in Example 1.18, "cuda-gdb List Source Code":

Example 1.18

```
(cuda-gdb) l fill
11      int tid = blockIdx.x*blockDim.x + threadIdx.x;
12      if (tid < n) a[tid] = tid;
13    }
14
15    void fill(int* d_a, int n)
16    {
17      int nThreadsPerBlock= 512;
18      int nBlocks= n/nThreadsPerBlock + ((n%nThreadsPerBlock)?1:0);
19
20      fillKernel <<< nBlocks, nThreadsPerBlock >>> (d_a, n);
```

Set a breakpoint at line 12 and run the program. We see that a thrust kernel runs and then the breakpoint is hit in **fillkernel()**, as shown in Example 1.19, "cuda-gdb Set a Breakpoint":

Example 1.19

```
(cuda-gdb) b 12
Breakpoint 1 at 0x401e30: file seqRuntime.cu, line 12.
(cuda-gdb) r
Starting program: /home/rmfarber/foo/ex1-3
[Thread debugging using libthread_db enabled]
[New process 3107]
[New Thread 139660862195488 (LWP 3107)]
[Context Create of context 0x1ed03a0 on Device 0]
Breakpoint 1 at 0x20848a8: file seqRuntime.cu, line 12.
[Launch of CUDA Kernel 0 (thrust::detail::device::cuda::detail::
launch_closure_by_value<thrust::detail::device::cuda::for_each_n_
closure<thrust::device_ptr<unsigned long long>, unsigned int, thrust::
detail::generate_functor<thrust::detail::fill_functor<unsigned long
long> > > ><<<(28,1,1),(768,1,1)>>>) on Device 0]
[Launch of CUDA Kernel 1 (fillKernel<<<(1954,1,1),(512,1,1)>>>) on
Device 0]
[Switching focus to CUDA kernel 1, grid 2, block (0,0,0), thread (0,0,0),
device 0, sm 0, warp 0, lane 0]

Breakpoint 1, fillKernel<<<(1954,1,1),(512,1,1)>>> (a=0x200100000,
n=50000)
    at seqRuntime.cu:12
12      if (tid < n) a[tid] = tid;
```

Print the value of the thread Id, **tid**, as in Example 1.20, "cuda-gdb Print a Variable":

Example 1.20

```
(cuda-gdb) p tid
$1 = 0
```

Switch to thread 403 and print the value of **tid** again. The value of **tid** is correct, as shown in Example 1.21, "cuda-gdb Change Thread and Print a Variable":

Example 1.21

```
(cuda-gdb) cuda thread(403)
[Switching focus to CUDA kernel 1, grid 2, block (0,0,0),
thread (403,0,0), device 0, sm 0, warp 12, lane 19]
12      if (tid < n) a[tid] = tid;
(cuda-gdb) p tid
$2 = 403
```

Exit cuda-gdb (Example 1.22, "cuda-gdb Exit"):

Example 1.22

```
(cuda-gdb) quit
The program is running.    Exit anyway? (y or n) y
```

This demonstrated only a minimal set of **cuda-gdb** capabilities. Much more information can be found in the manual "CUDA-GDB NVIDIA CUDA Debugger for Linux and Mac," which is updated and provided with each release of the CUDA tools. Parts 14 and 17 of my *Doctor Dobb's Journal* tutorials discuss **cuda-gdb** techniques and capabilities in much greater depth. Also, any good **gdb** or **ddd** tutorial will also help novice readers learn the details of **cuda-gdb**.

The CUDA Memory Checker

Unfortunately, it is very easy to make a mistake when specifying the size of a dynamically allocated region of memory. In many cases, such errors are difficult to find. Programming with many threads compounds the problem because an error in thread usage can cause an out-of-bounds memory access. For example, neglecting to check whether **tid** is less than the size of the vector in the fill routine will cause an out-of-bounds memory access. This is a subtle bug because the number of threads utilized is specified in a different program location in the execution configuration. See Example 1.23, "Modified Kernel to Cause an Out-of-Bounds Error":

Example 1.23

```
__global__ void fillKernel(int *a, int n)
{
  int tid = blockIdx.x*blockDim.x + threadIdx.x;
  // if(tid < n) // Removing this comparision introduces an out-of-bounds error
  a[tid] = tid;
}
```

The CUDA tool suite provides a standalone memory check utility called **cuda-memcheck**. As seen in Example 1.24, "Example Showing the Program Can Run with an Out-of-Bounds Error," the program appears to run correctly:

Example 1.24

```
$ cuda-memcheck badRuntime
Test Succeeded!
```

However **cuda-memcheck** correctly flags that there is an out-of-bounds error, as shown in Example 1.25, "Out-of-Bounds Error Reported by cuda-memcheck":

Example 1.25

```
$ cuda-memcheck badRuntime
========= CUDA-MEMCHECK
Test Succeeded!
========= Invalid __global__ write of size 4
=========     at 0x000000e0 in badRuntime.cu:14:fillKernel
=========     by thread (336,0,0) in block (97,0,0)
=========     Address 0x200130d40 is out of bounds
=========
========= ERROR SUMMARY: 1 error
```

Notice that no special compilation flags were required to use **cuda-memcheck**.

Use cuda-gdb with the UNIX ddd Interface

The GNU **ddd** (Data Display Debugger) provides a visual interface for **cuda-gdb** (or **gdb**). Many people prefer a visual debugger to a plain-text interface. To use **cuda-gdb**, **ddd** must be told to use a different debugger with the

"-debugger" command-line flag as shown in Example 1.26, "Command to Start ddd with cuda-gdb":

Example 1.26

```
ddd -debugger cuda-gdb badRuntime
```

Break points can be set visually, and all **cuda-gdb** commands can be manually entered. The following screenshot shows how to find an out-of-bounds error by first specifying **set cuda memcheck on**. As will be demonstrated in Chapter 3, **ddd** also provides a useful machine instruction window to examine and step through the actual instructions the GPU is using. See Example 1.27, "Using cuda-gdb Inside ddd to Find the Out-of-Bounds Error":

```
File  Edit  View  Program  Commands  Status  Source  Data                                    Help

(): main                                         Lookup Find> Break Watch Print Display Plot  Set

    int tid = blockIdx.x*blockDim.x + threadIdx.x;
    //if (tid < n)
⬦   a[tid] = tid;
    }

void fill(int* d_a, int n)
{
    int nThreadsPerBlock= 512;
    int nBlocks= n/nThreadsPerBlock + ((n%nThreadsPerBlock)?1:0);

    fillKernel <<< nBlocks, nThreadsPerBlock >>> (d_a, n);
}

int main()
{
    const int N=50000;

    // task 1: create the array
    thrust::device_vector<int> a(N);

    // task 2: fill the array using the runtime
    fill(thrust::raw_pointer_cast(&a[0]),N);

    // task 3: calculate the sum of the array
    int sumA= thrust::reduce(a.begin(),a.end(), 0);

    // task 4: calculate the sum of 0 .. N-1
    int sumCheck=0;
    for(int i=0; i < N; i++) sumCheck += i;

    // task 5: check the results agree

Copyright © 2001 Universität des Saarlandes, Germany.
Copyright © 2001-2004 Free Software Foundation, Inc.
Using host libthread_db library "/lib/libthread_db.so.1".
(gdb) set cuda memcheck on
(gdb) run
[Thread debugging using libthread_db enabled]
[New process 23055]
[New Thread 139865744762656 (LWP 23055)]
[Context Create of context 0x2571200 on Device 0]
[Launch of CUDA Kernel 0
(thrust::detail::device::cuda::detail::launch_closure_by_value<thrust::detail::device::cuda::for_each_n_
closure<thrust::device_ptr<unsigned long long>, unsigned int,
thrust::detail::generate_functor<thrust::detail::fill_functor<unsigned long long> > >
><<<(28,1,1),(768,1,1)>>>) on Device 0]
[Launch of CUDA Kernel 1 (fillKernel<<<(98,1,1),(512,1,1)>>>) on Device 0]

Program received signal CUDA_EXCEPTION_1, Lane Illegal Address.
[Switching focus to CUDA kernel 1, grid 2, block (97,0,0), thread (480,0,0), device 0, sm 5, warp 31,
lane 0]
0x00000000027b5050 in fillKernel (a=0x200100000, n=50000) at badRuntime.cu:14
(gdb)

⬦ Disassembling location 0x27b5050 to 0x27b5150...done.
```

WINDOWS DEBUGGING WITH PARALLEL NSIGHT

Parallel Nsight also provides a debugging experience familiar to Microsoft Visual Studio users yet includes powerful GPU features like thread-level debugging and the CUDA memory checker. It installs as a plug-in within Microsoft Visual Studio. Parallel insight also provides a number of features:

- Integrated into Visual Studio 2008 SP1 or Visual Studio 2010.
- CUDA C/C++ debugging.
- DirectX 10/11 shader debugging.
- DirectX 10/11 frame debugging.
- DirectX 10/11 frame profiling.
- CUDA kernel trace/profiling.
- OpenCL kernel trace/profiling.
- DirectX 10/11 API & HW trace.
- Data breakpoints for CUDA C/C++ code.
- Analyzer/system trace.
- Tesla Compute Cluster (TCC) support.

Parallel Nsight allows both debugging and analysis on the machine as well as on remote machines that can be located at a customer's site. The capabilities of Parallel Nsight vary with the hardware configuration seen in Table 1.3.

Figure 1.6 shows Parallel Nsight stopped at a breakpoint on the GPU when running the **fillkernel()** kernel in *seqRuntime.cu*. The *locals* window shows the values of various variables on the GPU.

A screenshot does not convey the interactive nature of Parallel Nsight, as many of the fields on the screen are interactive and can be clicked to gain more information. Visual Studio users should find the Parallel Nsight comfortable, as it reflects and utilized the look and feel of other aspects of Visual Studio. Parallel Nsight is an extensive package that is growing and maturing quickly. The most current information, including videos and the user forums, can be found on the Parallel Nsight web portal at http://www.nvidia.com/ParallelNsight as well as the help section in Visual Studio.

Table 1.3 Parallel Nsight Capabilities According to Machine Configuration

Hardware Configuration	Single GPU System	Dual GPU System	Two Systems, Each with a GPU	Dual-GPU System SLI MultiOS
CUDA C/C++ parallel debugger		☑	☑	☑
Direct3D shader debugger			☑	☑
Direct3D graphics inspector	☑	☑	☑	☑
Analyzer	☑	☑	☑	☑

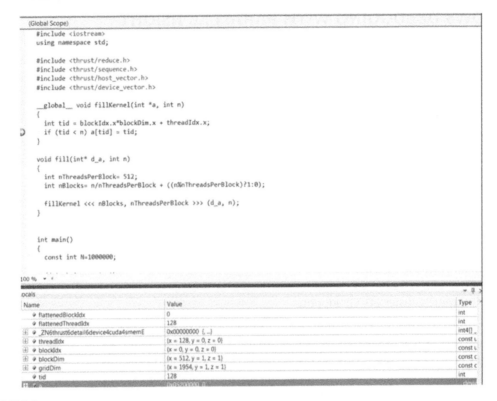

FIGURE 1.6

A Parallel Nsight debug screen.

SUMMARY

This chapter covered a number of important applied topics such as how to write, compile, and run CUDA applications on the GPGPU using both the runtime and Thrust APIs. With the tools and syntax discussed in this chapter, it is possible to write and experiment with CUDA using the basics of the Thrust and runtime APIs. Audacious readers may even attempt to write real applications, which is encouraged, as they can be refactored based on the contents of later chapters and feedback from the performance profiling tools. Remember, the goal is to become a proficient CUDA programmer and writing code is the fastest path to that goal. Just keep the three basic rules of GPGPU programming in mind:

1. Get the data on the GPGPU and keep it there.
2. Give the GPGPU enough work to do.
3. Focus on data reuse within the GPGPU to avoid memory bandwidth limitations.

Understanding basic computer science concepts is also essential to achieving high performance and improving yourself as a computer scientist. Keep Amdahl's law in mind to minimize serial bottlenecks as well as exploiting both task and data parallelism. Always try to understand the big-O implications of the algorithms that you use and seek out alternative algorithms that exhibit better scaling behavior. Always attempt to combine operations to achieve the highest computational density on the GPU while minimizing slow PCIe bus transfers.

## CHAPTER 2

CUDA for Machine Learning and Optimization

GPGPUs are powerful tools that are well-suited to unraveling complex real-world problems. Using only the simple CUDA capabilities introduced in Chapter 1, this chapter demonstrates how to greatly accelerate nonlinear optimization problems using the derivative-free Nelder-Mead and Levenberg-Marquardt optimization algorithms. Single- and double-precision application performance will be measured and compared between an Intel Xeon e5630 processor and an NVIDIA C2070 GPU as well as an older 10-series NVIDIA GTX 280 gaming GPU. Working example code is provided that can train the classic nonlinear XOR machine-learning problem 85 times faster than a modern quad-core Intel Xeon processor (341 times faster than single-core performance) under Linux with comparable performance under Windows 7.

At the end of the chapter, the reader will have a basic understanding of:

- Two popular optimization techniques, including GPU scalability limitations of the Levenberg-Marquardt algorithm
- How a CUDA-literate programmer can make significant contributions to modeling and data-mining efforts
- Machine learning and why the XOR problem is important to computationally universal devices
- C++ functors and how to write a single Thrust functor using __host__ and __device__ qualifiers that can run on both host and GPGPU devices
- Some example programs that demonstrate orders-of-magnitude increased performance over a conventional processor on techniques that can be applied to problems in machine learning, signal processing, statistics, and many other fields

MODELING AND SIMULATION

Mathematical modeling and numerical simulation are two important, distinct, and closely linked aspects of applied mathematics. A mathematical model is an abstraction of reality that can be used for analysis and prediction. Numerical simulation is based on applications that map mathematical models onto the computer. In combination, modeling and simulation are powerful techniques to advance human understanding of complex phenomena.

This book does not attempt to duplicate or shed new insight on the tremendous volume of work that has already been published concerning modeling and simulation. Depending on your particular area of interest, there are a number of excellent texts available that provide both precise and detailed introductions. Our focus is to provide the tools needed to exploit massively parallel hardware with CUDA so that readers can make their own contributions in their field of choice.

Two general approaches are utilized to create models:

1. Human-derived models based on first-principle analysis and other techniques

When available, these models provide deep insight into the phenomena being investigated. A literate CUDA programmer can contribute by efficiently mapping the calculations to the parallel hardware to achieve the highest performance and scale to the largest number of processing elements possible. The literature shows that a well-designed and written CUDA application can provide two orders of magnitude increased performance (Hwu, 2011; Stone et al., 2010). Such performance is disruptive, as simulations that previously would have taken a year can finish in a few days. Greater simulation accuracy is also possible as more accurate and detailed approximations can be utilized. Nonlinear problems particularly benefit from the NVIDIA Special Function Units (SFU) that calculate several transcendental functions (such as **log()**, **exp()**, **sin()**, **cos()**, and others) approximately 25 times faster than conventional processors.

2. Parameterized models derived by fitting data

Computationally derived models from data are relatively simple to construct compared to human-derived models. Many techniques exist that can create accurate models that generalize well. Neural networks are one example (Lapedes & Farber, 1987b). In general, the process of fitting a model to data is a computationally expensive process, with runtimes that grow by $O(N^2)$ and higher, where N is the number of data items. Parallelism can make many of these methods tractable and even interactive by reducing the runtime by some factor close to the number of processing elements. Containing hundreds of processing elements, a single GPU has the potential to reduce runtimes by two or more orders of magnitude. Clever partitioning of the problem across multiple GPUs can scale the number of available processing element by the number of GPUs.

Particular challenges arise when modeling systems that exhibit *nonlinear* behavior. A nonlinear system does not always respond proportionally to an input stimulus, which means their behavior cannot be modeled solely on the basis of some linear combination of the input or system stimulus. Although challenging, nonlinear systems give rise to many interesting phenomena including self-organizing systems, chaotic behavior, and life.

Fitting Parameterized Models

Model fitting can be phrased as a form of function optimization in which a set of model parameters, *P*, are adjusted to fit some data set with a minimum error. The error is determined by an *objective function*, sometimes called a *cost function*, which evaluates how well a model fits a data set for some set of model parameters. A common technique is to fit a curve to a set of *N* data points to minimize the sum of the squares of the distances between the predicted and known points on the curve. See Equation 2.1, "Sum of squares of differences error."

$$\text{Error} = \sum_{i}^{N} (\text{Known}_i - \text{Predicted}_i)^2 \qquad (2.1)$$

Because the sum of the squares of the differences is always positive, a perfect fit will result in a zero error. Unfortunately, this rarely occurs because most numerical techniques are subject to *local minima*, which means that the numerical technique somehow gets stuck at a low point in the cost function from which it cannot escape. As a result, no guarantee can be made that the *global minimum* or best overall fit has been found.

There are a number of popular libraries and tools that can be used to find the minimum of a function over many variables. The book *Numerical Recipes* is an excellent source of information (Press et al., 2007), which also provides working source code.[1] Many free and licensed numerical toolkits are available, including SLATEC, NAG (Numerical Algorithms Group), MIN-PACK, the GNU scientific library, MATLAB, Octave, scipy, gnuplot, SAS, Maple, Mathematica, STATLIB, and a plethora of others.

---

[1] The *Numerical Recipes* source code is copyrighted and will not be used, as we prefer to provide complete working examples.

Nelder-Mead Method

The Nelder-Mead method is a commonly used *direct search* nonlinear optimization technique (Nelder & Mead, 1965). The algorithm performs a search using a *simplex*, which is a generalized triangle in N dimensions. The method evaluates a user-provided function at each of the vertices and then iteratively shrinks the simplex as better points are found. The method terminates when a desired bound or other termination condition is reached.

With some limitations (McKinnon & McKinnon, 1999; Kolda, Lewis, & Torczon, 2007), the Nelder-Mead method has proven to be effective over time plus it is computationally compact. The original FORTRAN implementation was made available through STATLIB. John Burkhardt created a clean C-language implementation that he made freely available on his website.[2] The C++ template adaption of his code at the end of this chapter allows easy comparison of both single- and double-precision host and GPU performance.

Levenberg-Marquardt Method

The Levenberg-Marquardt algorithm (LMA) is a popular *trust region* algorithm that is used to find a minimum of a function (either linear or nonlinear) over a space of parameters. Essentially, a trusted region of the objective function is internally modeled with some function such as a quadratic. When an adequate fit is found, the trust region is expanded. As with many numerical techniques, the Levenberg-Marquardt method can be sensitive to the initial starting parameters. An excellent technical overview on the Levenberg-Marquardt with references is on the levmar website.[3] Another excellent resource is *Numerical Recipes*.

In traditional Levenberg-Marquardt implementations, *finite differences* are used to approximate the *Jacobian*. The Jacobian is a matrix of all first-order partial derivatives of the function being optimized. This matrix is convenient, as the user need only supply a single function to the library.

The original FORTRAN public domain MINPACK routine lmdif has proven to be a reliable piece of software over the decades—so much so that a variety of implementations has been created in many computer languages. Two excellent C/C++ implementations are levmar and lmfit.

For comparison purposes, the levmar library has been used in the examples because it provides both single- and double-precision routines. The reader will have to download and install the levmar package to run those examples. The levmar website provides installation instructions for both Microsoft and UNIX-based systems.

---

[2] http://people.sc.fsu.edu/~jburkardt/cpp_src/asa047/asa047.html.
[3] http://www.ics.forth.gr/~lourakis/levmar/index.html#download.

To support both single- and double-precision performance testing, wrappers were created that utilize C++ *polymorphism* to make the appropriate library call depending on type of the parameters passed to the wrapper. These wrappers also provide the necessary interface to pass an objective function to the levmar library, which expects a pointer to a function. See Example 2.1, "Using a Wrapper to Account for Variable Type."

Example 2.1

```
//wrapper around the levmar single- and double-precision calls
inline int levmar_dif( void (*func)(float *, float *, int, int, void *),
                float *p, float *x, int m, int n, int itmax,
                float *opts, float *info, float *work,
                float *covar, void* data)
{
  return slevmar_dif(func, p, x, m, n, itmax, opts, info, work,
                covar, data);
}
inline int levmar_dif( void (*func)(double *, double *, int, int, void *),
                double *p, double *x, int m, int n, int itmax,
                double *opts, double *info, double *work,
                double *covar, void* data)
{
  return dlevmar_dif(func, p, x, m, n, itmax, opts, info, work,
                covar, data);
}
```

Algorithmic Speedups

For the purposes of this book, only the evaluation of the objective function will be discussed. The reader should note that approximating the gradient numerically can impose a time to solution penalty.

Many optimization techniques, such as conjugate gradient, can greatly accelerate the process of finding a minimum by using a function, **dfunc()**, that calculates the derivative of the objective function. Saunders, Simon, and Yip pointed out that conjugate gradient is guaranteed to terminate after a finite number of steps (in exact arithmetic), that some measure of the error is decreased at every step of the method, and that the computational requirements for each step are constant (Saunders, Simon, & Yip, 1988). In practice, accumulated floating-point roundoff errors cause a gradual loss of accuracy, which affects the convergence rate. Even so, conjugate gradient is widely used for problems that are out of reach of exact algorithms.

Many symbolic differentiation tools exist to help the programmer write or automatically generate derivatives using symbolic math. One example is

GiNaC (GiNaC stands for GiNaC is Not a CAS, where CAS stands for Computer Algebra System). GiNaC is a freely downloadable C++ library that programmers can use to incorporate symbolic math into their applications. Unlike other symbolic mathematical packages, GiNaC takes C++ as input. The programmer can then use the algebraic capabilities of the library to perform useful tasks such as symbolic differentiation. The GiNaC website (http://www.gniac.de) claims it was designed to be a drop-in replacement for the symbolic math engine that powers the popular Maple CAS. Other packages include Maple and Mathematica.

MACHINE LEARNING AND NEURAL NETWORKS

Artificial Neural Networks (ANN) is a machine-learning technique that infers a function (a form of parameterized model) based on observed data. *Supervised learning* occurs when a teacher associates known values that reflect a desired or known outcome with each training example. *Unsupervised learning* occurs when a metric of goodness or fit is provided.

Functions inferred by neural networks have predictive power, meaning they can correctly forecast future values in a time series, respond and adapt to complex and unforeseen stimuli, and perform classification tasks. A famous early example is nettalk, which trained a neural network to read English text aloud (Sejnowski & Rosenberg, 1987). The nettalk data is still available for download.[4]

Training artificial neural networks can be expressed as a function optimization problem that seeks to determine the best network parameters (e.g., the internal network weights and biases) that will minimize the error on an initial data set. The fitting or training process is computationally expensive, as it requires repeatedly calling an objective function with sets of parameters that are evaluated over every example in the training data. The runtime is $O(N_{param} \times N_{data})$ for each objective function evaluation. In most cases, the number of parameters is small relative to the size of the training data, which means the overall runtime is dominated by the size of the data set.

During the training process, the neural net is attempting to fit a multidimensional surface to the training data (Lapedes & Farber, 1987a). Unfortunately, *the curse of dimensionality* tells us that the volume of space that must be searched, sampled, and modeled increases exponentially with the dimension of the data. For example, uniformly sampling a 1D unit interval between 0 and 1 at steps of 0.01 requires 100 samples, and sampling a 10-dimensional unit hypercube would require $(100)^{10}$ or 10^{20} samples.[5] Even with sparse sampling,

---

[4] http://archive.ics.uci.edu/ml/datasets/Connectionist+Bench+(Nettalk+Corpus).
[5] This example was adapted from the Wikipedia.org "Curse of Dimensionality" example. http://en.wikipedia.org/wiki/Curse_of_dimensionality)

smooth high-dimensional surfaces can require many data points. Many interesting phenomena require fitting convoluted, bumpy, high-dimensional surfaces, which can dramatically increase the amount of training data needed to fit a model that can approximate the multidimensional surface with acceptable accuracy.

Expensive objective functions tend to dominate the runtime when using popular optimization techniques like Nelder-Mead, Levenberg-Marquardt, Powell's method, conjugate gradient, and others. Under these circumstances, it is best to focus on reducing the runtime of the objective function. Mapping the problem efficiently to a GPGPU with hundreds of parallel threads can potentially reduce the runtime by two orders of magnitude over a single-threaded system, as shown by Equation 2.2, "Parallel runtime of an ANN-based objective function." Conversely, a quad-core processor can reduce the runtime only by a factor of 4 at best over a serial implementation.

$$O\left(\frac{N_{data} * N_{param}}{N_{processors}}\right) \qquad (2.2)$$

The examples in this chapter demonstrate that CUDA can reduce the runtime by 50 to 100 times over an implementation that runs on a conventional mult-core processor even when taking into account all of the GPU communications overhead. Although this is a known result for parallel systems in general (Farber, 1992; Thearling, 1995), it is amazing that this level of performance can be achieved even using a gaming GPU.

XOR: AN IMPORTANT NONLINEAR MACHINE-LEARNING PROBLEM

Andreas Weigend noted in *Introduction to the Theory of Neural Computation*:

> To contrast "learning" without generalization from learning with generalization, let us consider the widely and wildly celebrated fact that neural networks can learn to implement exclusive OR (XOR). But—what kind of learning is this? When four out of four cases are specified, no generalization exists! Learning a truth table is nothing but rote memorization: learning XOR is as interesting as memorizing the phone book. More interesting—and more realistic—are real-world problems, such as the prediction of financial data. In forecasting, nobody cares how well a model fits the training data—only the quality of future predictions counts, i.e., the performance on novel data or the generalization ability. Learning means extracting regularities from training examples that transfer to new examples. (Hertz, Krogh, & Palmer, 1991, p. 5)

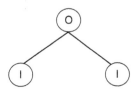

FIGURE 2.1

An example of a perceptron.

In 1969, a famous book entitled *Perceptrons* (Minsky & Papert, 1969) showed that it was not possible for a single-layer network, at that time called a *perceptron* (Figure 2.1), to represent the fundamental XOR logical function. The impact was devastating, as funding and interest in the nascent field of neural networks evaporated.

More the ten years passed until neural network research suddenly experienced a resurgence of interest. In the mid-1980s, a paper demonstrated that neural models could solve the Traveling Salesman Problem (Hopfield & Tank, 1985). Shortly thereafter, the backpropagation algorithm was created (Rummelhardt, Hinton, & Williams, 1986; Rummelhart, McClelland, & the PDP Research Group, 1987). A key demonstration showed it was possible to train a multilevel ANN to replicate an XOR truth table. In the following years, the field of neural network research and other related machine-learning fields exploded.

The importance of being able to learn and simulate the XOR truth table lies in understanding the concept of a *computationally universal* device. Universal Turing machines are an example of a computationally universal device (Hopcroft & Ullman, 2006) because they can, in theory, be used to simulate any other computational device.

Distinguishing ANN from perceptrons, Andreas Weigend observes:

> The computational power drastically increases when an intermediate layer of nonlinear units is inserted between inputs and outputs. The example of XOR nicely emphasizes the importance of such hidden units: they re-represent the input such that the problem becomes linearly separable. Networks without hidden units cannot learn to memorize XOR, whereas networks with hidden units can implement any Boolean function. (Hertz, Krogh, & Palmer, 1991, p. 6)

In other words, the ability to simulate XOR is essential to making the argument that multilayer ANNs are universal computational devices and perceptrons without any hidden neurons are limited computational devices. It is the extra nonlinear hidden layers that give ANNs the ability to simulate

FIGURE 2.2

An XOR network.

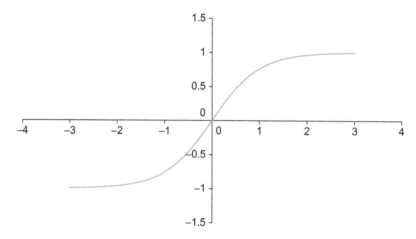

FIGURE 2.3

An example sigmoidal G function: tanh(x).

other computational devices. In fact, only two layers are required to perform modeling and prediction tasks as well as symbolic learning (Lapedes & Farber, 1987a). However, clever human-aided design can create smaller networks that utilize fewer parameters, albeit with more than two hidden layers (Farber et al., 1993). Figure 2.2 shows an XOR neural network with one hidden neuron that implements a sigmoid as shown in Figure 2.3.

An Example Objective Function

The **thrust::transform_reduce** template makes the implementation of an objective function both straight-forward and easy. For example, an ANN least means squares objective function requires the definition of a transform operator that calculates the square of the error that the network makes on each example in the training data. A reduction operation then calculates the sum of the squared errors.

Thrust utilizes *functors* to perform the work of the transform and reduction operations as well as other generic methods. In C++, a functor overloads the function call operator "()" so that an object may be used in place of an ordinary function. This has several important implications:

1. Functors can be passed to generic algorithms like **thrust::transform_reduce** much like C-language programmers utilize pointers to functions.
2. Passing and using functors is efficient, as C++ can inline the functor code. This eliminates function call overhead and allows the compiler to perform more extensive optimizations.
3. C++ functors can maintain a persistent internal state. As you will see, this approach can be very useful when working with different device, GPU, and thread memory spaces.

Inlining of functors is essential to performance because common functors such as **thrust::plus** only perform tiny amounts of computation. Without the ability to inline functors, generic methods like **thrust::transform_reduce** would not be possible because function call overhead would consume nearly as much (or more) time than the functor itself.

The Thrust documentation speaks of *kernel fusion*, which combines multiple functors into a single kernel. Per our second rule of GPGPU coding, kernel fusion increases GPGPU utilization per kernel invocation, which can avoid kernel startup latencies. Just as important, many generic methods like the **thrust::transform_reduce** template avoid performance robbing storage of intermediate values to memory as the functor calculations are performed on the fly. The latter point meets the requirements of our third rule of GPGPU programming: focus on data reuse within the GPGPU to avoid memory bandwidth limitations. The SAXPY example in the thrust Quick Start guide provides a clear and lucid demonstration of the performance benefits of kernel fusion.

A Complete Functor for Multiple GPU Devices and the Host Processors

The following example, Example 2.2, "An XOR functor for CalcError.h," is a complete XOR functor. The section in bold shows the simplicity to code to calculate the XOR neural network illustrated in Figure 2.2 plus error for each example in the training set.

Example 2.2

```
// The CalcError functor for XOR
static const int nInput = 2;
static const int nH1 = 1;
```

```
static const int nOutput = 1;
static const int nParam =
  (nOutput+nH1) // Neuron Offsets
  + (nInput*nH1) // connections from I to H1
  + (nH1*nOutput) // connections from H1 to O
  + (nInput*nOutput); // connections from I to O
static const int exLen = nInput + nOutput;

struct CalcError {
  const Real* examples;
  const Real* p;
  const int nInput;
  const int exLen;

CalcError( const Real* _examples, const Real* _p,
           const int _nInput, const int _exLen)
: examples(_examples), p(_p), nInput(_nInput), exLen(_exLen) {};

  __device__ __host__
  Real operator()(unsigned int tid)
  {
    const register Real* in = &examples[tid * exLen];
    register int index=0;
    register Real h1 = p[index++];
    register Real o = p[index++];

    h1 += in[0] * p[index++];
    h1 += in[1] * p[index++];
    h1 = G(h1);

    o += in[0] * p[index++];
    o += in[1] * p[index++];
    o += h1 * p[index++];

    // calculate the square of the diffs
    o -= in[nInput];
    return o * o;
  }
};
```

The nonlinear transfer function, **G**, in the previous example utilizes a hyperbolic **tanh** to define a sigmoid as illustrated in Figure 2.3. Other popular sigmoidal functions include the logistic function, piece-wise linear, and many others. It is easy to change the definition of **G** to experiment with these other functions.

It is important to note that two CUDA function qualifiers, __**device**__ and __**host**__, highlighted in the previous code snippet, specify a functor that can run on both the host processor and one or more GPU devices. This dual use of the functor makes it convenient to create hybrid CPU/GPU applications that can run on all the available computing resources in a system. It also makes performance comparisons between GPU- and host-based implementations easier.

This functor also uses persistence to encapsulate the data on the device, which ties the data to the calculation and allows work to be distributed across multiple devices and types of devices. Of course, the pointers to the vectors used by the functor should also reside on the device running the functor or undesired memory transfers will be required. CUDA 4.0 provides a unified virtual address space that allows the runtime to identify the device that contains a region of memory solely from the memory pointer. Data can then be directly transferred among devices. While the direct transfer is efficient, it still imposes PCIe bandwidth limitations.

Brief Discussion of a Complete Nelder-Mead Optimization Code

The following discussion will walk through a complete Nelder-Mead thrust API GPU example that provies single- and double-precision object instantiation, data generation, runtime configuration of the Nelder-Mead method, and a test function to verify that the network trained correctly. If desired, the code snippets in this section can be combined to create a complete *xorNM.cu* source file. Alternatively, a complete version of this example can be downloaded from the book's website.[6]

The objective function calculates the energy. In this example, the energy is the sum of the square of the errors made by the model for a given set of parameters as shown in Equation 2.3.

$$\text{energy} = \text{objfunc}(p_1, p_2, \dots p_n) \tag{2.3}$$

An optimization method is utilized to fit the parameters to the data with minimal error. In this example, the Nelder-Mead method is utilized, but many other numerical techniques can be used, such as Powell's method. If the derivative of the objective function can be coded, more efficient numerical algorithms such as conjugate gradient can be used to speed the minimization process. Some of these algorithms can, in the ideal case, reduce the runtime by a factor equal to the number of parameters.

---

[6] http://booksite.mkp.com/9780123884268

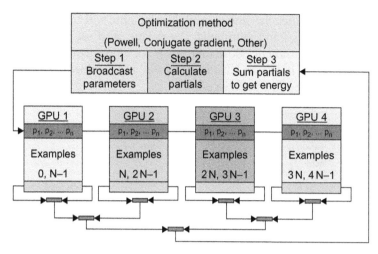

FIGURE 2.4
Optimization mapping.

The calculation performs three steps as illustrated in Figure 2.4. For generality, multiple GPUs are shown, although the example in this chapter will work on only one GPU:

1. Broadcast the parameters from the host to the GPU(s).
2. Evaluate the objective function on the GPU. If the run utilizes multiple GPUs, then each GPU calculates a partial sum of the errors. The data set is initially partitioned across all the GPUs, where the number of examples per GPU can be used to load-balance across devices with different performance characteristics.
3. The sum (or sum of the partial sums in the multi-GPU case) is calculated via a reduce operation. In this case, **thrust::transform_reduce** is used to sum the errors in one operation.

The following example source code uses preprocessor conditional statements to specify the type of machine and precision of the run, which can be specified via the command line at compile time. Though conditional compilation does complicate the source code and interfere with code readability, it is a fact of life in real applications, as it facilitates code reuse and supporting multiple machine types. For this reason, conditional compilation is utilized in this book.

The following conditionals are utilized in Example 2.3, "Part 1 of xorNM.cu":

- **USE_HOST**: Selects the code that will run the objective function on the host processor. The default is to run on the GPU.

- **USE_DBL**: Specifies that the compiled executable will use double-precision variables and arithmetic. The default is to use single-precision variables and arithmetic. Note that this is for convenience because C++ templates make it easy to have both single- and double-precision tests compiled by the same source code.

Example 2.3

```
#include <iostream>
#include <iomanip>
#include <cmath>

#include <thrust/host_vector.h>
#include <thrust/device_vector.h>
#include <thrust/copy.h>

// define USE_HOST for a host-based version
// define USE_DBL for double precision
using namespace std;

#include "nelmin.h"
```

C++ polymorphism is used to make the appropriate single- and double-precision call to **tanh()**. See Example 2.4, "Part 2 of xorNM.cu":

Example 2.4

```
// Define the sigmoidal function
__device__ __host__
inline float G(float x) {return(tanhf(x)) ;}
__device__ __host__
inline double G(double x) {return(tanh(x));}
```

For convenience, a simple class, **ObjFunc**, was defined to combine the functor with some simple data management methods.[7] C++ templates are utilized in the example code, so the performance of the functor and overall application using single- or double-precision floating point can be evaluated. The **CalcError** functor defined previously is included after the comment. This use of a C-preprocessor include is not recommended for production applications. For training purposes, the functor was purposely isolated to make it easy to modify by the reader.

Notice in this code section that **CalcError** is called directly in an OpenMP reduction loop when running on the host processor when **USE_HOST** is

---

[7] C++ objects encapsulate both data and methods that operate on the data into a single convenient package.

defined, which demonstrates the ability of Thrust to generate code for both GPU- and host-based functors. See Example 2.5, "Part 3 of xorNM.cu":

Example 2.5

```
// This is a convenience class to hold all the examples and
// architecture information. Most is boilerplate. CalcError
// is where all the work happens.
template<typename Real>
class ObjFunc {
  private:
    double objFuncCallTime;
    unsigned int objFuncCallCount;
  protected:
    int nExamples;
#ifdef USE_HOST
    thrust::host_vector<Real> h_data;
#else
    thrust::device_vector<Real> d_data;
#endif
    thrust::device_vector<Real> d_param;

  public:
    // The CalcError functor goes here
#include "CalcError.h"

    // Boilerplate constructor and helper classes
    ObjFunc() {nExamples = 0; objFuncCallCount=0; objFuncCallTime=0.;}

    double aveObjFuncWallTime() {return(objFuncCallTime/
    objFuncCallCount);}
    double totalObjFuncWallTime() {return(objFuncCallTime);}
    int get_nExamples() {return(nExamples);}

    void setExamples(thrust::host_vector<Real>& _h_data) {
#ifdef USE_HOST
      h_data = _h_data;
#else
      d_data = _h_data;
#endif
      nExamples = _h_data.size()/exLen;
      d_param = thrust::device_vector<Real>(nParam);
    }

#ifdef USE_HOST
    Real objFunc(Real *p) {
      if(nExamples == 0) {cerr << "data not set" << endl; exit(1);}

      double startTime=omp_get_wtime();
```

```
      Real sum = 0.;
      CalcError getError(&h_data[0], p, nInput, exLen);
#pragma omp parallel for reduction(+ : sum)
      for(int i=0; i < nExamples; ++i) {
        Real d = getError(i);
        sum += d;
      }

      objFuncCallTime += (omp_get_wtime() - startTime);
      objFuncCallCount++;
      return(sum);
   }
#else
    Real objFunc(Real *p)
    {
      if(nExamples == 0)  {cerr << "data not set" <<  endl; exit(1);}

      double startTime=omp_get_wtime();

      thrust::copy(p, p+nParam, d_param.begin());

      CalcError getError(thrust::raw_pointer_cast(&d_data[0]),
                    thrust::raw_pointer_cast(&d_param[0]),
                    nInput, exLen);
      Real sum = thrust::transform_reduce(
                    thrust::counting_iterator<unsigned int>(0),
                    thrust::counting_iterator<unsigned int>
                    (nExamples),
                    getError,
                    (Real) 0.,
                    thrust::plus<Real>());
      objFuncCallTime += (omp_get_wtime() - startTime);
      objFuncCallCount++;
      return(sum);
    }
 #endif
 };
```

The call to the objective function must be wrapped to return the appropriate type (e.g., **float** or **double**) as seen in Example 2.6, "Part 4 of xorNM.cu." C++ *polymorphism* selects the appropriate method depending on type of the parameters passed to the wrapper.

Example 2.6

```
// Wrapper so the objective function can be called
// as a pointer to function for C-style libraries.
// Note: polymorphism allows easy use of
```

```
// either float or double types.
void* objFunc_object=NULL;
float func(float* param)
{
  if(objFunc_object)
    return ((ObjFunc<float>*) objFunc_object)->objFunc(param);
  return(0.);
}
double func(double* param)
{
  if(objFunc_object)
    return ((ObjFunc<double>*) objFunc_object)->objFunc(param);
  return(0.);
}

// get a uniform random number between −1 and 1
inline float f_rand() {
  return 2.*(rand()/((float)RAND_MAX)) −1.;
}
```

A test function is defined to calculate the output of the function based on a set of input values. See Example 2.7, "Part 5 of xorNM.cu":

Example 2.7

```
template <typename Real, int nInput>
void testNN(const Real *p, const Real *in, Real *out)
{
  int index=0;
  Real h1 = p[index++];
  Real o = p[index++];

  h1 += in[0] * p[index++];
  h1 += in[1] * p[index++];
  h1 = G(h1);

  o += in[0] * p[index++];
  o += in[1] * p[index++];
  o += h1 * p[index++];

  out[0]=o;
}
```

For simplicity, the XOR truth table is duplicated to verify that the code works with large data sets and to provide the basis for a reasonable performance comparison between the GPGPU and host processor(s). As shown in the Example 2.8, a small amount of uniformly distributed noise with a variance of 0.01 has been added to each training example as most training data sets are noisy.

By simply defining an alternative functor and data generator, this same code framework will be adapted in Chapter 3 to solve other optimization problems. See Example 2.8, "Part 6 of xorNM.cu":

Example 2.8

```
template <typename Real>
void genData(thrust::host_vector<Real> &h_data, int nVec, Real xVar)
{
  // Initialize the data via replication of the XOR truth table
  Real dat[] = {
    0.1, 0.1, 0.1,
    0.1, 0.9, 0.9,
    0.9, 0.1, 0.9,
    0.9, 0.9, 0.1};

  for(int i=0; i < nVec; i++)
    for(int j=0; j < 12; j++) h_data.push_back(dat[j] + xVar * f_rand());
}
```

The **testTraining()** method defined in Example 2.9, "Part 7 of xorNM.cu," sets up the Nelder-Mead optimization and calls the test function to verify the results:

Example 2.9

```
template <typename Real>
void testTraining()
{
  ObjFunc<Real> testObj;
  const int nParam = testObj.nParam;
  cout << "nParam" << nParam << endl;

  // generate the test data
  const int nVec=1000 * 1000 * 10;
  thrust::host_vector<Real> h_data;
  genData<Real>(h_data, nVec, 0.01);
  testObj.setExamples(h_data);
  int nExamples = testObj.get_nExamples();
  cout << "GB data" << (h_data.size()*sizeof(Real)/1e9) << endl;

  // set the Nelder-Mead starting conditions
  int icount, ifault, numres;
  vector<Real> start(nParam);
  vector<Real> step(nParam,1.);
  vector<Real> xmin(nParam);

  srand(0);
  for(int i=0; i < start.size(); i++) start[i] = 0.2 * f_rand();
```

```
Real ynewlo = testObj.objFunc(&start[0]);
Real reqmin = 1.0E-18;
int konvge = 10;
int kcount = 5000;

objFunc_object = &testObj;
double optStartTime=omp_get_wtime();
nelmin<Real> (func, nParam, &start[0], &xmin[0], &ynewlo, reqmin,
              &step[0], konvge, kcount, &icount, &numres, &ifault);
double optTime=omp_get_wtime()-optStartTime;

cout << endl <<"  Return code IFAULT = " << ifault << endl << endl;
cout << "  Estimate of minimizing value X*:" << endl << endl;
cout << "  F(X*) = " << ynewlo << endl;
cout << "  Number of iterations = " << icount << endl;
cout << "  Number of restarts =    " << numres << endl << endl;

cout << "Average wall time for ObjFunc"
     << testObj.aveObjFuncWallTime() << endl;
cout << "Total wall time in optimization method" << optTime << endl;
cout << "Percent time in objective function" <<
  (100.*(testObj.totalObjFuncWallTime()/optTime)) << endl;

int index=0, nTest=4;
cout << "pred known" << endl;
thrust::host_vector<Real> h_test;
thrust::host_vector<Real> h_in(testObj.nInput);
thrust::host_vector<Real> h_out(testObj.nOutput);
genData<Real>(h_test, nTest, 0.0); // note: no variance for the test
for(int i=0; i< nTest; i++) {
  h_in[0] = h_test[index++];
  h_in[1] = h_test[index++];

  testNN<Real,2>(&xmin[0],&h_in[0],&h_out[0]);
  cout << setprecision(1) << setw(4)
       << h_out[0] << " "
       << h_test[index] << endl;
  index++;
  }
}
```

The call to **main()** is very simple; see Example 2.10, "Part 8 of xorNM.cu":

Example 2.10

```
int main ()
{
#ifdef USE_DBL
  testTraining<double> ();
```

```
#else
  testTraining<float> ();
#endif
  return 0;
}
```

Before building, put the Nelder-Mead template from the end of this chapter into the file *nelmin.h* in the same directory as the *xorNM.cu* source code. Also ensure that *CalcError.h* is in the same directory.

Building all variants of *xorNM.cu* is straightforward. The option **-use_fast_math** tells the compiler to use native GPU functions such as **exp()** that are fast but might not be as accurate as the software routines. Make certain that the file *nelmin.h* is in the same directory.

Under Linux type the code in Example 2.11, "Compiling xorNM.cu under Linux":

Example 2.11

```
# single-precision GPU test
nvcc -O3 -Xcompiler -fopenmp -use_fast_math xorNM.cu -o xorNM_GPU32
# single-precision HOST test
nvcc -D USE_HOST -O3 -Xcompiler -fopenmp xorNM.cu -o xorNM_CPU32

# double-precision HOST test
nvcc -D USE_DBL -O3 -Xcompiler -fopenmp -use_fast_math xorNM.cu -o
xorNM_GPU64
# double-precision HOST test
nvcc -D USE_DBL -D USE_HOST -O3 -Xcompiler -fopenmp xorNM.cu -o
xorNM_CPU64
```

Windows- and MacOS-based computers can utilize similar commands once **nvcc** is installed and the build environment is correctly configured. It is also straightforward to compile this example with Microsoft Visual Studio. Please utilize one of the many tutorials available on the Internet to import and compile CUDA applications using the Visual Studio GUI (graphical user interface).

Example 2.12, "Compiling xorNM.cu under cygwin," is an example command to build a single-precision version of *xorNM.cu* for a 20-series GPU under cygwin:

Example 2.12

```
nvcc -arch=sm_20 -Xcompiler "/openmp /O2" -use_fast_math xorNM.cu -o
xor_gpu32.exe
```

Running the program shows that an ANN network is indeed trained to solve the XOR problem as illustrated by the golden test results highlighted in Example 2.13, "Example Output," which shows that the XOR truth table is correctly predicted using the optimized parameters:

Example 2.13

```
sizeof(Real) 4
Gigabytes in training vector 0.48

  Return code IFAULT = 2

  Estimate of minimizing value X*:

  F(X*) = 4.55191e-08
  Number of iterations = 5001
  Number of restarts =   0

Average wall time for ObjFunc 0.00583164
Total wall time in optimization method 29.5887
Percent time in objective function 98.5844
  -- XOR Golden test --
pred known
  0.1 0.1
  0.9 0.9
  0.9 0.9
  0.1 0.1
```

PERFORMANCE RESULTS ON XOR

Table 2.1 provides a sorted list of the average time to calculate the XOR objective function under a variety of precision, optimization technique, and operating system configurations. Performance was measured using a 2.53 GHz quad-core Xeon e5630 and an NVIDIA C2070 (with ECC turned off. ECC, or Error Checking and Correcting memory, means that the memory subsystem check for memory errors, which can slow performance.). The performance of an inexpensive GeForce GTX280 gaming GPU performing single-precision Nelder-Mead optimization is also shown in the table.

PERFORMANCE DISCUSSION

The average times to calculate the XOR objective function reported in Table 2.1 are based on *wall clock time* collected with a call to the OpenMP **omp_get_wtime()** method. Wall clock time is an unreliable performance measuring tool, as any other process running on the host can affect the

Table 2.1 Observed Timings when Training an XOR Neural Network

OS	Machine	Opt Method	Precision	Average Obj Func Time	% Func Time	Speedup over Quad-Core	Speedup over Single-Core
Linux	NVIDIA C2070	Nelder-Mead	32	0.00532	100.0	85	341
Win7	NVIDIA C2070	Nelder-Mead	32	0.00566	100.0	81	323
Linux	NVIDIA GTX280	Nelder-Mead	32	0.01109	99.2	41	163
Linux	NVIDIA C2070	Nelder-Mead	64	0.01364	100.0	40	158
Win7	NVIDIA C2070	Nelder-Mead	64	0.01612	100.0	22	87
Linux	NVIDIA C2070	Levenberg-Marquardt	32	0.04313	2.7	10	38
Linux	NVIDIA C2070	Levenberg-Marquardt	64	0.08480	4.4	6	23
Linux	Intel e5630	Levenberg-Marquardt	32	0.41512	21.1		
Linux	Intel e5630	Levenberg-Marquardt	64	0.49745	20.8		
Linux	Intel e5630	Nelder-Mead	32	0.45312	100.0		
Linux	Intel e5630	Nelder-Mead	64	0.53872	100.0		

accuracy of the timing.[8] Chapter 3 discusses more advanced CUDA performance analysis tools such as the NVIDIA visual profiler for Linux and Parallel Nsight for Windows.

All tests ran on an idle system to attain the most accurate results. Reported speedups are based on the average wall clock time consumed during the calculation of the objective function, including all host and GPU data transfers required by the objective function. OpenMP was used to multithread the host-only tests to utilize all four cores of the Xeon processor.

As Table 2.1 shows, the best performance was achieved under Linux when running a single-precision test on an NVIDIA C2070 GPGPU. Improvements in the 20-series Fermi architecture have increased double-precision performance within a factor of 2 of single-precision performance, which is significantly better than the previous generations of NVIDIA GPGPUs. Still, these older GPUs are quite powerful, as demonstrated by the 41-times-faster single-precision performance of an NVIDIA 10-series GeForce GTX280 gaming GPU over all four

---

[8] It is worth noting that even tiny delays incurred by other processes briefly starting and stopping can introduce significant performance degradation in large programs running at scale, as discussed in the paper "The Case of the Missing Supercomputer Performance" (Petrini, Kerbyson, & Pakin, 2003). Cloud-based computing environments—especially those that utilize virtual machines—are especially sensitive to jitter.

cores of a quad-core Xeon processor. This same midlevel gaming GPU also delivers roughly half the single-precision performance of the C2070.

The Levenberg-Marquardt results are interesting because the order of magnitude performance decrease compared to the Nelder-Mead results highlights the cost of transferring the measurement vector from the GPU to the host, as well as the performance of host-based computations needed by Levenberg-Marquardt.

This particular partitioning of a Levenberg-Marquardt optimization problem requires a large data transfer. The size of the transfer scales with the size of the data and thus introduces a scaling barrier that can make it too expensive for larger problems and multi-GPU data sets. Still, the Levenberg-Marquardt is a valid technique for GPU computing, as it can find good minima when other techniques fail. Counterintuitively, it can also run faster because it may find a minimum with just a few function calls.

In contrast, Nelder-Mead does not impose a scalability limitation, as it requires only that the GPU return a single floating-point value. Other optimization techniques such as Powell's method and conjugate gradient share this desirable characteristic.

Using alternative optimization methods such as Powell's method and conjugate gradient, variants of this example code have been shown to scale to more than 500 GPGPUs on the TACC Longhorn GPGPU cluster and to tens of thousands of processors on both the TACC Ranger and Thinking Machines supercomputers (Farber, 1992; Thearling, 1995). Figure 2.5 shows the minimum and maximum speedup observed when running on 500 GPUs. It is believed that the network connecting the distributed nodes on the Longhorn

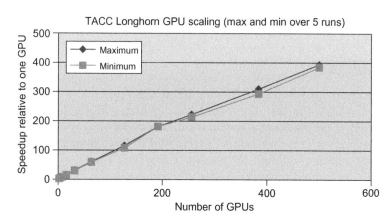

FIGURE 2.5

Scaling results to 500 GPUs.

GPU cluster is responsible for the variation. The benchmark was run on an idle system. More about multi-GPU applications will be discussed in Chapter 7 and the application Chapters 9–12 at the end of this book.

The advantage of the generic approach utilized by many numerical libraries is that by simply defining a new function of interest an application programmer can use the library to solve many problems. For example, the source code in this chapter will be modified in Chapter 3 to use a different functor that will perform a PCA (Principle Components Analysis). PCA along with the nonlinear variant NLPCA (Nonlinear Principle Components Analysis) has wide applicability in vision research and handwriting analysis (Hinton & Salakhutdinov, 2006)[9] as well as biological modeling (Scholz, 2011), financial modeling, Internet search, and many other commercial and academic fields.

Other powerful machine-learning techniques such as Hidden Markov Models (HMM), genetic algorithms, Bayesian networks, and many others parallelize very well on GPGPU hardware. As with neural networks, each has various strengths and weaknesses. By redefining the objective function, this same example code can implement other popular techniques such as:

- Optimization
- Locally weighted linear regression (LWLR)
- Naive Bayes (NB)
- Gaussian Discriminative Analysis (GDA)
- K-means
- Logistic regression (LR)
- Independent component analysis (ICA)
- Expectation maximization (EM)
- Support vector machine (SVM)
- Others, such as multidimension scaling (MDS), ordinal MDS, and other variants

SUMMARY

GPGPUs today possess a peak floating-point capability that was beyond the machines available in even the most advanced high-performance computing (HPC) centers until a Sandia National Laboratory supercomputer performed a trillion floating-point operations per second in December 1996. Many of those proposals for leading-edge research using such a teraflop supercomputer can be performed today by students anywhere in the world using a few GPGPUs in a workstation combined with a fast RAID (Redundant Array of Independent Disks) disk subsystem.

---

[9] Available online at http://www.cs.toronto.edu/~hinton/science.pdf.

The techniques and examples discussed in this chapter can be applied to a multitude of data fitting, data analysis, dimension reduction, vision, and classification problems. Conveniently, they are able to scale from laptops to efficiently utilize the largest supercomputers in the world.

CUDA-literate programmers can bring this new world of computational power to legacy projects. Along with faster application speeds, GPGPU technology can advance the state of the art by allowing more accurate approximations and computational techniques to be utilized and ultimately to create more accurate models.

Competition is fierce in both commercial and academic circles, which is why GPU computing is making such a huge impact on both commercial products and scientific research. The competition is global; this hardware is accessible to anyone in the world who wishes to compete, as opposed to the past where competition was restricted to a relatively small community of individuals with access to big, parallel machines.

THE C++ NELDER-MEAD TEMPLATE

```
#ifndef NELMIN_H
#define NELMIN_H

// Nelder-Mead Minimization Algorithm ASA047
// from the Applied Statistics Algorithms available
// in STATLIB. Adapted from the C version by J. Burkhardt
// http://people.sc.fsu.edu/~jburkardt/c_src/asa047/asa047.html

template <typename Real>
void nelmin ( Real (*fn)(Real*), int n, Real start[], Real xmin[],
             Real *ynewlo, Real reqmin, Real step[], int konvge,
             int kcount, int *icount, int *numres, int *ifault )
{
  const Real ccoeff = 0.5;
  const Real ecoeff = 2.0;
  const Real eps = 0.001;
  const Real rcoeff = 1.0;
  int ihi,ilo,jcount,l,nn;
  Real del,dn,dnn;
  Real rq,x,y2star,ylo,ystar,z;

  //  Check the input parameters.
  if ( reqmin <= 0.0 ) { *ifault = 1; return; }
  if ( n < 1 ) { *ifault = 1; return; }
  if ( konvge < 1 ) { *ifault = 1; return; }
```

```
vector<Real> p(n*(n+1));
vector<Real> pstar(n);
vector<Real> p2star(n);
vector<Real> pbar(n);
vector<Real> y(n+1);

*icount = 0;
*numres = 0;

jcount = konvge;
dn = ( Real ) ( n );
nn = n + 1;
dnn = ( Real ) ( nn );
del = 1.0;
rq = reqmin * dn;
//  Initial or restarted loop.
for ( ; ; ) {
  for (int i = 0; i < n; i++ ) { p[i+n*n] = start[i]; }
  y[n] = (*fn)( start );
  *icount = *icount + 1;

  for (int j = 0; j < n; j++ ) {
    x = start[j];
    start[j] = start[j] + step[j] * del;
    for (int i = 0; i < n; i++ ) { p[i+j*n] = start[i]; }
    y[j] = (*fn)( start );
    *icount = *icount + 1;
    start[j] = x;
  }
  //  The simplex construction is complete.
  //
  //  Find highest and lowest Y values.   YNEWLO = Y(IHI) indicates
  //   the vertex of the simplex to be replaced.
  ylo = y[0];
  ilo = 0;

  for (int i = 1; i < nn; i++ ) {
    if ( y[i] < ylo ) { ylo = y[i]; ilo = i; }
  }
  //  Inner loop.
  for ( ; ; ) {
    if ( kcount <= *icount ) {break; }
    *ynewlo = y[0];
    ihi = 0;

    for (int i = 1; i < nn; i++ ) {
      if ( *ynewlo < y[i] ) { *ynewlo = y[i]; ihi = i; }
    }
    //  Calculate PBAR, the centroid of the simplex vertices
```

```
//   excepting the vertex with Y value YNEWLO.
for ( int i = 0; i < n; i++ ) {
  z = 0.0;
  for ( int j = 0; j < nn; j++ ) { z = z + p[i+j*n]; }
  z = z - p[i+ihi*n];
  pbar[i] = z / dn;
}
//   Reflection through the centroid.
for ( int i = 0; i < n; i++ ) {
  pstar[i] = pbar[i] + rcoeff * ( pbar[i] - p[i+ihi*n] );
}
ystar = (*fn)( &pstar[0] );
*icount = *icount + 1;
//   Successful reflection, so extension.
if ( ystar < ylo ) {
  for ( int i = 0; i < n; i++ ) {
    p2star[i] = pbar[i] + ecoeff * ( pstar[i] - pbar[i] );
  }
  y2star = (*fn)( &p2star[0] );
  *icount = *icount + 1;
//   Check extension.
  if ( ystar < y2star ) {
    for ( int i = 0; i < n; i++ ) { p[i+ihi*n] = pstar[i]; }
    y[ihi] = ystar;
  } else { //   Retain extension or contraction.
    for ( int i = 0; i < n; i++ ) { p[i+ihi*n] = p2star[i]; }
    y[ihi] = y2star;
  }
} else { //   No extension.
  l = 0;
  for ( int i = 0; i < nn; i++ ) {
    if ( ystar < y[i] ) l += 1;
  }

  if ( 1 < l ) {
    for ( int i = 0; i < n; i++ ) { p[i+ihi*n] = pstar[i]; }
    y[ihi] = ystar;
  }
//   Contraction on the Y(IHI) side of the centroid.
  else if ( l == 0 ) {
    for ( int i = 0; i < n; i++ ) {
      p2star[i] = pbar[i] + ccoeff * ( p[i+ihi*n] - pbar[i] );
    }
    y2star = (*fn)( &p2star[0] );
    *icount = *icount + 1;
//   Contract the whole simplex.
    if ( y[ihi] < y2star ) {
```

```
        for (int j = 0; j < nn; j++ ) {
          for (int i = 0; i < n; i++ ) {
            p[i+j*n] = ( p[i+j*n] + p[i+ilo*n] ) * 0.5;
            xmin[i] = p[i+j*n];
          }
          y[j] = (*fn)( xmin );
          *icount = *icount + 1;
        }
        ylo = y[0];
        ilo = 0;

        for (int i = 1; i < nn; i++ ) {
          if ( y[i] < ylo ) { ylo = y[i]; ilo = i; }
        }
        continue;
      }
    //  Retain contraction.
      else {
        for (int i = 0; i < n; i++ ) {
          p[i+ihi*n] = p2star[i];
        }
        y[ihi] = y2star;
      }
    }
  //  Contraction on the reflection side of the centroid.
    else if ( l == 1 ) {
      for (int i = 0; i < n; i++ ) {
        p2star[i] = pbar[i] + ccoeff * ( pstar[i] - pbar[i] );
      }
      y2star = (*fn)( &p2star[0] );
      *icount = *icount + 1;
    //
    //  Retain reflection?
    //
      if ( y2star <= ystar ) {
        for (int i = 0; i < n; i++ ) { p[i+ihi*n] = p2star[i]; }
        y[ihi] = y2star;
      }
      else {
        for (int i = 0; i < n; i++ ) { p[i+ihi*n] = pstar[i]; }
        y[ihi] = ystar;
      }
    }
  }
  //  Check if YLO improved.
  if ( y[ihi] < ylo ) { ylo = y[ihi]; ilo = ihi; }
  jcount = jcount - 1;
```

```
      if ( 0 < jcount ) { continue; }
      //  Check to see if minimum reached.
      if ( *icount <= kcount ) {
        jcount = konvge;

        z = 0.0;
        for (int i = 0; i < nn; i++ ) { z = z + y[i]; }
        x = z / dnn;

        z = 0.0;
        for (int i = 0; i < nn; i++ ) {
          z = z + pow ( y[i] - x, 2 );
        }

        if ( z <= rq ) {break;}
      }
    }
    //  Factorial tests to check that YNEWLO is a local minimum.
    for (int i = 0; i < n; i++ ) { xmin[i] = p[i+ilo*n]; }
    *ynewlo = y[ilo];

    if ( kcount < *icount ) { *ifault = 2; break; }

    *ifault = 0;

    for (int i = 0; i < n; i++ ) {
      del = step[i] * eps;
      xmin[i] = xmin[i] + del;
      z = (*fn)( xmin );
      *icount = *icount + 1;
      if ( z < *ynewlo ) { *ifault = 2; break; }
      xmin[i] = xmin[i] - del - del;
      z = (*fn)( xmin );
      *icount = *icount + 1;
      if ( z < *ynewlo ) { *ifault = 2; break; }
      xmin[i] = xmin[i] + del;
    }

    if ( *ifault == 0 ) { break; }
    //  Restart the procedure.
    for (int i = 0; i < n; i++ ) { start[i] = xmin[i]; }
    del = eps;
    *numres = *numres + 1;
  }
  return;
}
#endif
```

## CHAPTER 3

The CUDA Tool Suite: Profiling a PCA/NLPCA Functor

CUDA enables efficient GPGPU computing with just a few simple additions to the C language. Simplicity of expression, however, does not equate to simplicity of program execution. As when developing applications for any computer, identifying performance bottlenecks can be complicated. Following the same economy of change used to adapt C and C++, NVIDIA has extended several popular profiling tools to support GPU computing. These are tools that most Windows and UNIX developers are already proficient and comfortable using such as **gprof** and Visual Studio. Additional tools such as hardware-level GPU profiling and a visual profiler have been added. Those familiar with building, debugging, and profiling software under Windows and UNIX should find the transition to CUDA straightforward. All CUDA tools are freely available on the NVIDIA website including the professional edition of Parallel Nsight for Microsoft Visual Studio.

In this chapter, the Microsoft and UNIX profiling tools for CUDA will be used to analyze the performance and scaling of the Nelder-Mead optimization technique when optimizing a PCA and NLPCA functor.

At the end of the chapter, the reader will have a basic understanding of:

- PCA and NPLCA analysis, including the applicability of this technique to data mining, dimension reduction, feature extraction, and other data analysis and pattern recognition problems.
- How the CUDA profiling tools can be used to identify bottlenecks and scaling issues in algorithms.
- Scalability issues and how even a simple dynamic memory allocation can have dramatic performance implications on an application.

PCA AND NLPCA

Principle Components Analysis (PCA) is extensively used in data mining and data analysis to (1) reduce the dimensionality of a data set and (2) extract features from a data set. *Feature extraction* refers to the identification of the salient aspects or properties of data to facilitate its use in a subsequent task, such as regression or classification (Duda & Hart, 1973). Obviously, extracting the principal features of a data set can help with interpretation, analysis, and understanding.

PCA analysis accounts for the maximum amount of variance in a data set using a set of straight lines where each line is defined by a weighted linear combination of the observed variables. The first line, or principle component, accounts for the greatest amount of variance; each succeeding component accounts for as much variance as possible while remaining orthogonal to (uncorrelated with) the preceding components. For example, a cigar-shaped distribution would require a single line (or principal component) to account for most of the variance in the data set illustrated in Figure 3.1.

PCA utilizes straight lines; NLPCA can utilize continuous open or closed curves to account for variance in data (Hsieh, 2004). A circle is one example of a *closed curve* that joins itself so there are no end points. Figure 3.2 illustrates an open curve. As a result, NLPCA has the ability to represent nonlinear problems in a lower dimensional space. Figure 3.2 illustrates one data set in which a single curve could account for most of the variance.

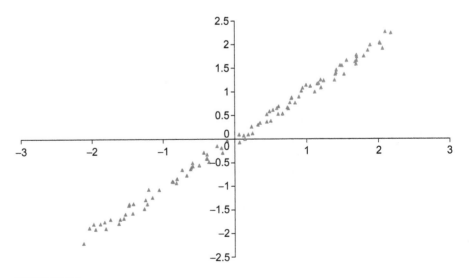

FIGURE 3.1

A linear PCA data set.

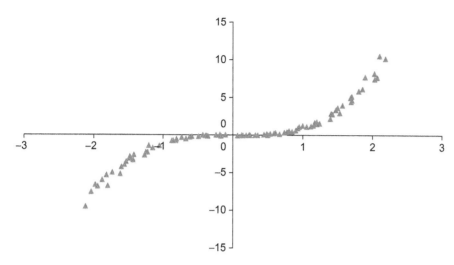

FIGURE 3.2
An NLPCA data set.

NLPCA has wide applicability to numerous challenging problems, including image and handwriting analysis (Hinton & Salakhutdinov, 2006; Schölkopf & Klaus-Robert Müller, 1998) as well as biological modeling (Scholz, 2007), climate (Hsieh, 2001; Monahan, 2000), and chemistry (Kramer, 1991). Geoffrey E. Hinton has an excellent set of tutorials on his website at the University of Toronto (Hinton, 2011). Chapter 10 expands this use of MPI (Message Passing Interface) so that it can run across hundreds of GPUs. Chapter 12 provides a working framework for real-time vision analysis that can be used as a starting point to explore these and more advanced techniques.

Autoencoders

In 1982, Erkki Oja proposed the use of a restricted number of linear hidden neurons, or bottleneck neurons, in a neural network to perform PCA analysis (Oja, 1982). Figure 3.3 illustrates a simple linear network with two inputs and one hidden neuron.

Such networks were later generalized to perform NLPCA. Figure 3.1 illustrates an architecture recommended by Kramer (1991) that uses multiple hidden layers with a sigmoidal nonlinear operator. The bottleneck neuron can be either linear or nonlinear. Hsieh extended this architecture to closed curves by using a circular node at the bottleneck (2001).

During training, the ANN essentially teaches itself because the input vectors are utilized as the known output vectors, which forces the lower half of the network to transform each input vector from a high- to low-dimensional space (from two dimensions to one in Figure 3.4) in such a way that the upper half

FIGURE 3.3
A two-input PCA network.

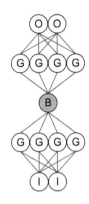

FIGURE 3.4
An NPLCA network with one bottleneck neuron.

of the network can correctly reconstruct the original high-dimensional input vector at the output neurons. A least-means-squared error is commonly used to determine the error over all the vectors. Such networks are sometimes called *autoencoders*. A perfect encoding would result in a zero error on the training set, as each vector would be exactly reconstructed at the output neurons. During analysis, the lower half of the network is used to calculate the low-dimensional encoding. Autoencoders have been studied extensively in the literature (Hinton & Salakhutdinov, 2006; Kramer, 1991) and are part of several common toolkits including MATLAB. One example is the nlpca toolkit on nlpca.org.

An Example Functor for PCA Analysis

Example 3.1, "A PCA Functor Implementing the Network in Figure 3.3," demonstrates the simplicity of the functor that describes the PCA network illustrated in Figure 3.3. This functor is designed to be substituted into the Nelder-Mead optimization source code from Chapter 2, which contains the typename definition for **Real** and variables used in this calculation.

Example 3.1

```
static const int nInput = 2;
static const int nH1 = 1;
static const int nOutput = nInput;
static const int nParam =
  (nOutput+nH1) // Neuron Offsets
  + (nInput*nH1) // connections from I to H1
  + (nH1*nOutput); // connections from H1 to O
static const int exLen = nInput;

struct CalcError {
  const Real* examples;
```

```
    const Real* p;
    const int nInput;
    const int exLen;

CalcError( const Real* _examples, const    Real* _p,
              const int _nInput, const int _exLen)
  : examples(_examples), p(_p), nInput(_nInput), exLen(_exLen) {};

    __device__ __host__
    Real operator()(unsigned int tid)
    {
      const register Real* in = &examples[tid * exLen];
      register int index=0;

      register Real h0 = p[index++];

      for(int i=0; i < nInput; i++) {
        register Real input=in[i];
        h0 += input * p[index++];
      }

      register Real sum = 0.;
      for(int i=0; i < nInput; i++) {
        register Real o = p[index++];
        o += h0 * p[index++];
        o -= in[i];
        sum += o*o;
      }
      return sum;
    }
};
```

Example 3.2, "A Linear Data Generator," defines the subroutine **genData()**, which creates a two-dimensional data set based on the linear relationship between two variables $z1$ and $z2$ shown in Equation 3.1. Noise is superimposed onto t according to two uniformly distributed sequences, $e1$ and $e2$ with zero mean. A variance of 0.1 was used to generate the training data and for Figure 3.1.

Example 3.2

```
template <typename Real>
void genData(thrust::host_vector<Real> &h_data, int nVec, Real xVar)
{
  Real xMax = 1.1; Real xMin = -xMax;
  Real xRange = (xMax - xMin);
  for(int i=0; i < nVec; i++) {
    Real t = xRange * f_rand();
```

```
    Real z1 = t +    xVar * f_rand();
    Real z2 = t +    xVar * f_rand();
    h_data.push_back( z1 );
    h_data.push_back( z2 );
  }
}
```

$$z1 = t + e1, \; e1 = N\{0, 0.1\}$$
$$z2 = t + e2, \; e2 = N\{0, 0.1\}$$
(3.1)

Figure 3.5 shows how the PCA network was able to reconstruct 100 randomly generated data points using **genData** with a zero variance (*xVar* equals zero).

The complete source code for this example can be downloaded from the book's website. Those who wish to adapt the *xorNM.cu* example from Chapter 2 can use the functor in Example 3.1 and data generator in Example 3.2. In addition, the test for correctness will need to be modified. To attain high-accuracy, this example required that **kcount** be set to 50000.

An Example Functor for NLPCA Analysis

The NLPCA functor in Example 3.3 implements the network shown in Figure 3.4. This functor is designed to be substituted into the Nelder-Mead

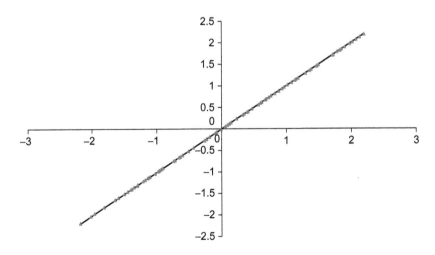

FIGURE 3.5
Nelder-Mead-trained PCA network reconstructing 100 random points.

optimization source code from Chapter 2, which contains the typename definition for **Real** and variables used in this calculation.

Example 3.3

```
static const int nInput = 2;
static const int nH1 = 4;
static const int nH2 = 1;
static const int nH3 = 4;
static const int nOutput = nInput;
static const int nParam =
  (nOutput+nH1+nH2+nH3) // Neuron Offsets
  + (nInput*nH1)       // connections from I to H1
  + (nH1*nH2)          // connections from H1 to H2
  + (nH2*nH3)          // connections from H2 to H3
  + (nH3*nOutput);     // connections from H3 to 0
static const int exLen = nInput;

struct CalcError {
  const Real* examples;
  const Real* p;
  const int nInput;
  const int exLen;

CalcError( const Real* _examples, constReal* _p,
           const int _nInput, const int _exLen)
: examples(_examples), p(_p), nInput(_nInput), exLen(_exLen) {};

  __device__ __host__
  Real operator()(unsigned int tid)
  {
    const register Real* in = &examples[tid * exLen];
    register int index=0;

    register Real h2_0 = p[index++]; // bottleneck neuron
    {
      register Real h1_0 = p[index++];
      register Real h1_1 = p[index++];
      register Real h1_2 = p[index++];
      register Real h1_3 = p[index++];
      for(int i=0; i < nInput; i++) {
        register Real input=in[i];
        h1_0 += input * p[index++]; h1_1 += input * p[index++];
        h1_2 += input * p[index++]; h1_3 += input * p[index++];
      }
      h1_0 = G(h1_0); h1_1 = G(h1_1);
      h1_2 = G(h1_2); h1_3 = G(h1_3);

      h2_0 += p[index++] * h1_0; h2_0 += p[index++] * h1_1;
```

```
      h2_0 += p[index++] * h1_2; h2_0 += p[index++] * h1_3;
    }
    register Real h3_0 = p[index++];
    register Real h3_1 = p[index++];
    register Real h3_2 = p[index++];
    register Real h3_3 = p[index++];
    h3_0 += p[index++] * h2_0; h3_1 += p[index++] * h2_0;
    h3_2 += p[index++] * h2_0; h3_3 += p[index++] * h2_0;
    h3_0 = G(h3_0); h3_1 = G(h3_1);
    h3_2 = G(h3_2); h3_3 = G(h3_3);

    register Real sum = 0.;
    for(int i=0; i < nOutput; i++) {
      register Real o = p[index++];
      o += h3_0 * p[index++]; o += h3_1 * p[index++];
      o += h3_2 * p[index++]; o += h3_3 * p[index++];
      o -= in[i];
      sum += o*o;
    }
    return sum;
  }
};
```

The **genData** method is modified to define a nonlinear relationship between $z1$ and $z2$ with $e1$ and $e2$ as described previously for the PCA data generator. Example 3.4 implements a nonlinear data generator using Equation 3.2.

$$z1 = t + e1$$
$$z2 = t^3 + e2$$
(3.2)

Example 3.4

```
template <typename Real>
void genData(thrust::host_vector<Real> &h_data, int nVec, Real xVar)
{
  Real xMax = 1.1; Real xMin = -xMax;
  Real xRange = (xMax - xMin);
  for(int i=0; i < nVec; i++) {
    Real t = xRange * f_rand();
    Real z1 = t +    xVar * f_rand();
    Real z2 = t*t*t +    xVar * f_rand();
    h_data.push_back( z1 );
    h_data.push_back( z2 );
  }
}
```

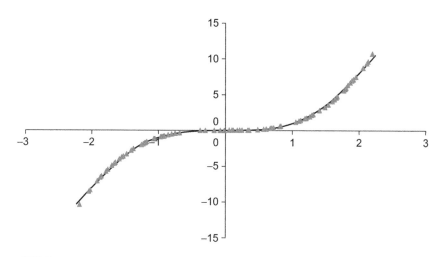

FIGURE 3.6
NLPCA Nelder-Mead-trained curve overlaid with 100 random test points.

Figure 3.6 shows that the network found a reasonable solution with a bottleneck of one neuron. The scatterplot reconstructs the high-dimensional data for 100 randomly chosen points on the curve.

The complete source code can be downloaded from the book's website.

OBTAINING BASIC PROFILE INFORMATION

The collection of low-level GPU profiling information can be enabled through use of the environmental variable **CUDA_PROFILE**. Setting this variable to 1 tells CUDA to collect runtime profiling information from hardware counters on the GPU. Gathering this information does not require special compiler flags, nor does it affect application performance. Setting **CUDA_PROFILE** to 0 disables the collection of the profile information.

By default, the CUDA profiler writes information to the file *cuda_profile_0.log* in the current directory. The name of the destination file can be changed through the environment variable **CUDA_PROFILE_LOG**. Further, the user can specify an options file to select the specific information that is to be gathered from the hardware counters with the environmental variable **CUDA_PROFILE_CONFIG**. The types and amounts of profile information that can be collected differ between GPU generations. Please consult the NVIDIA profiler documentation to see what information can be gathered from your GPGPU.

Examining the contents of *cuda_profile_0.log* after running **nlpcaNM_GPU32** with **CUDA_PROFILE**=1 shows that indeed this is the raw profiler output.

Just looking at the first few lines, one can see that several data transfers occurred from the host to device after the application started, which we can infer are the movement of the training set, parameters, and other information to the GPGPU. Highlighted in Example 3.5, "CUDA GPU Profile for Single-Precision Nelder-Mead NLPCA Optimization," is a reported *occupancy* value, which is a measure of GPU thread-level parallelization (TLP). High occupancy is generally good, but high application performance can also be achieved by applications with lower occupancy that attain high instruction-level parallelism (ILP). To understand occupancy, you need to understand some basics about the GPU hardware and execution model as discussed in the next chapter.

Example 3.5

```
# CUDA_PROFILE_LOG_VERSION 2.0
# CUDA_DEVICE 0 Tesla C2070
# TIMESTAMPFACTOR fffff6faa0f3f368
method,gputime,cputime,occupancy
method=[ memcpyHtoD ] gputime=[ 1752.224 ] cputime=[ 1873.000 ]
method=[ memcpyDtoD ] gputime=[ 179.296 ] cputime=[ 20.000 ]
method=[ _ZN6thrust6detail6device4cuda6detail23launch_closure_by_
valueINS2_18for_each_n_closureINS_10device_ptrIyEEjNS0_16generate_
functorINS0_12fill_functorIyEEEEEEEEvT_ ] gputime=[ 5.056 ] cputime=
[ 7.000 ] occupancy=[ 0.500 ]
method=[ _ZN6thrust6detail6device4cuda6detail23launch_closure_by_
valueINS2_18for_each_n_closureINS_10device_ptrIfEEjNS0_16generate_
functorINS0_12fill_functorIfEEEEEEEEvT_ ] gputime=[ 2.144 ] cputime=
[ 5.000 ] occupancy=[ 0.500 ]
method=[ memcpyDtoD ] gputime=[ 2.048 ] cputime=[ 5.000 ]
method=[ memcpyHtoD ] gputime=[ 1.120 ] cputime=[ 5.000 ]
method=[ memcpyHtoD ] gputime=[ 1.088 ] cputime=[ 3.000 ]
method=[ _ZN6thrust6detail6device4cuda6detail23launch_closure_by_
valueINS3_21reduce_n_smem_closureINS_18transform_iteratorIN7Obj
FuncIfE9CalcErrorENS_17counting_iteratorIjNS_11use_defaultESB_
SB_EEfSB_EElfNS_4plusIfEEEEEEvT_ ] gputime=[ 850.144 ] cputime=
[ 5.000 ] occupancy=[ 0.625 ]
method=[ _ZN6thrust6detail6device4cuda6detail23launch_closure_by_
valueINS3_21reduce_n_smem_closureINS0_15normal_iteratorINS_
10device_ptrIfEEEElfNS_4plusIfEEEEEEvT_ ] gputime=[ 5.952 ] cputime=
[ 4.000 ] occupancy=[ 0.500 ]
method=[ memcpyDtoH ] gputime=[ 1.952 ] cputime=[ 856.000 ]
method=[ memcpyHtoD ] gputime=[ 1.120 ] cputime=[ 4.000 ]
method=[ memcpyHtoD ] gputime=[ 1.088 ] cputime=[ 4.000 ]
...
```

GPROF: A COMMON UNIX PROFILER

To gain insight into host side performance, a CUDA application can be compiled with the **-profile** command-line option as seen in the **nvcc** command in Example 3.6:

Example 3.6

```
nvcc -profile -arch=sm_20 -O3 -Xcompiler -fopenmp nlpcaNM.cu
```

The Linux **gprof** profiler can then be used to examine the host-side behavior. The following output shows that the Nelder-Mead optimization method **nelmin** (highlighted in the following example), consumed only 10.79% of the runtime. The next largest consumer of host-only time is the allocation of the four STL (Standard Template library) vectors in **nelmin()** aside from two host-side methods supporting thrust on the GPU. Gprof reports that **nelmin()** is only called once, allowing us to conclude that the Nelder-Mead optimization code does not make significant demands on the host processor. See Example 3.7, "Example gprof Output":

Example 3.7

```
Flat profile:

Each sample counts as 0.01 seconds.
  %   cumulative   self              self     total
 time   seconds   seconds    calls  s/call   s/call  name
10.79     0.22      0.22        1    0.22     1.08   void nelmin
<float>(float (*)(float*), int, float*, float*, float*, float,
float*, int, int, int*, int*, int*)
 9.80     0.42      0.20   10508880   0.00     0.00   unsigned
long thrust::detail::util::divide_ri<unsigned long, unsigned long>
(unsigned long, unsigned long)
 8.33     0.59      0.17    3502960   0.00     0.00   thrust::
detail::device::cuda::arch::max_active_blocks_per_multiprocessor
(cudaDeviceProp const&, cudaFuncAttributes const&, unsigned long,
unsigned long)
 4.41     0.68      0.09   12001144   0.00     0.00      void
thrust::advance<thrust::detail::normal_iterator<float*>, unsigned
long>(thrust::detail::normal_iterator<float*>&, unsigned long)
 3.92     0.76      0.08   69730562   0.00     0.00      std::
vector<float, std::allocator<float> >::operator[](unsigned long)
...
```

The combined output of both the CUDA profiler and **gprof** demonstrate that the optimization functor dominates the runtime of this application. Although much useful information can be gathered with **gprof** and the CUDA profiler, it still takes considerable work and some guesswork to extract and analyze the information.

More information about can be found in the **gprof** manual. The NVIDIA documentation on the visual profiler is an excellent source of information about the low-level CUDA profiler.

THE NVIDIA VISUAL PROFILER: NVVP

NVIDIA provides the visual profiler **nvvp** or **NVidia Visual Profiler** for UNIX, Windows, and Mac to collect and analyze the low-level GPU profiler output for the user. As with the low-level profiler, the application does not need to be compiled with any special flags. By default, the visual profiler runs the application 15 times for 30 seconds per run to gather an ensemble of measurements.

The visual profiler is simple to use. The following instructions are for CUDA 4.1. Please see the instructions for later versions.

- Launch the CUDA visual profiler using the **nvvp** command.
- In the dialog that comes up, press the "Profile application" button in the "Session" pane.
- In the next dialog that comes up, type in the full path to your compiled CUDA program in the "Launch" text area.
- Provide any arguments to your program in the "Arguments" text area. Leave this blank if your code doesn't take any arguments.
- Make sure the "Enable profiling at application launch" and "CUDA API Trace" settings are checked.
- Press the "Launch" button at the bottom of the dialog to begin profiling.

Table 3.1 shows the information presented by default on the visual profiler summary screen after profiling the binary for *nlpcaNM.cu*.

Thrust generates some obscure names, but we can infer that **launch_closure_by_value-2** is **transform_reduce** performing a transform with the **CalcError** functor. The **launch_closure_by_value-3** method is the following reduction operation. The number of transform and reduce operations should be the same. We can infer that the different number of calls in the report (58 vs. 57) was caused by termination of the application by the visual profiler after 30 seconds of runtime.

According to the three rules of efficient GPGPU programming introduced in Chapter 1, Table 3.1 shows that our application is very efficient:

1. Get the data on the GPGPU and keep it there.

Table 3.1 Output Summary from the Visual Profiler on the nlpcaNM.cu Binary

Method	#Calls	GPU Time (us)	CPU Time (us)	%GPU Time	Glob Mem Read Throughput	Glob Mem Write Throughput	IPC	l1 Gld Hit Rate %
launch_closure_by_value-2	58	49919.4	50240.4	83.86	10.6109	0.10275	1.77138	94.4175
launch_closure_by_value-3	57	325.248	572.552	0.54	33.4966	12.1854	0.658475	0
launch_closure_by_value-0	1	5.312	8	0	27.3012	0.0783133	0.240059	0
launch_closure_by_value-1	1	2.144	6	0	64.3582	0.134328	0.541946	0
memcpyHtoD	117	1897.09	2406	3.18				
memcpyDtoD	2	181.792	208.744	0.3				
memcpyDtoH	57	88.896	48717	0.14				

This application is not limited by PCIe bus speed, as less than 4% of the runtime is consumed by the combined data transfer operations (**memcpyHtoD()**, **memcpyDtoD()**, and **memcpyDtoH()**).

2. Give the GPGPU enough work to do.

This application is not bound by kernel startup legacy, as the dominant method consumes 83.38% of the runtime and takes an average 49,919 microseconds to complete—far beyond the nominal kernel startup time of four microseconds.

3. Focus on data reuse within the GPGPU to avoid memory bandwidth limitations.

The runtime is dominated by a method that has an instructions per clock count (IPC) of 1.77, which is close to the peak theoretical limit of two instructions per clock for a 20-series Fermi GPGPU like the C2070. Further, this kernel is not limited by memory bandwidth, as the global memory bandwidth usage of 10.63 GB/s is less than 10% of the 143 GB/s the C2070 memory subsystem can provide. Further the l1 gld (Global Load) hit rate shows that the cache is being utilized effectively 94% of the time.

The visual profiler will automatically perform much of the preceding analysis for the user by clicking on a method name in the *Method* field. The report in Example 3.8, "Visual Profiler Kernel Analysis," was generated after clicking on *launch_closure_by_value-2*:

Example 3.8

```
Analysis for kernel launch_closure_by_value-2 on device Tesla C2070

Summary profiling information for the kernel:
Number of calls:    58
```

```
Minimum GPU time(us):    794.37
Maximum GPU time(us):    951.78
Average GPU time(us):    860.68
GPU time (%):   83.86
Grid size:    [14    1    1]
Block size:   [960    1    1]

Limiting Factor
Achieved Instruction Per Byte Ratio:  45.92 ( Balanced Instruction Per
Byte Ratio: 3.58 )
Achieved Occupancy:  0.63 ( Theoretical Occupancy: 0.62 )
IPC: 1.77 ( Maximum IPC: 2 )
Achieved global memory throughput:  10.71 ( Peak global memory
throughput(GB/s): 143.42 )

Hint(s)
The achieved instructions per byte ratio for the kernel is greater than
the balanced  instruction per byte ratio for the device. Hence, the
kernel is likely compute bound. For details, click on Instruction
Throughput Analysis.
```

Clicking the "Instruction Throughput Analysis" button shows that this kernel is indeed achieving a very high instruction throughput. There is some branching in the kernel that most likely happens inside the **tanh()** function, which suggests using another sigmoidal function to increase performance. See Example 3.9, "Visual Profiler Instruction Analysis":

Example 3.9

```
IPC: 1.77
Maximum IPC: 2
Divergent branches(%): 13.47
Control flow divergence(%): 12.62
Replayed Instructions(%): 1.08
Global memory replay(%): 0.55
Local memory replays(%): 0.00
Shared bank conflict replay(%): 0.00
Shared memory bank conflict per shared memory instruction(%): 0.00
```

The NVIDIA visual profiler (**nvvp**) collects and provides a wealth of additional information and analysis not discussed here. The Visual Profiler manual is an excellent source of information,[1] as is the help tab on the startup screen. Just type **nvvp** and click on *help* in the GUI. Later chapters will reference important

---

[1] Downloadable along with CUDA at http://developer.nvidia.com/cuda-downloads.

nvvp profiler measurements to aid in the understanding and interpretation of GPU performance. Because the Visual Profiler runs on all CUDA-enabled operating systems (Windows, UNIX, and Mac OS X), these discussions should benefit all readers.

PARALLEL NSIGHT FOR MICROSOFT VISUAL STUDIO

Parallel Nsight is the debugging and analysis tool that NVIDIA provides for Microsoft developers; it installs as a plug-in within Microsoft Visual Studio. Parallel Nsight allows both debugging and analysis on the machine as well as on remote machines, which can be located at a customer's site. Be aware that the capabilities of Parallel Nsight vary with the hardware configuration, as can be seen in Table 3.2.

Table 3.2 Parallel Nsight Capabilities According to Machine Configuration

Hardware Configuration	Single-GPU System	Dual-GPU System	Two Systems, Each with a GPU	Dual-GPU System SLI MultiOS
CUDA C/C++ Parallel Debugger		☑	☑	☑
Direct3D Shader Debugger			☑	☑
Direct3D Graphics Inspector	☑	☑	☑	☑
Analyzer	☑	☑	☑	☑

The following discussion highlights only a few features of Parallel Nsight as part of our analysis of *nlpcaNM.cu*. Parallel Nsight is an extensive package that is growing and maturing quickly. The most current information— including videos and user forums—can be found on the Parallel Nsight web portal (http://www.nvidia.com/ParallelNsight) as well as in the help section in Visual Studio.

The Nsight Timeline Analysis

As can be seen in Trace timeline in Figure 3.7, Parallel Nsight provides a tre-mendous amount of information that is easily accessible via mouseover and zooming operations, as well as various filtering operations. Given the volume of information available in these traces, it is essential to know that regions of the timeline can be selected by clicking the mouse on the screen at a desired starting point of time. A vertical line will appear on the screen.

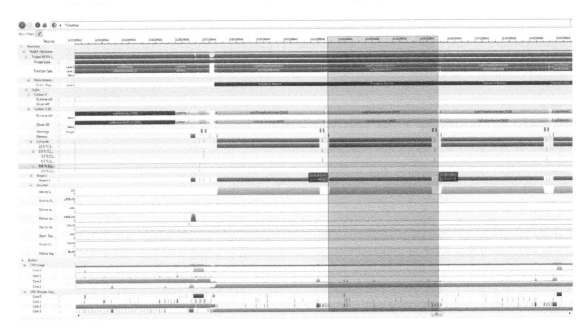

FIGURE 3.7

Parallel Nsight timeline.

Then press the Shift key and move the mouse (with the button pressed) to the end region of interest. This action will result in a gray overlay, as shown in Figure 3.7. A nice feature is that the time interval for the region is calculated and displayed.

The timeline can be used to determine if the application is CPU-bound, memory-bound, or kernel-bound:

- **CPU-bound:** There will be large areas where the kernel is shown to be running.
- **PCIe transfer–limited:** Kernel execution is blocked while waiting on memory transfers to or from the device, which can be seen by looking at the Memory row. If much time is being spent waiting on memory copies, consider using the Streams API to pipeline the application. This API allows data transfers and kernel execution to overlap. Before modifying code, compare the duration of the transfers and kernels to ensure that a performance gain will be realized.
- **Kernel-bound:** If the majority of the application time is spent waiting on kernels to complete, then switch to the "Profile CUDA" activity and rerun the application to collect information from the hardware counters. This information can help guide the optimization of kernel performance.

Zooming into a region of the timeline view allows Parallel Nsight to provide the names of the functions and methods as sufficient space becomes available in each region, which really helps the readability of the traces.

The NVTX Tracing Library

The NVTX library provides a powerful way to label sections of the computation to provide an easy-to-follow link to what the actual code is doing. Annotating Parallel Nsight traces can greatly help in understanding what is going on and provide information that will be missed by other CUDA tracing tools.

The simplest two NVTX methods are:

- **nvtxRangePushA**(char*): This method pushes a string on the NVTX stack that will be visible in the timeline. Nested labels are allowed to annotate asynchronous events.
- **nvtxRangePop**(): Pop the topmost label off the stack so that it is no longer visible on the timeline trace.

The *nvToolsExt.h* header file is included in those source files that use the NVTX library. In addition, the 32- or 64-bit version of the nvToolsExt library must be linked with the executable. The simplicity of these library calls is shown in Example 3.10, "NVTX Instrumented Transform_Reduce," to annotate the **thrust::transform_reduce** call in *nlpcaNM.cu*:

Example 3.10

```
nvtxRangePushA("Transform Reduce");
Real sum = thrust::transform_reduce(
            thrust::counting_iterator<unsigned int>(0),
            thrust::counting_iterator<unsigned int>(nExamples),
            getError,
            (Real) 0.,
            thrust::plus<Real>());
nvtxRangePop();
```

Figure 3.7 is a screenshot showing the amount of detail that is available on a timeline trace. This timeline shows three **transform_reduce** operations. The middle operation has been highlighted in gray to help separate the three annotated operations. The traces at the top show GPU activity and API calls; the bottom traces show activity on the system and related to the application on all the multiprocessor cores.

Parallel Nsight makes excellent use of color to help with interpretations, which is not shown in this grayscale image. A large monitor is suggested when using Parallel Nsight, as the timeline contains much information, including labels and scrollable, interactive regions.

Scaling Behavior of the CUDA API

Looking at the timeline for the NLPCA example (Figure 3.8), we see that the functor occupies most of the GPU runtime. For three runs—using a full-size and a 10x and a 100x smaller data set—the timelines show that the repeated allocation and deallocation of a small scratch region of memory for the reduction consumes an ever greater percentage of the runtime. This consumption represents a scaling challenge in the current CUDA 4.0 implantation. The NVTX library was used to annotate the timeline.

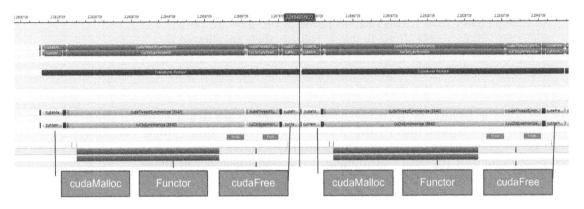

FIGURE 3.8

nlpcaNM.cu full data size.

Reducing the data by a factor of 10 times (Figure 3.9) shows that **cudaMalloc()** occupies more of the **transform_reduce** runtime.

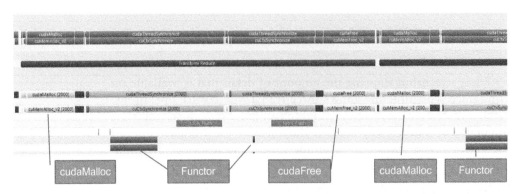

FIGURE 3.9

nlpcaNM.cu 1/10 data size.

At 100 times smaller, when using 10,000 examples (Figure 3.10), the time to allocate and free temporary space for **transform_reduce** consumes a significant amount of the runtime.

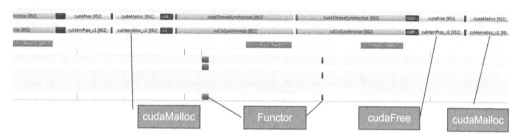

FIGURE 3.10
nlpcaNM.cu 10k examples.

Even with the inefficiency of the allocation, Parallel Nsight graphically shows that the NLPCA functor achieves very high efficiency, as it performs nearly two operations per clock on all the multiprocessors of a C2050 (Figure 3.11).

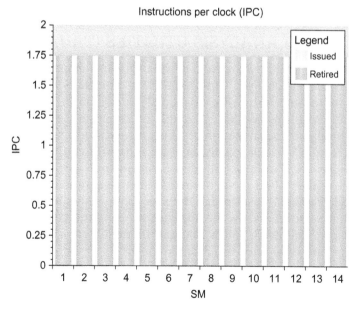

FIGURE 3.11
Parallel Nsight instructions per clock for nlpcaNM.cu.

Parallel Nsight also reports that all the multiprocessors on the GPU are fully utilized (Figure 3.12), which rounds out the analysis that the **CalcError** functor is good use of the GPU capabilities.

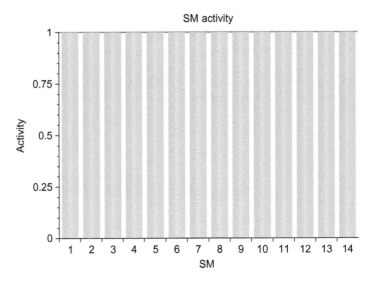

FIGURE 3.12
Multiprocessor activity on the GPU for nlpcaNM.cu.

TUNING AND ANALYSIS UTILITIES (TAU)

NIVIDA is not the only provider of analysis and debugging tools for CUDA. Tuning and Analysis Utilities (TAU) is a program and performance analysis tool framework being developed for the Department of Energy (DOE) Office of Sciences that is capable of gathering performance information through instrumentation of functions, methods, basic blocks, and statements. All C++ language features are supported, including templates and namespaces. TAU's profile visualization tool, **paraprof**, provides graphical displays of all the performance analysis results in aggregate and single node/context/thread forms. The user can quickly identify sources of performance bottlenecks in the application using the GUI. In addition, TAU can generate event traces that can be displayed with the Vampir, Paraver, or JumpShot trace visualization tools.

The paper "Parallel Performance Measurement of Heterogeneous Parallel Systems with GPUs" is the latest publication about the CUDA implementation (Malony et al., 2011; Malony, Biersdorff, Spear, & Mayanglamba, 2010). The software is available for free download from the Performance Research Laboratory (PRL).[2]

---

[2] http://www.cs.uoregon.edu/research/tau.

SUMMARY

With this accessible computational power, many past supercomputing techniques are now available for everyone to use—even on a laptop. In the 2006 paper "Reducing the Dimensionality of Data with Neural Networks," Hinton and Salakhutdinov noted:

> It has been obvious since the 1980s that backpropagation through deep autoencoders would be very effective for nonlinear dimensionality reduction, provided that computers were fast enough, data sets were big enough, and the initial weights were close enough to a good solution. All three conditions are now satisfied. (Hinton & Salakhutdinov, 2006, p. 506)

The techniques discussed in this chapter, including autoencoders, can be applied to a host of data fitting, data analysis, dimension reduction, vision, and classification problems. Conveniently, they are able to scale from laptops to the largest supercomputers in the world.

As this chapter showed, achieving high performance inside a functor does not guarantee good performance across all problem sizes. Sometimes the bottlenecks that limit performance are as subtle as the dynamic memory allocation of temporary space, as identified in the **thrust::transform_reduce** method.

Without being able to see what the GPU is doing, performance monitoring is guesswork. Having the right performance analysis tool is key to finding performance limitations. For this reason, the CUDA tool suite contains a number of common profiling and debugging tools that have been adapted to GPU computing. These are tools that Windows, UNIX, and Max developers are already comfortable with. Although each tool has both strengths and weaknesses, they all provide a useful view into GPU performance while requiring only a minimal learning investment. In this way, CUDA offers a smooth transition to massively parallel GPU programming.

## CHAPTER 4

The CUDA Execution Model

The heart of CUDA performance and scalability lies in the execution model and the simple partitioning of a computation into fixed-sized blocks of threads in the execution configuration. CUDA was created to map naturally the parallelism within an application to the massive parallelism of the GPGPU hardware. From the high-level language expression of the kernel to the replication of the lowest-level hardware units, on-board GPU scalability is preserved while many common parallel programming pitfalls are avoided. The result is massive thread scalability and high application performance across GPGPU hardware generations. The CUDA toolkit provides the programmer with those tools needed to exploit parallelism at both the thread level and the instruction level within the processing cores. Even the first CUDA program presented in Chapter 1 has the potential to run a million concurrent hardware threads of execution on some future generation of GPU. Meanwhile, the functor in Chapter 2 demonstrated high performance across multiple types and generations of GPUs.

At the end of this chapter, the reader will have a basic understanding of:

- How CUDA expresses massive parallelism without imposing scaling limitations.
- The meaning and importance of a warp and half-warp.
- Scheduling, warp divergence, and why GPUs are considered a SIMT architecture.
- How to use both TLP and ILP in a CUDA program.
- The advantages and disadvantages of TLP and ILP for arithmetic and memory transactions.
- The impact of warp divergence and general rules on how to avoid it.
- The application of Little's law to streaming multiprocessors.
- The **nvcc** compiler, SM related command-line options, and **cuobjdump**.
- Those profiler measurements relevant to occupancy, TLP, ILP, and the SM.

GPU ARCHITECTURE OVERVIEW

The heart of CUDA performance and scalability lies in the simple partitioning of a computation into fixed sized blocks of threads in the execution configuration. These thread blocks provide the mapping between the parallelism of the application and the massive replication of the GPGPU hardware.

Massive GPU hardware parallelism is achieved through replication of a common architectural building block called a *streaming multiprocessor* (SM). By altering the number of SMs, GPU designers can create products to meet market needs at various price and performance points. The block diagram in Figure 4.1 illustrates the massive replication of multiprocessors on a GF100 (Fermi) series GPGPU.

The software abstraction of a thread block translates into a natural mapping of the kernel onto an arbitrary number of SM on a GPGPU. Thread blocks also act as a container of thread cooperation, as only threads in a thread block can share data.[1] Thus a thread block becomes both a natural expression of the parallelism in an application and of partitioning the parallelism into multiple containers that run independently of each other.

The translation of the thread block abstraction is straightforward; each SM can be scheduled to run one or more thread blocks. Subject only to device limitations, this mapping:

- Scales transparently to an arbitrary number of SM.
- Places no restriction on the location of the SM (potentially allowing CUDA applications to transparently scale across multiple devices in the future).
- Gives the hardware the ability to broadcast both the kernel executable and user parameters to the hardware. A parallel broadcast is the most scalable and generally the fastest communication mechanism that can move data to a large number of processing elements.

Because all the threads in a thread block execute on an SM, GPGPU designers are able to provide high-speed memory inside the SM called *shared memory* for data sharing. This elegant solution also avoids known scaling issues with maintaining coherent caches in multicore processors. A coherent cache is guaranteed to reflect the latest state of all the variables in the cache regardless of how many processing elements may be reading or updating a variable.

---

[1] For some problems and with good reason, a developer may choose to use atomic operations to communicate between threads of different thread blocks. This approach breaks the assumption of independence between thread blocks and may introduce programming errors, scalability, and performance issues.

In toto, the abstraction of a thread block and replication of SM hardware work in concert to transparently provide unlimited and efficient scalability. The challenge for the CUDA programmer is to express their application kernels in such a way to exploit this parallelism and scalability.

Thread Scheduling: Orchestrating Performance and Parallelism via the Execution Configuration

Distributing work to the streaming multiprocessors is the job of the Giga-Thread global scheduler (highlighted in Figure 4.1). Based on the number of blocks and number of threads per block defined in the kernel execution configuration, this scheduler allocates one or more blocks to each SM. How many blocks are assigned to each SM depends on how many resident threads and thread blocks a SM can support.

NVIDIA categorizes their CUDA-enabled devices by *compute capability*. An important specification in the compute capability is the *maximum number of resident threads per multiprocessor*. For example, an older G80 compute capability 1.0 device has the ability to manage 768 total resident threads per multiprocessor. Valid block combinations for these devices include three blocks of 256 threads, six blocks of 128 threads, and other combinations not exceeding 768 threads per SM. A newer GF100, or compute capability 2.0 GPU, can support 1,536 resident threads or twice the number of a compute 1.0 multiprocessor.

The GigaThread global scheduler was enhanced in compute 2.0 devices to support concurrent kernels. As a result, compute 2.0 devices can better utilize the GPU hardware when confronted with a mix of small kernels or kernels with unbalanced workloads that stop using SM over time. In other words, multiple kernels may run at the same time on a single GPU as long as they are issued into different streams. Kernels are executed in the order in which they were issued and only if there are SM resources still available after all thread blocks for preceding kernels have been scheduled.

Each SM is independently responsible for scheduling its internal resources, cores, and other execution units to perform the work of the threads in its assigned thread blocks. This decoupled interaction is highly scalable, as the GigaThread scheduler needs to know only when an SM is busy.

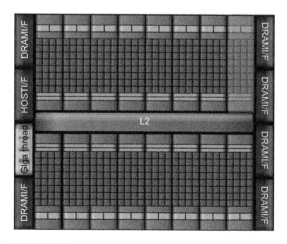

FIGURE 4.1

Block diagram of a GF100 (Fermi) GPU.

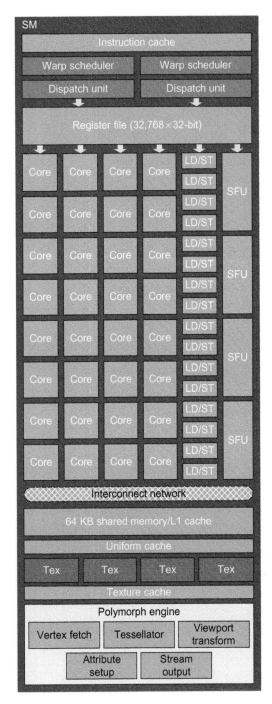

FIGURE 4.2

Block diagram of a GF100 SM.

On each clock tick, the SM warp schedulers decide which warp to execute next, choosing from those not waiting for:

- Data to come from device memory.
- Completion of earlier instructions.

As illustrated in Figure 4.2, each GF100 SM has 32 SIMD (Single Instruction Multiple Data) cores. The use of a SIMD execution model means that the scheduler on the SM dictates that all the cores it controls will run the same instruction. Each core, however, may use different data. Basing the design of the streaming multiprocessors on a SIMD execution model is a beautiful example of "just enough and no more" in processor design because SIMD cores require less space and consume less power than non-SIMD designs. These benefits are multiplied by the massive replication of SM inside the GPU.

GPU hardware architects have been able to capitalize on the SIMD savings by devoting more power and space by adding ALU (Arithmetic and Logic Units), floating-point, and Special Function Units for transcendental functions. As a result, GPGPU devices have a high flop per watt ratio compared to conventional processors (Vuduc, 2010) as seen in Table 4.1.

To this point, we have correctly spoken about programming a GPU in terms of individual threads. From a performance perspective, it is necessary to start thinking in terms of the number of SIMD threads inside a warp or a half-warp on GF100 SM with dual schedulers. A *warp* is a block of 32 SIMD threads on most GPUs. Just like a thread block for the GigaThread scheduler, a warp is the basic unit for scheduling work inside a SM.

Because each warp is by definition a block of SIMD threads, the scheduler does not need to check for dependencies within the instruction stream. Figure 4.2 shows that each GF100 SM has two warp schedulers and two instruction dispatch units, which allows two warps to be issued and executed concurrently. Using this dual-issue model, GF100

Table 4.1 Flops Per Watt for Various Devices

Architecture	Intel Nehalem x5550	NVIDIA T10P C1060	NVIDIA GT200 GTX 285	NVIDIA Fermi C2050
GHz	2.66	1.44	1.47	1.15
Sockets	2	1	1	1
Cores/socket (SM/GPU)	4	(30)	(30)	(14)
Peak Gflop (single)	170.6	933	1060	1030
Peak Gflop (double)	85.3	78	88	515
Peak GB/s	51.2	102	159	144
Sockets only watts	200	200	204	247
64-bit flops/watt	0.4265	0.39	0.431372549	2.08502
32-bit flops/watt	0.853	4.665	5.196078431	4.17004

streaming multiprocessors can achieve two operations per clock by selecting two warps and issuing one instruction from each warp to a group of sixteen cores, sixteen load/store units, or four SFUs.

Most instructions can be dual-issued: two integer instructions, two floating-point instructions, or a mix of integer, floating-point, load, store, and SFU instructions. For example:

- The first unit can execute 16 FMA FP32s while the second concurrently processes 16 ADD INT32s, which appears to the scheduler as if they executed in one cycle.
- The quadruple SFU unit is decoupled, and the scheduler can therefore send instructions to two SIMD units once it is engaged, which means that the SFUs and SIMD units can be working concurrently. This setup can provide a big performance win for applications that use transcendental functions.

GF100 GPUs do not support dual-dispatch of double-precision instructions, but a high IPC is still possible when running double-precision instructions because integer and other instructions can execute when double-precision operations are stalled waiting for data.

Utilizing a decoupled global and local scheduling mechanism based on thread blocks has a number of advantages:

- It does not limit on-board scalability, as only the active state of the SMs must be monitored by the global scheduler.
- Scheduling a thread block per SM limits the complexity of thread resource allocation and any interthread communication to the SM, which partitions each CUDA kernel in a scalable fashion so that no other SM or even the global scheduler needs to know what is happening within any other SM.
- Future SM can be smarter and do more as technology and manufacturing improve with time.

Relevant computeprof Values for a Warp

active warps/ active cycle	The average number of warps that are active on a multiprocessor per cycle, which is calculated as: (active warps)/(active cycles)

Warp Divergence

SIMD execution does have drawbacks, but it affects only code running inside an SM. GPGPUs are not true SIMD machines because they are composed of many SMs, each of which may be running one or more different instructions. For this reason, GPGPU devices are classified as SIMT (Single Instruction Multiple Thread) devices.

Programmers must be aware that conditionals (*if* statements) can greatly decrease performance inside an SM, as each branch of each conditional must be evaluated. Long code paths in a conditional can cause a 2-times slowdown for each conditional within a warp and a 2^N slowdown for N nested loops. A maximum 32-time slowdown can occur when each thread in a warp executes a separate condition.

Fermi architecture GPUs utilize *predication* to run short conditional code segments efficiently with no branch instruction overhead. Predication removes branches from the code by executing both the *if* and *else* parts of a branch in parallel, which avoids the problem of mispredicted branches and warp divergence.

Section 6.2 of "The CUDA C Best Practices Guide" notes:

> When using branch predication, none of the instructions whose execution depends on the controlling condition is skipped. Instead, each such instruction is associated with a per-thread condition code or predicate that is set to true or false according to the controlling condition. Although each of these instructions is scheduled for execution, only the instructions with a true predicate are actually executed. Instructions with a false predicate do not write results, and they also do not evaluate addresses or read operands. (NVIDIA, CUDA C Best Practices Guide, May 2011, p. 56)

The code in Example 4.1, "A Short Code Snippet Containing a Conditional," contains a conditional that would run on all threads computing the logical predicate and two predicated instructions as shown in Example 4.2:

Example 4.1

```
if (x<0.0) z = x-2.0;
else z = sqrt(x);
```

The **sqrt** has a false predicate when **x** < 0 so no error occurs from attempting to take the square root of zero.

Example 4.2

```
p = (x<0.0);        // logical predicate
 p: z = x-2.0;      // True predicated instruction
!p: z = sqrt(x);    // False predicated instruction
```

Per section 6.2 of "The CUDA C Best Practices Guide," the length of the predicated instructions is important:

> The compiler replaces a branch instruction with predicated instructions only if the number of instructions controlled by the branch condition is less than or equal to a certain threshold: If the compiler determines that the condition is likely to produce many divergent warps, this threshold is 7; otherwise it is 4. (NVIDIA, CUDA C Best Practices Guide, May 2011, p. 56)

If the code in the branches is too long, the **nvcc** compiler inserts code to perform *warp voting* to see if all the threads in a warp take the same branch. If all the threads in a warp vote the same way, there is no performance slowdown.

In some cases, the compiler can determine at compile time that all the threads in the warp will go the same way. In Example 4.3, "Example When Voting Is Not Needed," there is no need to vote even though **case** is a non-constant variable:

Example 4.3

```
//The variable case has the same value across all threads
if (case==1)
  z = x*x;
else
  z = x+2.3;
```

Guidelines for Warp Divergence

Sometimes warp divergence is unavoidable. Common application examples include PDEs (Partial Differential Equations) with boundary conditions, graphs, trees, and other irregular data structures. In the worst case, a 32-time slowdown can occur when:

- One thread needs to perform an expensive computational task.
- Each thread performs a separate task.

Avoiding warp divergence is a challenge. Though there are many possible solutions, none will work for every situation. Following are some guidelines:

- Try to reformulate the problem to use a different algorithm that either does not cause warp divergence or expresses the problem so that the compiler can reduce or eliminate warp divergence.
- Consider creating separate lists of expensive vs. inexpensive operations and using each list in a separate kernel. Hopefully, the bulk of the work will occur in the inexpensive kernel. Perhaps some of the expensive work can be performed on the CPU.
- Order the computation (or list of computations) to group computations into blocks that are multiples of a half-warp.
    - If possible, use asynchronous kernel execution to exploit the GPU SIMT execution model.
    - Utilize the host processor(s) to perform part of the work that would cause a load imbalance on the GPU.

The book *GPU CUDA Gems* (Hwu, 2011) is a single-source reference to see how many applications handle problems with irregular data structures and warp divergence. Each chapter contains detailed descriptions of the problem, solutions, and reported speedups. Examples include:

- Conventional and novel approaches to accelerate an irregular tree-based data structure on GPGPUs.
- Avoiding conditional operations that limit parallelism in a string similarity algorithm.
- Using GPUs to accelerate a dynamic quadrature grid method and avoid warp divergence as grid points move over the course of the calculation.
- Approached to irregular meshes that involve conditional operations and approaches to regularize computation.

Relevant computeprof Values for Warp Divergence

Divergent branches (%)	The percentage of branches that are causing divergence within a warp amongst all the branches present in the kernel. Divergence within a warp causes serialization in execution. This is calculated as: (100 * divergent branch)/(divergent branch + branch)
Control flow divergence (%)	Control flow divergence gives the percentage of thread instructions that were not executed by all threads in the warp, hence causing divergence. This should be as low as possible. This is calculated as: 100 * ((32 * instructions executed)—threads instruction executed)/ (32 * instructions executed))

WARP SCHEDULING AND TLP

Running multiple warps per SM is the only way a GPU can hide both ALU and memory latencies to keep the execution units busy.

From a software perspective, the hardware SM scheduler is fast enough that it basically has no overhead. Inside the SM, the hardware can detect those warps whose next instruction is ready to run because all resource and data dependencies have been resolved. From this pool of eligible warps, the SM scheduler selects one based on an internal prioritized schedule. It then issues the instruction from that warp to the SIMD cores. If all the warps are *stalled*, meaning they all have some unresolved dependency, then no instruction can be issued resulting in idle hardware and decreased performance.

The idea behind TLP is to give the scheduler as many threads as possible to choose from to minimize the potential for a performance loss. *Occupancy* is a measure of TLP, which is defined as the number of warps running concurrently on a multiprocessor divided by maximum number of warps that can be resident on an SM. A high occupancy implies that the scheduler on the SM has many warps to choose from and thus hide both ALU and data latencies. Chances are at lease one warp should be ready to run because all the dependencies are resolved.

Though simple in concept, occupancy is complicated in practice, as it can be limited by on-chip SM memory resources such as registers and shared memory. NVIDIA provides the CUDA Occupancy calculator to help choose execution configurations.

Common execution configuration (block per grid) heuristics include:

- Specify more blocks than number of SM so all the multiprocessors have at least one block to execute.
  - This is a lower bound, as specifying fewer blocks than SM will clearly not utilize all the resources of the GPU.
  - To exploit asynchronous kernel execution for small problems, the developer may purposely underutilize the GPU. GF100 and later architectures can utilize concurrent kernel execution to increase application performance by running blocks from different kernels on unused SM. These GPUs accelerate those applications that have multiple kernels that are too small to run on all the SM of the GPU but take too much time to export to the host processor.
- Specify multiple blocks per SM to run concurrently inside a SM.
  - Choose the number of blocks to be a multiple of the number of SM on the GPU to fully utilize all the SM. This approach ensures that all the SM have a balanced workload.
  - Blocks that are not waiting at a __syncthreads will keep the hardware busy.
  - The numbers of blocks that can run are subject to resource availability on the SM including register and shared memory space.

- When possible, specify a very large number of blocks per grid (e.g., thousands).
    - Doing so will help the application across multiple GPGPU generations.
    - It will also keep the SM fully loaded with resident thread blocks.

Relevant computeprof Values for Occupancy

Achieved kernel occupancy	This ratio provides the actual occupancy of the kernel based on the number of warps executing per cycle on the SM. It is the ratio of active warps and active cycles divided by the max number of warps that can execute on an SM. This is calculated as: (active warps/active cycles)/4

ILP: HIGHER PERFORMANCE AT LOWER OCCUPANCY

High occupancy does not necessarily translate into the fastest application performance. Instruction-level parallelism (ILP) can be equally effective in hiding arithmetic latency by keeping the SIMD cores busy with fewer threads that consume fewer resources and introduce less overhead.

The reasoning for ILP is simple and powerful: using fewer threads means that more registers can be used per thread. Registers are a precious resource, as they are the only memory fast enough to attain peak GPU performance. The larger the bandwidth gap between the register store and other memory, the more data that must come from registers to achieve high performance.

Sometimes having a few more registers per thread can prevent register spilling and preserve high performance. Although necessary, register spilling violates the programmer's expectation of high performance from register memory and can cause catastrophic performance decreases. Utilizing fewer threads also benefit kernels that use shared memory by reducing the number of shared memory accesses and by allowing data reuse within a thread (Volkov, 2010). A minor benefit includes a reduction in some of the work that the GPU must perform per thread.

The following loop, for example, would consume 2048 bytes of register storage and require that the loop counter, i, be incremented 512 times in a block with 512 threads. A thread block containing only 64 threads would require only 256 bytes of register storage and reduce the number of integer increment in place operations by a factor of 4. See Example 4.4, "Simple for Loop to Demonstrate ILP Benefits":

Example 4.4

```
for(int i=0; i < n; i++) ...
```

Reading horizontally across the columns, Table 4.2 encapsulates how the number of registers per threads increases as the occupancy decreases for various compute generations.

Table 4.2 Increasing Registers Per Thread as Occupancy Decreases

	Maximum Occupancy	Maximum Registers	Increase
GF100	20 at 100% occupancy	63 at 33% occupancy	3x more registers per thread
GF200	16 at 100% occupancy	≈128 at 12.5% occupancy	8x more registers per thread

ILP Hides Arithmetic Latency

As with TLP, multiple threads provide the needed parallelism. For example, the shaded row in Figure 4.3 highlights four independent operations that happen in parallel across three threads.

Table 4.3 A Set of TLP Arithmetic Operations

Thread 1	Thread 2	Thread 3	Thread 4
$x = x + c$	$y = y + c$	$z = z + c$	$w = w + c$
$x = x + b$	$y = y + b$	$z = z + b$	$w = w + b$
$x = x + a$	$y = y + a$	$z = z + a$	$w = w + a$

Due to warp scheduling, parallelism can also happen among the instructions within a thread, as long as there are enough threads to create two or more warps within a block.

Table 4.4 Instruction Rearranged for ILP

	Thread	
Instructions–>	$w = w + b$ $z = z + b$ $y = y + b$ $x = x + b$	Four independent operations
	$w = w + a$ $z = z + a$ $y = y + a$ $x = x + a$	Four independent operations

The following example demonstrates ILP by creating two or more warps that run on a single SM. As can be seen in Example 4.5, "Arithmetic ILP Benchmark," the execution configuration specifies only one block. The number of warps resident on the SM is increased as the number of threads within the block is increased from 32 to 1024, and the performance is reported. This example will run to completion on a compute 2.0 device that can support 1024 threads per block. Earlier devices will detect a runtime error via the call to **cudaGetLastError**, which will stop the test when the maximum number of threads per block exceeds the number that the GPU can support. Because kernel launches are asynchronous, **cudaSynchronizeThread** is used to wait for kernel completion.

Example 4.5

```
#include <omp.h>
#include <iostream>
using namespace std;
#include <cmath>

//create storage on the device in gmem
__device__ float d_a[32], d_d[32];
__device__ float d_e[32], d_f[32];

#define NUM_ITERATIONS ( 1024 * 1024)

#ifdef ILP4
// test instruction level parallelism
#define OP_COUNT 4*2*NUM_ITERATIONS
__global__ void kernel(float a, float b, float c)

{
  register float d=a, e=a, f=a;
#pragma unroll 16
  for(int i=0; i < NUM_ITERATIONS; i++) {
    a = a * b + c;
    d = d * b + c;
    e = e * b + c;
    f = f * b + c;
  }

    // write to gmem so the work is not optimized out by the compiler
    d_a[threadIdx.x] = a; d_d[threadIdx.x] = d;
    d_e[threadIdx.x] = e; d_f[threadIdx.x] = f;
}
#else
// test thread level parallelism
#define OP_COUNT 1*2*NUM_ITERATIONS
__global__ void kernel(float a, float b, float c)
{
#pragma unroll 16
  for(int i=0; i < NUM_ITERATIONS; i++) {
    a = a * b + c;
  }

  // write to gmem so the work is not optimized out by the compiler
  d_a[threadIdx.x] = a;
```

```
}
#endif
int main()
{
  // iterate over number of threads in a block
  for(int nThreads=32; nThreads <= 1024; nThreads += 32) {
    double start=omp_get_wtime();
    kernel<<<1, nThreads>>>(1., 2., 3.); // async kernel launch
    if(cudaGetLastError() != cudaSuccess) {
      cerr << "Launch error" << endl;
      return(1);
    }
    cudaThreadSynchronize(); // need to wait for the kernel to complete
    double end=omp_get_wtime();
    cout << "warps" << ceil(nThreads/32) << " "
         << nThreads << " " << (nThreads*(OP_COUNT/1.e9)/(end - start))
         << " Gflops " << endl;
  }
  return(0);
}
```

As seen in Figure 4.3, ILP increases performance just by increasing the number of independent instructions per thread. The best performance on a compute 2.0 device occurs when 576 threads are resident on the SM. As noted in the presentation "Better Performance at Lower Occupancy," the upper bound currently appears to be an ILP of 4 (Volkov, 2010). It is suspected that the scoreboard on the SM that tracks memory usage is the limiting factor. The patent "Tracking Register Usage During Multithreaded Processing Using a Scoreboard" (Coon, Mills, Oberman, & Siu, 2008) might provide additional insight.

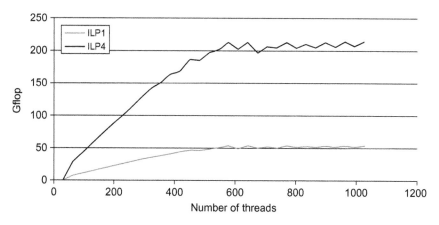

FIGURE 4.3

Comparison of ILP1 vs. ILP4 performance on a C2070.

Table 4.5 Minimum Parallelism to Achieve 100 Percent Utilization

Compute Generation	GPU Architecture	Latency (Cycles)	Throughput (Cores/SM)	Parallelism (Operations/SM)
Compute 1.x	G80-GT200	≈24	8	≈192
Compute 2.0	GF100	≈18	32	≈576
Compute 2.1	GF104	≈18	48	≈864

Table 4.5 shows the minimum arithmetic parallelism needed to achieve 100 percent throughput (Volkov, 2010).

ILP Hides Data Latency

It is important to note that threads don't stall in the SM on a memory access— only on data dependencies. From the perspective of a warp, a memory access requires issuing a load or store instruction to the LD/ST units.[2] The warp can then continue issuing other instructions until it reaches one that depends on the completion of a memory transaction. At that point, the warp will stall. To increase performance, the compiler can reorder instructions to:

- Keep the largest number of memory transactions "in flight" and thus best utilize memory bandwidth and the LD/ST units.
- Supply other, nondependent instructions required by the thread to keep the computational cores busy.
- Minimize the time that dependent instructions must remain in the queue by positioning the data-dependent instruction in the queue so that it reaches the top of the queue close to the expected data arrival time.

As a result of this complex choreography, ILP can also hide memory latency. Vasily Volkov notes that ILP can achieve 84 percent of peak memory bandwidth while requiring only 4 percent occupancy when copying 14 **float4** values per thread (Volkov, 2010). A *float4* is a structure of four 32-bit floating-point variables that fits perfectly into a 128-bit cache line. These structures exploit the bit-level parallelism of a cache line memory transaction as well as ILP parallelism.

ILP in the Future

The current GF100 architecture encourages the use of smaller blocks because it can schedule more blocks due to the additional resources per SM. This

---

[2] Although there is no difference in performing a store or load operation, the literature discusses ILP writes in terms of multiple outputs—meaning multiple write operations to memory.

approach presents a new way of thinking about problems to achieve both high utilization and performance. It is worth noting that compute 2.0 devices and even 1.x GPUs can sometimes issue a second instruction from the same warp in parallel to the special function unit.

CPU developers will recognize ILP as a form of *superscalar* execution that executes more than one instruction during a clock cycle by simultaneously dispatching multiple instructions to redundant functional units on the processor. NVIDIA has added superscalar execution to the scheduler in compute 2.1 devices. The warp scheduler in these devices has the ability to analyze the next instruction in a warp to determine if that instruction is ILP-safe and whether there is an execution unit available to handle it. The result is that compute 2.1 devices can execute a warp in a superscalar fashion for any CUDA code without requiring explicit programmer actions to force ILP.

ILP has been incorporated into the CUBLAS 2.0 and CUFFT 2.3 libraries. Performing an single-precision level-3 BLAS matrix multiply (SGEMM) on two large matrices demonstrates the following performance increases (Volkov, 2010):

Table 4.6 CUBLAS ILP Speedup Reported for SGEMM

	CUBLAS 1.1	CUBLAS 2.0	
Threads per block	512	64	8x smaller thread blocks
Occupancy (Compute 1.0)	67%	33%	2x lower occupancy
Performance (Compute 1.0)	128 Gflop/s	204 Gflop/s	1.6x faster performance

Similarly, ILP benefits batched 1024-point complex-to-complex single-precision Fast Fourier Transform (FFTs):

Table 4.7 CUFFT ILP Speedup Reported for Batched FFTs

	CUFFT 2.2	CUFFT 2.3	
Threads per block	256	64	4x smaller thread blocks
Occupancy (Compute 1.0)	33%	17%	2x lower occupancy
Performance (Compute 1.0)	45 Gflop/s	93 Gflop/s	2x faster performance

ILP benefits arithmetic problems: Current work on the MAGMA BLAS libraries demonstrates up to 838 Gflop/s using 33 percent occupancy and 2 thread blocks per SM (Volkov, 2010). The MAGMA team has made the conclusion that dense linear algebra methods are now a better fit on GPU architectures instead of traditional multicore architectures (Nath, Stanimire, & Dongerra, 2010).

ILP benefits memory bandwidth problems: To saturate the bus on a Fermi C2050 requires keeping 30–50 128-byte transactions in flight per SM (Micikevicius, 2010). Volkov recommends keeping 100 KB in flight to hide memory latency—less if the kernel is compute-bound.

Relevant computeprof Values for Instruction Rates

Instruction throughput	This value is the ratio of achieved instruction rate to peak single-issue instruction rate. The achieved instruction rate is calculated using the profiler counter "instructions." The peak instruction rate is calculated based on the GPU clock speed. In the case of instruction dual-issue coming into play, this ratio shoots up to greater than 1. This is calculated as: (instructions)/(gpu_time * clock_frequency)
Ideal instruction/ byte ratio	This value is a ratio of the peak instruction throughput and the peak memory throughput of the CUDA device. This is a property of the device and is independent of the kernel.
Instruction/byte	This value is the ratio of the total number of instructions issued by the kernel and the total number of bytes accessed by the kernel from global memory. If this ratio is greater than the ideal instruction/ byte ratio, then the kernel is compute-bound, and if it's less, then the kernel is memory-bound. This is calculated as: (32 * instructions issued * #SM)/{32 * (l2 read requests + l2 write requests + l2 read texture requests)}
IPC (instructions per cycle)	This value gives the number of instructions issued per cycle. This should be compared to maximum IPC possible for the device. The range provided is for single-precision floating-point instructions. This is calculated as: (instructions issued/active cycles)
Replayed instructions (%)	This value gives the percentage of instructions replayed during kernel execution. Replayed instructions are the difference between the numbers of instructions that are actually issued by the hardware to the number of instructions that are to be executed by the kernel. Ideally, this should be zero. This is calculated as: 100 * (instructions issued − instruction executed)/instruction issue

LITTLE'S LAW

Little's law (Little, 1961) is derived from general information theory but has important application to understanding the performance of memory hierarchies. Generalized to multiprocessor systems, Little's law for concurrency (Equation 4.1) can be expressed as:

$$Concurrency = bandwidth * latency \qquad (4.1)$$

where *concurrency* is the aggregate system concurrency and *bandwidth* is the aggregate memory bandwidth.

Nearly all CUDA applications will be limited by memory bandwidth. The performance of global memory is of particular concern, as can be seen in the bandwidths reported in "Better Performance at Lower Occupancy" (Volkov, 2010):

- Register memory (≈8 TB/s)
- Shared memory (≈1.6 TB/s)
- Global memory (177 GB/s)

From a TLP point of view, Little's law tells us that the number of memory transactions "in flight," N (see Equation 4.2, "TLP memory transactions in flight"), is the product of the arrival rate λ and the memory latency, L.

$$N = \lambda L \qquad (4.2)$$

where the arrival rate, λ, is the product of the IPC (the desired instruction rate) and the density of load instructions.

In other words, as additional threads are added and multiplexed over the same hardware resources, greater latency can be hidden. As we have observed, this is an overly simplistic view, as complex data dependencies introduce stalls plus hardware limitations create bottlenecks.

From an ILP point of view, independent memory transactions can be batched (Equation 4.3, "ILP-batched memory transactions in flight").

$$N = \lambda L - B \qquad (4.3)$$

where B is the batch size of the independent loads.

Saturating the bus on a Fermi C2050 requires keeping 30–50 128-byte transactions in flight per SM (Micikevicius, 2010). Volkov recommends the minimum parallelism for peak arithmetic performance on a C2050 be 576 threads per block and keeping 100 KB of data in flight for peak memory performance on memory-bound kernels. Table 4.8 summarizes these results.

Table 4.8 C2050 Minimum Parallelism for Peak Data and Arithmetic Performance

	Latency	Throughput	Parallelism
Arithmetic	≈18	32	≈576
Memory	<800 cycles	<177 GB.s	<100 KB

To increase the concurrency in your applications, consider the following:

- Increase occupancy.
- Maximize the available registers using the **nvcc** command-line option **-maxrregcount**, or giving the compiler additional per kernel help with the **__launch_bounds__** specification in the kernel declaration.
- Adjust the thread block dimensions to best utilize the SM warp scheduler(s).
- Modify the code to use ILP and process several elements per thread.

- Pay careful attention to the instruction "mix":
  - For example, the math-to-memory operation ratios.
  - Don't bottleneck on one function unit causing the other units to stall.
- Don't "traffic-jam" kernel code:
  - Try to create lots of small thread blocks containing a uniform distribution of operation densities (e.g., int, floating-point, memory, and SFU).
  - Don't bunch operations of a similar type in one section of a kernel, as doing so could cause a load imbalance in the SM.

CUDA TOOLS TO IDENTIFY LIMITING FACTORS

CUDA provides several tools to work with your code and the concurrency of your kernels.

The CUDA Occupancy Calculator is a good tool to use during the planning stages to understand occupancy across devices. As shown in Figure 4.4, "Screenshot of the CUDA Occupancy Calculator," this is a spreadsheet that the programmer can use to ask "what if" questions based on register and shared memory usage.

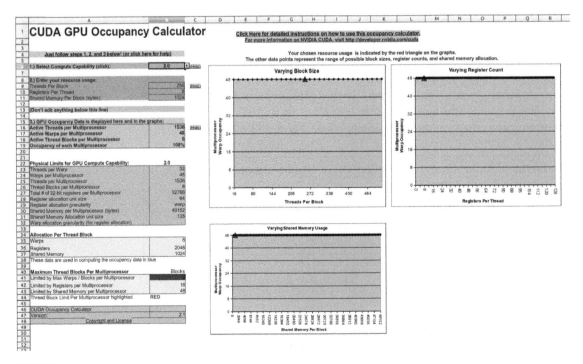

FIGURE 4.4
Screenshot of the CUDA Occupancy Calculator.

The nvcc Compiler

The **nvcc** compiler provides a common compilation framework for the UNIX, Windows, and Mac OS X operating systems.

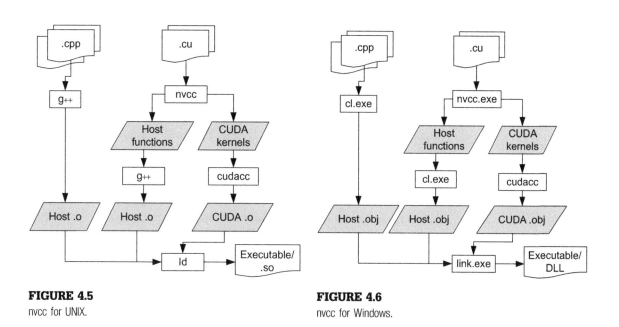

FIGURE 4.5
nvcc for UNIX.

FIGURE 4.6
nvcc for Windows.

As shown in Example 4.5, the **nvcc** compiler provides the **#pragma unroll** directive, which can be used to control unrolling of any given loop. It must be placed immediately before the loop and applies only to that loop. By default, the compiler unrolls small loops with a known trip count. If the loop is large or the trip count cannot be determined, the user can specify how many times the loop is to be unrolled.

The **#pragma unroll 16** used in Example 4.5 tells the compiler to unroll the loop 16 times to prevent the control logic of the **for** loop from interfering with the ILP test results.

The primary benefits gained from loop unrolling are:

- Reduced dynamic instruction count due to fewer number of compare and branch operations for the same amount of work done.
- Better scheduling opportunities due to the availability of additional independent instructions can improve ILP plus hide pipeline and memory access latencies.

- Opportunities for exploiting register and memory hierarchy locality when outer loops are unrolled and inner loops are fused (unroll-and-jam transformation).

Loop unrolling is not a panacea, as it can degrade performance due to excessive register usage and spilling to local memory.

The following **nvcc** command-line switches are also important for optimization and code generation:

- **-arch=sm_20** generates code for compute 2.0 devices.
- **-maxrregcount=N** specifies the maximum number of registers kernels can use at a per-file level.
- The **__launch_bounds__** qualifier can be inserted in the declaration of the kernel as shown in Example 4.6 to control the number of registers on a per-kernel basis.
- **--ptxas-options=-v** or **-Xptxas=-v** lists per-kernel register, shared, and constant memory usage.
- **-use_fast_math** coerces every **functionName()** call to the equivalent native hardware function call name, **__functionName()**. This approach makes the code run faster at the cost of slightly diminished precision and accuracy.

Launch Bounds

Controlling register usage is key to achieving high performance in CUDA. To minimize register usage, the compiler utilizes a set of *heuristics*. A heuristic is a rule-of-thumb guideline generally derived from observation and trial and error.

The developer can aid the compiler through the use of a **__launch_bounds__** qualifier in the definition of a **__global__** function as shown in Example 4.6, "Example Launch Bounds Usage" where:

Example 4.6

```
__global__ void
__launch_bounds__ (maxThreadsPerBlock, minBlocksPerMultiprocessor)
kernel(float a, float b, float c)
{
...
}
```

- **maxThreadsPerBlock** specifies the maximum number of threads per block with which the application will use.
- **minBlocksPerMultiprocessor** is optional and specifies the desired minimum number of resident blocks per multiprocessor. It compiles to the **.minnctapersm** PTX directive.

If launch bounds are specified, the compiler has the opportunity to increase register usage to better hide instruction latency. A kernel will fail to launch if the execution configuration specifies more threads per block than allowed by the launch bounds directive.

The Disassembler

The **cuobjdump** disassembler is a useful tool to examine the instructions generated by the compiler. It can be utilized to examine the mix of instructions provided in a warp to the SM as well as checking on what the compiler is doing. Example 4.7, "cuobjdump without loop unrolling," is the code for Example 4.5 without loop unrolling. The bold code shows that only one fused mult-add (FFMA) instruction is utilized.

Example 4.7

```
code for sm_20
        Function : _Z6kernelfff
/*0000*/   /*0x00005de428004404*/   MOV R1, c [0x1] [0x100];
/*0008*/   /*0x80001de428004000*/   MOV R0, c [0x0] [0x20];
/*0010*/   /*0xfc009de428000000*/   MOV R2, RZ;
/*0018*/   /*0x04209c034800c000*/   IADD R2, R2, 0x1;
/*0020*/   /*0x9000dde428004000*/   MOV R3, c [0x0] [0x24];
/*0028*/   /*0x0421dc231a8e4000*/   ISETP.NE.AND P0, pt, R2,
                                     c [0x10] [0x0], pt;
/*0030*/   /*0xa0301c0030008000*/   FFMA R0, R3, R0, c [0x0] [0x28];
/*0038*/   /*0x600001e74003ffff*/   @P0 BRA 0x18;
/*0040*/   /*0x84009c042c000000*/   S2R R2, SR_Tid_X;
/*0048*/   /*0x0000dde428007800*/   MOV R3, c [0xe] [0x0];
/*0050*/   /*0x10211c032007c000*/   IMAD.U32.U32 R4.CC,
                                     R2, 0x4, R3;
/*0058*/   /*0x10209c435000c000*/   IMUL.U32.U32.HI R2, R2, 0x4;
/*0060*/   /*0x10215c4348007800*/   IADD.X R5, R2, c [0xe] [0x4];
/*0068*/   /*0x00401c8594000000*/   ST.E [R4], R0;
/*0070*/   /*0x00001de780000000*/   EXIT;
        . . . . . . . . . . . . . . . . . . . . . .
```

The impact of the loop unrolling can be seen in Example 4.8, "cuobjdump showing loop unrolling," through the replication of the FFMA instruction:

Example 4.8

```
code for sm_20
        Function : _Z6kernelfff
/*0000*/   /*0x00005de428004404*/   MOV R1, c [0x1] [0x100];
/*0008*/   /*0x80001de428004000*/   MOV R0, c [0x0] [0x20];
```

```
/*0010*/    /*0xfc009de428000000*/    MOV R2, RZ;
/*0018*/    /*0x9000dde428004000*/    MOV R3, c [0x0] [0x24];
/*0020*/    /*0x40209c034800c000*/    IADD R2, R2, 0x10;
/*0028*/    /*0xa0301c0030008000*/    FFMA R0, R3, R0, c [0x0] [0x28];
/*0030*/    /*0x0421dc231a8e4000*/    ISETP.NE.AND P0, pt, R2, c [0x10]
                                        [0x0], pt;
/*0038*/    /*0xa0301c0030008000*/    FFMA R0, R3, R0, c [0x0] [0x28];
/*0040*/    /*0xa0301c0030008000*/    FFMA R0, R3, R0, c [0x0] [0x28];
/*0048*/    /*0xa0301c0030008000*/    FFMA R0, R3, R0, c [0x0] [0x28];
/*0050*/    /*0xa0301c0030008000*/    FFMA R0, R3, R0, c [0x0] [0x28];
/*0058*/    /*0xa0301c0030008000*/    FFMA R0, R3, R0, c [0x0] [0x28];
/*0060*/    /*0xa0301c0030008000*/    FFMA R0, R3, R0, c [0x0] [0x28];
/*0068*/    /*0xa0301c0030008000*/    FFMA R0, R3, R0, c [0x0] [0x28];
/*0070*/    /*0xa0301c0030008000*/    FFMA R0, R3, R0, c [0x0] [0x28];
/*0078*/    /*0xa0301c0030008000*/    FFMA R0, R3, R0, c [0x0] [0x28];
/*0080*/    /*0xa0301c0030008000*/    FFMA R0, R3, R0, c [0x0] [0x28];
/*0088*/    /*0xa0301c0030008000*/    FFMA R0, R3, R0, c [0x0] [0x28];
/*0090*/    /*0xa0301c0030008000*/    FFMA R0, R3, R0, c [0x0] [0x28];
/*0098*/    /*0xa0301c0030008000*/    FFMA R0, R3, R0, c [0x0] [0x28];
/*00a0*/    /*0xa0301c0030008000*/    FFMA R0, R3, R0, c [0x0] [0x28];
/*00a8*/    /*0xa0301c0030008000*/    FFMA R0, R3, R0, c [0x0] [0x28];
/*00b0*/    /*0x800001e74003fffd*/    @P0 BRA 0x18;
/*00b8*/    /*0x84009c042c000000*/    S2R R2, SR_Tid_X;
/*00c0*/    /*0x0000dde428007800*/    MOV R3, c [0xe] [0x0];
/*00c8*/    /*0x10211c032007c000*/    IMAD.U32.U32 R4.CC, R2, 0x4, R3;
/*00d0*/    /*0x10209c435000c000*/    IMUL.U32.U32.HI R2, R2, 0x4;
/*00d8*/    /*0x10215c4348007800*/    IADD.X R5, R2, c [0xe] [0x4];
/*00e0*/    /*0x00401c8594000000*/    ST.E [R4], R0;
/*00e8*/    /*0x00001de780000000*/    EXIT;
..........................
```

As of CUDA 4.0, the **nvcc** compiler has the ability to include inline PTX assembly language. PTX is the low-level parallel thread execution virtual machine and instruction set architecture (ISA). The most current information on PTX can be found in the document "PTX: Parallel Thread Execution ISA" that is included with each release.

PTX Kernels

Giving developers the ability to disassemble and create assembly language kernels provides everything an adventurous programmer needs to directly program the SM on a GPU. The PTX kernel in Example 4.9 was taken from the NVIDIA **ptxjit** sample provided with the SDK samples:

Example 4.9

```
/*
 * PTX is equivalent to the following kernel:
 *
 * __global__ void myKernel(int *data)
 * {
 *         int tid = blockIdx.x * blockDim.x + threadIdx.x;
 *         data[tid] = tid;
 * }
 *
 */
char myPtx[] = "\n\
        .version 1.4\n\
        .target sm_10, map_f64_to_f32\n\
        .entry _Z8myKernelPi (\n\
                .param .u64 __cudaparm__Z8myKernelPi_data)\n\
        {\n\
        .reg .u16 %rh<4>;\n\
        .reg .u32 %r<5>;\n\
        .reg .u64 %rd<6>;\n\
        cvt.u32.u16     %r1, %tid.x;\n\
        mov.u16         %rh1, %ctaid.x;\n\
        mov.u16         %rh2, %ntid.x;\n\
        mul.wide.u16    %r2, %rh1, %rh2;\n\
        add.u32         %r3, %r1, %r2;\n\
        ld.param.u64    %rd1, [__cudaparm__Z8myKernelPi_data];\n\
        cvt.s64.s32     %rd2, %r3;\n\
        mul.wide.s32    %rd3, %r3, 4;\n\
        add.u64         %rd4, %rd1, %rd3;\n\
        st.global.s32   [%rd4+0], %r3;\n\
        exit;\n\
        }\n\
";
```

GPU Emulators

GPU simulators such as ocelot have unique abilities to characterize the run-time behavior of CUDA kernels code that are not available to other tools in the GPU toolchain (Farooqui, Kerr, Diamos, Yalamanchili, & Schwan, 2011). Features include:

- Workload characterization
- Load imbalance
- "Hot-spots" in the PTX code

The ocelot tool that can be freely downloaded.

SUMMARY

Understanding the SM is the key to understanding GPGPU programming. The twin concepts of a thread block and warp of SIMD threads encompass the scalability, performance, and power efficiency of GPU computing. Knowing how instructions execute in parallel within an SM, as well as the factors that stall the instruction pipeline, is fundamental to understanding GPGPU application performance. Little's law, and queuing theory in general, provide the theoretical foundation upon which very detailed GPU and application models can be based. Empirical studies have shown that exploiting both ILP and TLP provides the highest application performance. The benefits have been so significant that both ILP and TLP are now utilized in the CUBLAS and CUFFT libraries, which are the keystone of many applications.

Knowledgeable CUDA programmers have the ability to incorporate both ILP and TLP in their applications. NVIDIA has provided the necessary tools so that UNIX, Windows, and Mac OS X developers can examine, experiment with, and alter the instruction mix in their kernels to best exploit ILP and capture TLP with controlled register usage. Exploiting these tools can make the difference between good and great performance. Similarly, understanding and avoiding warp divergence can make all the difference when programming with irregular data structures or for applications that have irregular boundaries.

## CHAPTER 5

CUDA Memory

High-performance GPGPU applications require reuse of data inside the SM. The reason is that on-board *global memory* is simply not fast enough to meet the needs of all the streaming multiprocessors on the GPU. Data transfers from the host and other GPGPUs further exacerbate the problem as all DMA (Direct Memory Access) operations go through global memory, which consumes additional memory bandwidth. CUDA exposes the memory spaces within the SM and provides configurable caches to give the developer the greatest opportunity for data reuse. Managing the significant performance difference between on-board and on-chip memory to attain high-performance needs is of paramount important to a CUDA programmer.

At the end of this chapter, the reader will have a basic understanding of:

- Why memory bandwidth is a key gating factor for application performance.
- The different CUDA memory types and how CUDA exposes the memory on the SM.
- The L1 cache and importance for register spilling, global memory accesses, recursion, and divide-and-conquer algorithms.
- Important memory-related profiler measurements.
- Limitations on hardware memory design.

THE CUDA MEMORY HIERARCHY

The CUDA programming model assumes that the all threads execute on a physically separate device from the host running the application. Implicit is the assumption that the host and all the devices maintain their own

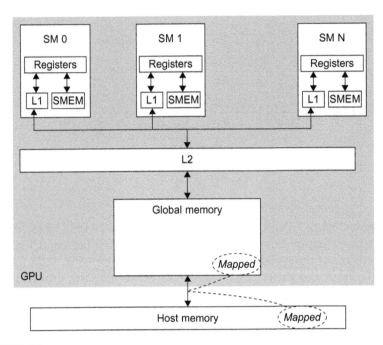

FIGURE 5.1

The CUDA memory hierarchy.

separate memory spaces, referred to as host and device memory,[1] and that some form of bulk transfer is the mechanism of data transport.

The line between the host and device memory becomes somewhat blurred when host memory is mapped into the address space of the GPU. In this way, modifications by either the device or host will be reflected in the memory space of all the devices mapping a region of memory. Pages are transparently transferred asynchronously between the host and GPU(s). Experienced programmers will recognize that mapped memory is analogous to the **mmap()** system call.

Uniform Virtual Addressing (UVA) is a CUDA 4.0 feature that simplifies multi-GPU programming by giving the runtime the ability to determine upon which device a region of memory resides purely on the basis of the pointer address. Semantically, UVA gives CUDA developers the ability to perform direct GPU-to-GPU data transfers with **cudaMemcpy()**. To use it, just register the memory region with **cudaHostRegister()**. Bulk data transfers can then occur between devices by calling **cudaMemcpy()**. The runtime will ensure that the appropriate source and destination devices are used in the transfer. The method **cudaHostUnregister(ptr)** terminates the use of UVA data transfers for that region of memory. See Figure 5.1.

---

[1] Some low-end devices actually share the same memory as the host, but they do not change the programming model.

Table 5.1 Bandwidth of Various GPU Memory	
Register memory	≈8,000 GB/s
Shared memory	≈1,600 GB/s
Global memory	177 GB/s
Mapped memory	≈8 GB/s one-way

GPU MEMORY

CUDA-enabled GPGPUs have both on-chip and on-board memory. The fastest and most scalable is the highly desirable on-chip SM memory. These are limited memory stores measured in kilobytes (KB) of storage. The on-board global memory is a shared memory system accessible by all the SM across the GPU. It is measured in gigabytes (GB) of memory, which is by far the largest, most commonly used, and slowest memory store on the GPU.

Benchmarks have shown the significant bandwidth differences between on-chip and off-chip memory systems (see Table 5.1). Only registers internal to the SM have the bandwidth needed to keep the SM fully loaded (without stalls) to achieve peak performance. Although the bandwidth of shared memory can greatly accelerate applications, it is still too slow to achieve peak performance (Volkov, 2010).

Managing the significant performance difference between on-board and on-chip memory is the primary concern of a CUDA programmer. To put the performance implications in perspective, consider how memory bandwidth limits the performance of the following simple calculation when it resides in global memory, in Example 5.1, "A Simple Memory-Bandwidith-Limited Calculation":

Example 5.1

```
for(i=0; i < N; i++) c[i] = a[i] * b[i];
```

Each floating-point multiply requires two memory reads and a write. Assuming that single-precision (32-bit or 4-byte) floating-point values are being used, a teraflop (trillion floating-point operations per second) GPU would require 12 terabytes per second (TB/s) of memory bandwidth for this calculation to run at full speed. Said another way, a GPU with 177 GB/s of memory bandwidth could only deliver 14 Gflop, or approximately 1.4 percent of the performance of a teraflop GPU. When the extra precision of 64-bit (8-byte) floating-point arithmetic is required, the reader can halve the effective computational rate.[2]

---

[2] Data reuse is important on conventional processors as well. The impact tends to be less dramatic when an application becomes memory-bound because conventional systems have fewer processing cores.

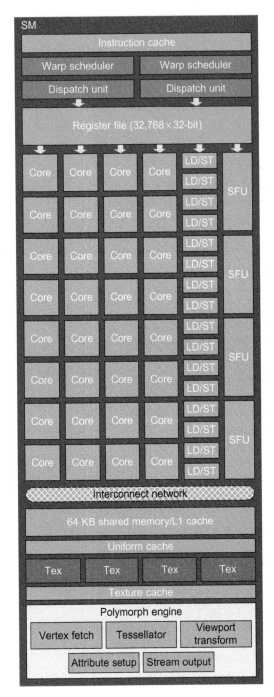

FIGURE 5.2

A GF100 streaming multiprocessor.

Clearly, it is necessary to reuse the data within the SM to achieve high performance. Only by exploiting data *locality* can a programmer minimize global memory transactions and keep data in fast memory. GPGPUs support two types of locality as they accelerate both computational and rendering applications:

- Temporal locality: assumes that a recently accessed data item is likely to be used again in the near future. Many computational applications demonstrate this LRU (Least Recently Used) behavior.
- Spatial locality: neighboring data is cached with the expectation that spatially adjacent memory locations will be used in the near future. Rendering operations tend to have high 2D spatial locality.

As can be seen in Figure 5.2, the SM also contains constant (labeled Uniform cache in the figure) and texture memory caches. Though desirable, the L1 and L2 caches in compute 2.0 devices have subsumed much of the capability of these memory spaces. When programming compute 1.x devices, constant memory must be used when data needs to be efficiently broadcast to all the threads. Texture memory can be used as a form of cache to avoid global memory bandwidth limitations and handle some small irregular memory accesses (Haixiang, Schmidt, Weiguo, & Müller-Wittig, 2010). However, the texture cache is relatively small—on the order of 8 KB. Of course, visualization is the intended usage and greatest value for texture memory across all compute device generations.

Compute 2.0 devices added an L1 cache to each SM and a unified L2 cache that fits between all the SM and global memory, as shown in Figure 5.1.

L2 CACHE

The unified L2 (Level 2) cache is a tremendous labor-saving device that works as a fast data store accessible by all the SM on the GPU. A great many applications will suddenly run faster on compute 2.0 devices because of the L2 cache. Two reasons are:

- Without requiring any intervention by the CUDA programmer, the L2 will cache data in an LRU fashion that allows many CUDA kernels avoid global memory bandwidth bottlenecks.
- The L2 cache greatly speeds irregular memory access patterns that otherwise would exhibit extremely poor GPU performance. For many algorithms, this characteristic will determine whether an application can be used on compute 1.x hardware.

Fermi GPUs provide a 768 KB unified L2 cache that is guaranteed to present a coherent view to all SMs. In other words, any thread can modify a value held in the L2 cache. At a later time, any other thread on the GPU can read that particular memory address and receive the correct, updated value. Of course, atomic operations must be used to guarantee that the store (or write) transaction completes before other threads are allowed read access.

Previous GPGPU architectures had challenges with this very common read/update operation because two separate data paths were utilized—specifically, the read-only texture load path and the write-only pixel data output path. To ensure data correctness, older GPU architectures required that all participating caches along the read path be potentially invalidated and flushed after any thread modified the value of an in-cache memory location. The Fermi architecture eliminated this bottleneck with the unified L2 cache along with the need for the texture and Raster Output (ROP) caches in earlier-generation GPUs.

All data loads and stores go through the L2 cache *including CPU/GPU memory copies*, emphasized to stress that host data transfers might unexpectedly affect cache hits and thus application performance. Similarly, asynchronous kernel execution can also pollute the cache.

Relevant computeprof Values for the L2 Cache

Table 5.2 Visual Profiler Values for the L2 Cache

L2 cache texture memory read throughput (GB/s)	This value gives the throughput achieved while reading data from L2 cache when a request for data residing in texture memory is made. This is calculated as (l2 read tex requests * 32)/(gpu time * 1000)
L2 cache global memory read throughput (GB/s)	This value gives the throughput achieved while reading data from L2 cache when a request for data residing in global memory is made by L1. This is calculated as (l2 read requests * 32)/(gpu time * 1000)
L2 cache global memory write throughput (GB/s)	This value gives the throughput achieved while writing data to L2 cache when a request to store data in global memory is made by L1. This is calculated as (l2 write requests * 32)/(gpu time * 1000)

(continued)

Table 5.2 Visual Profiler Values for the L2 Cache—cont'd

L2 cache global memory throughput (GB/s)	This value is the combined L2 cache read and write memory throughput. This is calculated as (L2 cache global memory read throughput + L2 cache global memory write throughput)
L2 cache read hit ratio (%)	Percentage of hits that occur in L2 cache while reading from global memory. This is calculated as 100 * (L2 cache global memory read throughput – glob mem read throughput)/ (L2 cache global memory read throughput)
L2 cache write hit ratio (%)	Percentage of hits that occur in L2 cache while writing to global memory. This is calculated as 100 * (L2 cache global memory write throughput – glob mem write throughput)/ (L2 cache global memory write throughput)

L1 CACHE

Compute 2.0 devices have 64 KB of L1 memory that can be partitioned to favor shared memory or dynamic read/write operations. Note that the L1 cache:

- Is designed for *spatial and not temporal reuse*. Most developers expect processor caches that behave as an LRU cache. On a GPU, this mistaken assumption can lead to unexpected cache misses, as frequently accessing a cached L1 memory location does not guarantee that the memory location will stay in the cache.
- Will not be affected by stores to global memory, as store operations bypass the L1 cache.
- Is not coherent. The volatile keyword must be used when declaring shared memory that can be modified by threads in other blocks to guarantee that the compiler will not load the shared memory location into a register. Private data (registers, stack, etc.) can be used without concern.
- Has a latency of 10–20 cycles.

The L1 caches per-thread local data structures such the per-thread stack. The addition of a stack allows compute 2.0 devices to support recursive routines (routines that call themselves). Many problems can be naturally expressed in a recursive form. For example, *divide-and-conquer* methods repeatedly break a larger problem into smaller subproblems. At some point, the problem becomes simple enough to solve directly. The solutions to the subproblems are combined to give a solution to the initial problem. The stack can consume up to 1 KB of the L1 cache.

CUDA also uses an abstract memory type called *local memory*. Local memory is not a separate memory system *per se* but rather a memory location used to hold spilled registers. Register spilling occurs when a thread block requires more register storage than is available on an SM. Pre-Fermi GPUs spilled registers to global memory, which caused a dramatic drop in application performance, as three-orders-of-magnitude-slower GB/s global memory accesses replaced TB/s register memory. Compute 2.0 and later devices spill registers to the L1 cache, which minimizes the performance impact of register spills.

If desired, the Fermi L1 cache can be deactivated with the **-Xptxas -dlcm=cg** command-line argument to **nvcc**. Even when deactivated, both the stack and local memory still reside in the L1 cache memory.

The beauty in this configurability is that applications that reuse data or have misaligned, unpredictable, or irregular memory access patterns can configure the L1 cache as a 48 KB dynamic cache (leaving 16 KB for shared memory) while applications that need to share more data amongst threads inside a thread block can assign 48 KB as shared memory (leaving 16 KB for the cache). In this way, the NVIDIA designers empowered the application developer to configure the memory within the SM to achieve the best performance.

The L1 cache is utilized when the compiler generates an LDU (LoaD Uniform) instruction to cache data that needs to be efficiently broadcast to all the threads within the SM. Previous generations of GPUs could broadcast information efficiently among all the threads in an application only from constant memory.

Compute 2.0 devices can broadcast data from global memory without requiring explicit programmer intervention, subject to the following conditions:

1. The pointer is prefixed with the **const** keyword.
2. The memory access is uniform across all the threads in the block as in Example 5.2, "A Uniform Memory Access Example":

> **Example 5.2**
> ```
> __global__ void kernel( float *g_dst, const float *g_src )
> {
>     g_dst = g_src[0] + g_src[blockIdx.x];
> }
> ```

Relevant computeprof Values for the L1 Cache

Table 5.3 Visual Profiler Values for the L1 Cache

L1 gld hit rate (%)	This value is calculated as 100*(L1 global load hit count)/((L1 global load hit count) + (L1 global load miss count))
L1 cache read throughput (GB/s)	This value gives the throughput achieved while accessing data from L1 cache. This is calculated as [(L1 global load hit + L1 local load hit) * 128 * #SM + L2 read requests * 32]/(gpu time * 1000)
L1 cache global hit ratio (%)	Percentage of hits that occur in L1 cache while accessing global memory. This statistic will be zero when L1 cache is disabled. This is calculated as (100 * L1 global load hit)/(L1 global load hit + L1 global load miss)

CUDA MEMORY TYPES

Table 5.4 summarizes the characteristics of the various CUDA memory spaces for compute 2.0 and later devices.

Table 5.4 CUDA Memory Types and Characteristics

Memory	Location	Cached	Access	Scope
Register	On-chip	No	Read/write	One thread
Local	On-chip	Yes	Read/write	One thread
Shared	On-chip	N/A	Read/write	All threads in a block
Global	Off-chip (unless cached)	Yes	Read/write	All threads + host
Constant	Off-chip (unless cached)	Yes	Read	All threads + host
Texture	Off-chip (unless cached)	Yes	Read/write	All threads + host

Registers

Registers are the fastest memory on the GPU. They are a very precious resource because they are the only memory on the GPU with enough bandwidth and a low enough latency to deliver peak performance.

Each GF100 SM supports 32 K 32-bit registers. The maximum number of registers that can be used by a CUDA kernel is 63, due to the limited number of bits available for indexing into the register store. The number of available registers varies on a Fermi SM:

- If the SM is running 1,536 threads, then only 21 registers can be used.
- The number of available registers degrades gracefully from 63 to 21 as the workload (and hence resource requirements) increases by number of threads.

Register spilling on GF100 SM increases the importance of the L1 cache because it can preserve high performance. Be aware that pressure from register spilling and the stack (which can consume 1 KB of L1 storage) can increase the cache miss rate by forcing data to be evicted.

Local memory

Local memory accesses occur for only some automatic variables. An automatic variable is declared in the device code without any of the __device__, __shared__, or __constant__ qualifiers. Generally, an automatic variable resides in a register except for the following:

- Arrays that the compiler cannot determine are indexed with constant quantities.
- Large structures or arrays that would consume too much register space.
- Any variable the compiler decides to spill to local memory when a kernel uses more registers than are available on the SM.

The **nvcc** compiler reports total local memory usage per kernel (lmem) when compiling with **the –ptxas-options=-v** option. These reported values may be affected by some mathematical functions that access local memory.

Relevant computeprof Values for Local Memory Cache

Table 5.5 Visual Profiler Values for the Local Memory
Local memory bus traffic (%)	Percentage of bus traffic caused due to accesses to local memory. This is calculated as $$(2*L1 \text{ local load miss}*128*100)/((L2 \text{ read requests} + L2 \text{ write requests})*32/\#SMs)$$

Shared Memory

Shared memory (also referred to as smem) can be either 16 KB or 48 KB per SM arranged in 32 banks that are 32 bits wide. Contrary to early NVIDIA documentation, shared memory is not as fast as register memory.

Shared memory can be allocated three different ways:

1. Statically within the kernel or globally within the file as shown in the declaration in Example 5.3, "A Static Shared Memory Declaration":

   Example 5.3
   ```
   __shared__ int s_data[256];
   ```

2. Dynamically within the kernel by calling the driver API function **cuFuncSetSharedSize**.
3. Dynamically via the execution configuration.

Only a single block of shared memory can be allocated via the execution configuration. Using more than one dynamically allocated shared memory variable in a kernel requires manually generating the offsets for each variable. Example 5.4, "Multiple Variables in a Dynamically Allocated Shared Memory Block," shows how to allocate and utilize two dynamically allocated shared memory vectors **a** and **b**:

   Example 5.4
   ```
   __global__ void kernel(int aSize)
   {
       extern __shared__ float sData[];
       float *a, *b;

       a = sData; // a starts at the beginning of the dynamically allocated
       smem block
   ```

```
    b = &a[aSize]; // b starts immediately following the end of a in the
    smem block
}
```

The kernel call would look like Example 5.5, "Execution Configuration that Dynamically Allocates Shared Memory":

Example 5.5

```
Kernel<<<nBlocks, nThreadPerBlock, nBytesSharedMemory>>>(aSize);
```

Shared memory is arranged in 32 four-byte-wide banks on the SM. Under ideal circumstances, 32 threads will be able to access shared memory in parallel without performance degradation. Unfortunately, *bank conflicts* occur when multiple requests are made by different threads for data within the same bank. These requests can either be for the same address or for multiple addresses that map to the same bank. When this happens, the hardware serializes the memory operations. If n threads within a warp cause a bank conflict, then n accesses are executed serially, causing an n-times slowdown on that SM.

The size of the memory request can also cause a bank conflict. Shared memory in compute 2.0 devices has been improved to support double-precision variables in shared memory without causing warp serialization. Previous-generation GPUs required a workaround that involved splitting 64-bit data into two 32-bit values and storing them separately in shared memory. Be aware that the majority of 128-bit memory accesses (e.g., **float4**) will still cause a two-way bank conflict in shared memory on compute 2.0 devices.

Padding shared memory to avoid bank conflicts represents a portability challenge. Example 5.6, "Shared Memory Padded for a GT200/Tesla C1060" illustratres an older code that

Example 5.6

```
__shared__ tile [16][17];
```

must change both tile size and padding to warp size for compute 2.0 devices, as in Example 5.7, "Shared Memory Padded for a Compute 2.0 Device":

Example 5.7

```
__shared__ tile [32][33];
```

Notice that a column was added in the previous example to prevent a bank conflict. In this case, wasting space is preferable to accepting the performance slowdown. Without the padding, every consecutive column index access within a warp would serialize.

Shared memory has the ability to multicast, which means that if *n* threads within a warp access the same word at the same time, then only a single shared memory fetch occurs. Compute 2.0 devices broadcast the entire word, which means that multiple threads can access different bytes within the broadcast word without affecting performance. Whole-word broadcast was available only in 1.x devices. Subword accesses within the broadcast word, or the same bank, caused serialization.

Threads can communicate via shared memory without using the _syncthreads barrier, as long as they all belong to the same warp. See Example 5.8, "A Barrier Is Not Required When Sharing Data within a Warp":

Example 5.8
```
if (tid < 32) { ... }
```

If shared memory is used to communicate between warps in a thread block, make certain to have **volatile** in front of the shared memory declaration. The **volatile** keyword eliminates the possibility that the compiler might silently cache the previously loaded shared memory value in a register and fail to reload it again on next reference. Due to architectural changes:

- Compute 1.x devices access shared memory only directly as an operand.
- Compute 2.0 devices have a load/store architecture that can bring data into registers.

Legacy codes need to add a **volatile** keyword to avoid errors when running on compute 2.0 devices. As shown in the following example, a simple __shared__ declaration was sufficient on compute 1.x devices. The legacy code needs to be changed, as shown in Example 5.9, "A Volatile Must Be Added to Codes that Communicate across Thread Blocks with Shared Memory":

Example 5.9
```
__shared__ int cross[32]; // acceptable for 1.x devices

// Compute 2.0 devices require a volatile
volatile __shared__ int cross[32];
```

Volkov notes that the trend in parallel architecture design is towards an inverse memory hierarchy where the number of registers is increasing compared to cache and shared memory. Scalability and performance are the reasons as registers can be replicated along with the SM (or the processor core in a multicore processor). More registers means that more data can be kept in high-speed memory, which means that more instructions can run without external dependencies resulting in higher performance (Volkov, 2010). He also notes that the performance gap between shared memory and arithmetic throughput has increased with Fermi, raising concerns that the current shared memory hardware on the Fermi architecture is a step backward (Volkov, 2010).

Table 5.6 shows the ratio of shared memory banks to thread processors compared to the number of registers per thread.

Table 5.6 Trends Toward an Inverse Memory Hierarchy			
Architecture	Banks vs. Thread Processors	Ratio of Banks to Thread Processors	Registers per Thread
G80-GT200	16 banks vs. 8 thread processors	2:1	128
GF100	32 banks vs. 32 thread processors	1:1	21–64

For portability, performance, and scalability reasons, it is highly recommended that registers be used instead of shared memory whenever possible.

Relevant computeprof Values for Shared Memory

Table 5.7 Visual Profiler Values for smem	
Shared memory bank conflict per shared memory instruction (%)	This value gives an indication of the number of bank conflicts caused per shared memory instruction. This value may exceed 100% if there are n-way bank conflicts or the data accessed is double precision. This is calculated as 100*(L1 shared bank conflict)/(shared load + shared store)
Shared bank conflict replay (%)	Percentage of replayed instructions caused due to shared memory bank conflicts. This is calculated as 100*(L1 shared conflict)/instructions issued

Constant Memory

For compute 1.x devices, constant memory is an excellent way to store and broadcast read-only data to all the threads on the GPU. The constant cache is limited to 64 KB. It can broadcast 32-bits per warp per two clocks per multiprocessor and should be used when all the threads in a warp read the same address. Otherwise, the accesses will serialize on compute 1.x devices.

Compute 2.0 and higher devices allow developers to access global memory with the efficiency of constant memory when the compiler can recognize and use the LDU instruction. Specifically, the data must:

- Reside in global memory.
- Be read-only in the kernel (programmer can enforce this using the **const** keyword).
- Must not depend on the thread ID.

See Example 5.10, "Examples of Uniform and Nonuniform Constant Memory Accesses":

Example 5.10

```
__global__ void kernel( const float *g_a )
{
    float x = g_a[15]; // uniform
    float y = g_a[blockIdx.x + 5] ; // uniform
    float z = g_a[threadIdx.x] ; // not uniform !
}
```

There is no need for **__constant__** declaration; plus, there is no fixed limit to the amount of data, as is the case with constant memory. Still, constant memory is useful on compute 2.0 devices when there is enough pressure on the cache to cause eviction of the data that is to be broadcast.

Constant memory is statically allocated within a file. Only the host can write to constant memory, which can be accessed via the runtime library methods: **cudaGetSymbolAddress()**, **cudaGetSymbolSize()**, **cudaMemcpyToSymbol()**, and **cudaMemcpyFromSymbol()**, plus **cuModuleGetGlobal()** from the driver API.

Texture Memory

Textures are bound to global memory and can provide both cache and some limited, 9-bit processing capabilities. How the global memory that the texture binds to is allocated dictates some of the capabilities the texture can provide. For this reason, it is important to distinguish between three memory types that can be bound to a texture (see Table 5.8).

For CUDA programmers, the most salient points about using texture memory are:

- Texture memory is generally used in visualization.
- The cache is optimized for 2D spatial locality.
- It contains only 8 KB of cache per SM.

Table 5.8 How Memory Was Created Defines the Texture Capability

Memory Type	How Created	Texture Capability	Texture Update
Linear memory	cudaMalloc()	• Acts as a linear cache	Free to write to the global memory from threads if the incoherence is safe.
CUDA arrays	cudaMallocArray(), cudaMalloc3D()	• Cache optimized for spatial locality • Interpolation, wrapping, and clamping	Writing to arrays from a kernel is not allowed.
2D pitch linear memory	cudaMallocPitch()	• Cache optimized for spatial locality • Interpolation, wrapping, and clamping	Free to write to the global memory from threads if the incoherence is safe.

- Textures have limited processing capabilities that can efficiently unpack and broadcast data. Thus, a single **float4** texture read is faster than four separate 32-bit reads.
- Textures have separate 9-bit computational units that perform out-of-bounds index handling, interpolation, and format conversion from integer types (char, short, int) to float.
- A thread can safely read some texture or surface memory location only if this memory location has been updated by a previous kernel call or memory copy, but not if it has been previously updated by the same thread or another thread from the same kernel call.

It is important to distinguish between textures bound to memory allocated with **cudaMalloc()** and those bound to padded memory allocated with **cudaMallocPitch()**.

- **When using the texture only as a cache:** In this case, programmers might consider binding the texture memory created with **cudaMalloc()**, because the texture unit cache is small and caching the padding added by **cudaMallocPitch()** would be wasteful.
- **When using the texture to perform some processing:** In this case, it is important to bind the texture to padded memory created with **cudaMallocPitch()** so that the texture unit boundary processing works correctly. In other words, don't bind linear memory created with **cudaMalloc()** and attempt to manually set the pitch to a texture because unexpected things might happen—especially across device generations.

Depending on how the global memory bound to the texture was created, there are several possible ways to fetch from the texture that might also invoke some form of texture processing by the texture.

The simplest way to fetch data from a texture is by using **tex1Dfetch()** because:

- Only integer addressing is supported.
- No additional filtering or addressing modes are provided.

Use of the methods **tex1D()**, **tex2D()**, and **tex3D()** are more complicated because the interpretation of the texture coordinates, what processing occurs during the texture fetch, and the return value delivered by the texture fetch are all controlled by setting the texture reference's mutable (runtime) and immutable (compile-time) attributes:

- Immutable parameters (compile-time).
  - Type: type returned when fetching
    - Basic integer and float types
    - CUDA 1-, 2-, 4-element vectors
  - Dimensionality:
    - Currently 1D, 2D, or 3D
  - Read mode:
    - cudaReadModeElementType
    - cudaReadModeNormalizedFloat (valid for 8- or 16-bit integers). It returns [−1,1] for signed, [0,1] for unsigned
- Mutable parameters (runtime, only for array textures and pitch linear memory).
  - Normalized:
    - Nonzero = addressing range [0,1]
  - Filter mode:
    - cudaFilterModePoint
    - cudaFilterModeLinear
  - Address mode:
    - cudaAddressModeClamp
    - cudaAddressModeWrap

By default, textures are referenced using floating-point coordinates in the range $[0,N)$ where N is the size of the texture in the dimension corresponding to the coordinate. Specifying that normalized texture coordinates will be used implies all references will be in the range $[0,1)$.

The *wrap mode* specifies what happens for out-of-bounds addressing:

- Wrap: out-of-bounds coordinates are wrapped (via modulo arithmetic), as shown in Figure 5.3.
- Clamp: out-of-bounds coordinates are replaced with the closest boundary, as shown in Figure 5.4.

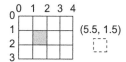

FIGURE 5.3

Example of a texture wrapping an out-of-bounds coordinate.

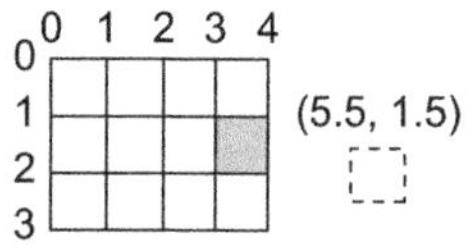

FIGURE 5.4

Example of a texture clamping an out-of-bounds coordinate.

Table 5.9 Visual Profiler Values for Texture Memory

Texture Hit Rate (%)	This Value Is Calculated as 100 *(tex_cache_requests – tex_cache_misses)/(tex_cache_requests)
Texture cache memory throughput (GB/s)	This value gives the memory throughput achieved while reading data from texture memory. This statistic will be zero when texture memory is not used. This is calculated as (#SM * tex cache sector queries * 32)/(gpu time * 1000)
Texture cache hit rate (%)	Percentage of hits that occur in texture cache while accessing data from texture memory. This statistic will be zero when texture memory is not used. This value is calculated as 100 * (tex cache requests – tex cache misses)/tex cache requests

Linear texture filtering may be performed only for textures that are configured to return floating-point data. A *texel*, short for "texture element," is an element of a texture array. Thus, linear texture filtering performs low-precision (9-bit fixed-point with 8-bits of fractional value) interpolation between neighboring texels. When enabled, the texels surrounding a texture fetch location are read and the return value of the texture fetch is interpolated by the texture hardware based on where the texture coordinates fell between the texels. Simple linear interpolation is performed for one-dimensional textures, as shown in Equation 5.1, "Texture linear interpolation."

$$tex(x) = (1 - \alpha)\, T[i] + \alpha T[i + 1] \tag{5.1}$$

Similarly, the dedicated texture hardware will perform bilinear and trilinear filtering for higher-dimensional data.

As long as the 9-bits of accuracy can be tolerated, the dedicated texture units offer an innovative opportunity to gain even greater performance from GPU computing. One example is "GRASSY: Leveraging GPU Texture Units for Asteroseismic Data Analysis" (Townsend, Sankaralingam, & Sinclair, 2011).

Relevant computeprof Values for Texture Memory

Complete working examples utilizing texture memory can be found in Part 13 of my *Doctor Dobb's Journal* tutorial series (http://drdobbs.com/cpp/218100902).

GLOBAL MEMORY

Understanding how to efficiently use global memory is an essential requirement to becoming an adept CUDA programmer. Focusing on data reuse within the SM and caches avoids memory bandwidth limitations. This is the third most important rule of high-performance GPGPU programming, as introduced in Chapter 1:

1. Get the data on the GPGPU and keep it there.

2. Give the GPGPU enough work to do.

3. Focus on data reuse within the GPGPU to avoid memory bandwidth limitations.

At some point, it is not possible to avoid global memory, in which case it is essential to understand how to use global memory effectively. In particular, the Fermi architecture made some important changes in how CUDA programmers need to think about and use global memory.

From the developer's perspective, it cannot be stressed too strongly that all global memory accesses need to be perfectly coalesced. A coalesced memory access means that the hardware can coalesce, or combine, the memory requests from the threads into a single wide memory transaction. Best performance occurs when:

- The memory address is aligned. The NVIDIA CUDA C Best Practices Guide points out that misaligned accesses can cause an 8 times reduction in global memory bandwidth on older devices. A Fermi GPU with caching enabled would see around a 15 percent drop (Micikevicius, 2010). The authors of the NVIDIA guide note that, "Memory allocated through the runtime API, such as via **cudaMalloc()**, is guaranteed to be aligned to at least 256 bytes. Therefore, choosing sensible thread block sizes, such as multiples of 16, facilitates memory accesses by half warps that are aligned to segments. In addition, the qualifiers **__align__(8)** and **__align__(16)** can be used when defining structures to ensure alignment to segments." (CUDA C Best Practices Guide p. 27)
- A warp accesses all the data within a contiguous region, which means that the wider memory transaction is 100 percent efficient because every byte retrieved is utilized.

As discussed in Chapter 4, try to keep enough memory requests in flight to fully utilize the global memory subsystem:

- From an ILP perspective, attempt to process several elements per threads to pipeline multiple loads. A side benefit is that indexing calculations can often be reused.
- From a TLP perspective, launch enough threads to maximize throughput.

Analyze the memory requests in your application via the source code and profiler output. Experiment with the caching configurations and shared memory vs. L1 cache configuration to see what works best.

From a hardware perspective memory requests are issued in groups of 32 threads (as opposed to 16 in previous architectures), which matches the instruction issue width. Thus, the 32 addresses of a warp should ideally address a contiguous, aligned region to stream data from global memory at the highest bandwidth.

There are two types of loads from global memory:

- **Caching loads:** This is the default mode. A memory fetch transaction attempts to find the data in the L1 and then the L2 caches. Failing that, a 128-byte cache line load is issued.

- **Noncaching loads:** When lots of data needs to be fetched but not from consecutive addresses, better performance might be achieved by turning off the L1 cache with the **nvcc** command-line option **-Xptxas -dlcm=gc**. In this case, the SM does not look to see whether the data is in the L1, but it will invalidate the cache line if it is already in the L1. If the data is not in the L2, then a 32-byte global memory load is issued. This can deliver better data utilization when a 128-byte cache line fetch would be wasteful.

Global memory store transactions occur by invalidating the L1 cache line and then writing to the L2. Only when it's evicted is the L2 data actually written to global memory.

Most applications will benefit from the cache because it performs coalesced global memory loads and stores in terms of a 128-byte cache line size. Once data is inside the L2 cache, applications can reuse data, perform irregular memory accesses, and spill registers without incurring the dramatic slowdown seen in older-generation GPUs caused by having to rely on round trips to the much slower global memory. For performance reasons and transparency reasons, the L1 and L2 caches in compute 2.0 devices are a very good thing.

Common Coalescing Use Cases

Some common use cases for accessing global memory are shown with caching enabled (Table 5.10) and disabled (Table 5.11).

Table 5.10 Common Cached Global Memory Use Cases

Cache Enabled	Case	Bytes Needed by the Warp	Bytes Fetched from Gmem	Efficiency
Y	Broadcast access consecutive 4-byte words to all threads in the warp ($N \le 32$)	N*128	128	3200%
Y	Warp accesses 32 aligned, consecutive 4-byte words	128	128	100%
Y	Warp accesses 32 aligned, permuted 4-byte words	128	128	100%
Y	Warp accesses 32 misaligned, consecutive 4-byte words	128	256	50%
Y	Warp accesses 32 misaligned, permuted 4-byte words	128	256	50%
Y	Warp accesses N scattered 4-byte words ($N \le 32$)	128	N*128	1/N or 3.125% worst case

Table 5.11 Common Noncached Global Memory Use Cases

Cache Enabled	Case	Bytes Needed by the Warp	Bytes Fetched from Gmem	Efficiency
N	Warp accesses 32 aligned, consecutive 4-byte words	128	128	100%
N	Warp accesses 32 aligned, permuted 4-byte words	128	128	100%
N	Warp accesses 32 misaligned, consecutive 4-byte words	128	128 or 256	80–100%, depending on pattern
N	Warp accesses N scattered 4-byte words ($N \leq 32$)	128	N^*32	4/N or 12.5% worst case

Global memory on the GPU was designed to quickly stream memory blocks of data into the SM. Unfortunately, loops that perform indirect indexing, utilize pointers to varying regions in memory, or that have an irregular or a large stride break this assumption. As can be seen in Table 5.10, scattered reads can reduce global memory throughput to only 3.125% of the hardware capability. Turning off the cache can provide a 4-times speed improvement, which is good but still starves the SM for data, as it provides only 12.5% of the potential global memory bandwidth.

Allocation of Global Memory

Memory can be statically allocated in device memory with a declaration:

Example 5.11

```
__device__ int gmemArray[SIZE];
```

When using the runtime API, linear (or 1D) regions of global memory can be dynamically allocated with **cudaMalloc()** and freed with **cudaFree()**. The Thrust API internally uses **cudaMalloc()**.

- Memory is aligned on 256-byte boundaries.
- For 2D accesses to be fully coalesced, both the width of the thread block and the width of the array must be a multiple of the warp size (or only half the warp size, for devices of compute capability 1.x). The runtime **cudaMallocPitch()** and driver API **cuMemAllocPitch()** methods pad the array allocation appropriately for the destination device. The associated memory copy functions described in the reference manual must be used with pitch linear memory.

Memory can be dynamically allocated in the kernel using the standard C-language **malloc()** and **free()**. It is aligned on 16-byte boundaries.

Dynamic global memory allocation on the device is supported only by devices of compute capability 2.x. Memory allocated by a given CUDA thread via **malloc()** remains allocated for the lifetime of the CUDA context, or until it is explicitly released by a call to **free()**. Any thread can use memory allocated by any other CUDA thread – even in later kernel launches. Be aware that any CUDA thread may free memory allocated by another thread, which means that care must be taken to ensure that the same pointer is not freed more than once. The CUDA memory checker, **cuda-memcheck**, is a useful tool to help find memory errors.

The device heap must be created before any kernel can dynamically allocate memory. By default, CUDA creates a heap of 8MB. Unlike the heap on a conventional processor, the heap on the GPU does not resize dynamically. Further, the size of the heap cannot be changed once a kernel module has loaded. Memory reserved for the device heap consumes space just like memory allocated through host-side CUDA API calls such as **cudaMalloc()**.

The following API functions get and set the heap size:

- Driver API:
    - **cuCtxGetLimit**(size_t* size, CU_LIMIT_MALLOC_HEAP_SIZE).
    - **cuCtxSetLimit**(CU_LIMIT_MALLOC_HEAP_SIZE, size_t size).
- Runtime API:
    - **cudaDeviceGetLimit**(size_t* size, cudaLimitMallocHeapSize).
    - **cudaDeviceSetLimit**(cudaLimitMallocHeapSize, size_t size).

The heap size granted will be at least **size** bytes. **cuCtxGetLimit** and **cudaDeviceGetLimit** return the currently requested heap size.

The *CUDA C Programming Guide Version 4.0* provides simple working examples of per-thread, per-threadblock, and allocation persistence across kernel invocations.

Limiting Factors in the Design of Global Memory

Global memory does represent a scaling challenge for GPGPU architects. Although multiple memory subsystems can be combined to deliver blocks of data at the aggregate performance of the combined memory systems, limiting factors such as cost, power, heat, space, and reliability prevent memory bandwidth from scaling as fast as computational throughput.

The Fermi memory subsystem provides the combined memory bandwidth of six partitions of GDDR5 memory on GF100 hardware. With this design, the GPGPU hardware architects were able to increase memory bandwidth by a factor of six over a single partition. There is no longer a linear mapping between addresses and partitions, so typical access patterns are unlikely to all fall into the same partition. This design avoids partition camping (bottle-necking on a subset or even a single controller).

The Fermi memory system supports ECC memory on high-end cards, but this feature is disabled on consumer cards. ECC is also used on memory internal to the SM. Using error correcting memory with ECC is a "must have" when deploying large numbers of GPUs in datacenter and supercomputer installations to ensure that data-sensitive applications like medical imaging, financial options pricing, and scientific simulations are protected from memory errors. ECC can be turned off at the driver level to gain an additional 20 percent in memory bandwidth and added memory capacity, which can benefit global memory bandwidth-limited applications and can be an acceptable optimization for noncritical applications. The Linux **nvidia-smi** command added a -**e** option for controlling ECC. There is a control panel option to enable or disable ECC in Windows.

There are three ways to increase the hardware bandwidth of memory in a system:

1. **Increase the memory clock rate.** Faster memory is more expensive, it consumes more power (which means that heat is generated), and faster memory can be more error-prone.
2. **Increase the bus width.** This option requires that the GPU chip have lots of pins for the memory interface. No matter how small the lithography of the manufacturing process, it is possible to fit only a limited number of physical pin connectors in a given space. More pins means that the size of the chip must be increased, which leads to a vicious cycle, as manufacturing larger chips means that fewer chips can be made per wafer, thereby driving up the cost. In a competitive market for consumer products, higher costs quickly make products unattractive so they do not sell well. Consumer products are the market that is really driving the economics of GPGPU development, which makes cost a critical factor. Optical connectors offer the potential to break this vicious cycle, but this technology has not yet matured enough to be commonly used in manufacturing.
3. **Transmit more data per pin per clock.** This is the magic behind GDDR5 (Graphics Double Data Rate version 5) memory and the hope behind optical connectors. Basically, the channel capacity can be calculated from the physical properties of the channel. For example, the Nyquist sampling theorem lets us determine the maximum possible data rate based on the frequency of the channel in the absence of noise. Increasing the frequency of a channel means that

more data can be transmitted per unit time. Unfortunately, high-frequency electrical signals are prone to noise. The Shannon theorem tells us the maximum theoretical information transfer rate in the presence of noise, but it is up to the engineers and standards committees to make the magic of higher bandwidth data transmission happen.

Relevant computeprof Values for Global Memory

Table 5.12 Visual Profiler Values for gmem	
glob mem read throughput (GB/s)	Global memory read throughput in gigabytes per second. For compute capability < 2.0, this is calculated as $$(((gld\_32*32) + (gld\_64*64) + (gld\_128*128)) * TPC)/(gputime * 1000)$$ For compute capability >= 2.0, this is calculated as $$((DRAM\ reads) * 32)/(gputime * 1000)$$
glob mem write throughput (GB/s)	Global memory write throughput in gigabytes per second. For compute capability < 2.0, this is calculated as $$(((gst\_32*32) + (gst\_64*64) + (gst\_128*128)) * TPC)/(gputime * 1000)$$ For compute capability >= 2.0, this is calculated as $$((DRAM\ writes) *32)/(gputime * 1000)$$ This derived statistic is also shown as "Achieved global memory write throughput (GB/s)" in the kernel analysis window for Fermi.
glob mem overall throughput (GB/s)	Global memory overall throughput in gigabytes per second. This is calculated as global memory read throughput + global memory write throughput
kernel-requested global memory read throughput (GB/s)	This is the actual number of bytes requested in terms of loads by the kernel from global memory divided by the kernel execution time. These requests are made in terms of global load instructions, which can be of varying word sizes of 8, 16, 32, 64, or 128 bits. This is calculated as $$(gld\ instructions\ 8bit + 2 * gld\ instructions\ 16bit + 4 * gld\ instructions\ 32bit + 8 * gld\ instructions\ 64bit + 16 * gld\ instructions\ 128bit)/(gpu\ time * 1000)$$
kernel-requested global memory write throughput (GB/s)	This is the actual number of bytes requested in terms of stores by the kernel from global memory divided by the kernel execution time. These requests are made in terms of global store instructions, which can be of varying word sizes of 8, 16, 32, 64, or 128 bits. This is calculated as $$(gst\ instructions\ 8bit + 2 * gst\ instructions\ 16bit + 4 * gst\ instructions\ 32bit + 8 * gst\ instructions\ 64bit)$$
kernel-requested global memory throughput (GB/s)	This is the combined kernel requested read and write memory throughput. This is calculated as $$(kernel\text{-}requested\ global\ memory\ read\ throughput + kernel\text{-}requested\ global\ memory\ write\ throughput)$$
global memory excess load (%)	This shows the percentage of excess data that is fetched while making global memory load transactions. Ideally 0% excess loads will be achieved when kernel requested global memory read throughput is equal to the L2 cache read throughput i.e. the number of bytes requested by the kernel in terms of reads are equal to the number of bytes actually fetched by the hardware during kernel execution to service the kernel. If this statistic is high, it implies that the access pattern for fetch is not coalesced, many extra bytes are getting fetched while serving the threads of the kernel. This is calculated as $$100 - (100 * kernel\ requested\ global\ memory\ read\ throughput/l2\ read\ throughput)$$

Table 5.12 Visual Profiler Values for gmem—cont'd

global memory excess store (%)	This value shows the percentage of excess data that is accessed while making global memory store transactions. Ideally, 0 percent excess stores will be achieved when kernel-requested global memory write throughput is equal to the L2 cache write throughput, that is, the number of bytes requested by the kernel in terms of stores are equal to the number of bytes actually accessed by the hardware during kernel execution to service the kernel. If this statistic is high, it implies that the access pattern for store is not coalesced and many extra bytes are getting accessed during execution of the threads of the kernel. This is calculated as 100 − (100 * kernel-requested global memory write throughput/L2 write throughput)
peak global memory throughput (GB/s)	This is the peak memory throughput or bandwidth that can be achieved on the present CUDA device. This is a device property and the kernel-achieved memory throughput should be as close as possible to this peak.
global memory replay (%)	Percentage of replayed instructions caused due to global memory accesses. This is calculated as 100 * (L1 global load miss)/instructions issued.

SUMMARY

CUDA makes various hardware spaces available to the programmer. It is essential that the CUDA programmer utilize the available memory spaces to best advantage given the three orders of magnitude difference in bandwidth (from 8 TB/s register bandwidth to 8 GB/s for PCIe-limited mapped memory) between the various CUDA memory types. Failure to do so can result in poor performance.

CUDA provides a number of excellent measured and derived profile information to help track down memory bottlenecks. Understanding the characteristics of each memory type is a prerequisite to adept CUDA programming. Automated analysis by the CUDA profilers can point the developer in the right direction. Knowing how to read the profiler output is a core skill in creating high-performance applications. Otherwise, finding application bottlenecks becomes a matter of guesswork. Similarly, the CUDA memory checker can help find errors in using memory.

## CHAPTER 6

Efficiently Using GPU Memory

The importance of efficiently using GPU memory cannot be overstated. With roughly three-orders-of-magnitude difference in speed between the fastest on-chip register memory and mapped host memory that must traverse the PCIe bus, literate CUDA developers must understand the most efficient ways to use memory. Latency hiding through ILP or TLP is essential to application performance. Prefetching can keep more memory transactions in flight to move data to fast memory and speed even memory bandwidth-limited reduction operations. Irregular data structures are a challenge with current GPU technology, but some techniques can preserve performance even with random memory accesses. However, finding more and better ways to utilize GPU memory is an area of active research as new libraries become available that support irregular data structures such as graphs and sparse matrices.

At the end of this chapter, the reader will have a basic understanding of:

- Using prefetch to better utilize global memory.
- Efficient use of registers, shared, and global memory in an ILP-based reduction kernel.
- How to write generic methods that utilize functors.
- Techniques to speed problems that have irregular and random memory accesses.
- Generic approaches and libraries for sparse matrices.
- Graph centrality metrics and codes that can provide 10- to 50-times speedups.
- Performance reasons to use SoA.
- Stencils and tiles.

REDUCTION

Reduction operations perform common tasks such as finding the minimum, maximum, or sum of a vector. Writing a high-performance reduction for GPU computing is surprisingly complex because it requires a detailed understanding of CUDA memory spaces and the execution model.

The thrust API provides a simple interface that hides all the complexity of a reduction, making it both flexible and easy to use. Thrust uses a reduction designed by Mark Harris at NVIDIA. The paper and example code demonstrating various optimizations for reduction are included with the NVIDIA SDK in the *reduction* directory. Both the paper and code are recommended reading.

This chapter provides a reduction example that ties together much of the discussion in previous chapters and extends the reduction created by Mark Harris:

- C++ templates extend the generality of the reduction code to use user-defined types such as floats, doubles, integers, long integers, and others.
- New features of compute 2.0 devices such as the PTX prefetch instruction and inline assembly code are used to increase global memory read performance.
- Temporary storage is passed to the reduction method so that the programmer can eliminate redundant **cudaMalloc()** and **cudaFree()** operations that slow the thrust implementation as noted in Chapter 3.
- The passing and use of inline functors is demonstrated to create a generic reduction operation that is applicable more than just finding the sum of a vector.
- ILP, discussed in Chapter 4, is utilized both to make the code more understandable and to free SM resources for complicated reductions such as the objective functions defined in Chapters 3 and 4.

The Reduction Template

The following walkthrough of the code for the generic reduction template *functionReduce.h* covers the key concepts and thinking behind each section of code. The code snippets can be combined to construct the complete *functionReduce.h* source file.

The #**ifndef** check of the preprocessor variable **REDUCE_H** protects against compiler errors, should the template file ever be included multiple times; see Example 6.1, "Part 1 of *functionReduce.h*":

Example 6.1

```
#ifndef REDUCE_H
#define REDUCE_H
```

For simplicity, the following section of the template defines the number of blocks and threads for use on a C2050 or C2070 GPU. These definitions can be set manually from the information determined by the NVIDIA SDK code **deviceQuery**. A production version of this template might query the device properties and set these values automatically, as in Example 6.2, "Part 2 of *functionReduce.h*":

Example 6.2

```
// Define the number of blocks as a multiple of the number of SM
// and the number of threads as the maximum resident on the SM
#define N_BLOCKS (1*14)
#define N_THREADS 1024
#define WARP_SIZE 32
```

Example 6.3 starts the definition of the **_functionReduce()** method:

Example 6.3

```
template <class T, typename UnaryFunction, typename BinaryFunction>
  __global__ void
  _functionReduce(T *g_odata, unsigned int n, T initVal,
            UnaryFunction fcn, BinaryFunction fcn1)
{
```

Notice that:

- All variables are defined in terms of the template variable type **T** for generality. For example, **T** can be defined as a **float**, **double**, **int**, or **char** type.
- A scratch region of memory is provided so that each SM can write a single partial result of type **T** to global memory. Passing a pointer allows reuse of the scratch space to avoid the repetitive allocate and free overhead observed in the thrust reduction operation in Chapter 3.
- The number of calls to the unary function **fcn()** is passed to via the variable **n**.
- The unary function **fcn()** can be defined to fetch data from memory or calculate some result on the fly. For example, the test code that follows this template defines **fcn()** as a functor that fetches data from a vector in global memory. Alternative functors can fetch data from complex data structures in global memory, calculate a result based on numerous data structures in memory, perform a table lookup, or avoid the use of global memory entirely by returning some constant or computed value.
- As with the thrust reduction call, an initial value is passed. This can be the starting value for a sum, or an initial value to use in a **minimum()** or **maximum()** reduction.

- The binary function **fcn1()** defines a generic operation on two of the values returned by **fcn()**. Examples include the **thrust::plus()** functor when a sum is desired. Similarly, the **thrust::minimum()** or **thrust::maximum()** functors can be used. Alternatively, the user can provide his or her own binary functor.

Each thread on the GPU starts out with the register variable **myVal** set to **initVal**. Then each thread iterates through and calculates a partial result in fast register memory. If **fcn1()** were a **plus()** operation and **fcn()** fetched data from a vector in global memory, then **myVal** would contain the partial sums of all the vector elements as shown in Figure 6.1. This step reduces the data from **n** values (which could be on the order of millions) to **N_BLOCKS*N_THREADS** partial values. Note that the loop traverses the vector in reverse order, starting at the end and working toward the beginning. This approach gives the author of **fcn()** the opportunity to confirm that any prefetching does not access data prior to the start of the vector. Thus **fcn()** does not need to know the end or length of the vector, which saves memory and a register. See Example 6.4, "Part 4 of *functionReduce.h*":

Example 6.4

```
T myVal = initVal;

{ // 1) Use fastest memory first.
  const int gridSize = blockDim.x*gridDim.x;
  for(int i = n-1 -(blockIdx.x * blockDim.x + threadIdx.x);
    i >= 0; i -= gridSize)
    myVal = fcn1(fcn(i), myVal);
}
```

After this loop completes, the register variable **myVal** contains **N_BLOCKS*N_THREADS** partial values. In CUDA, register variables are not accessible to other threads. For this reason, it is necessary to move the partial values stored in **myVal** to slower shared memory so that they can be accessed

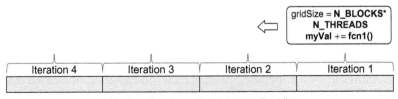

FIGURE 6.1

Iteratively fetching gridDim regions of data from global memory.

by other threads. The transfer from register to shared memory happens in step 2 shown in Example 6.5. This is a parallel transfer all the threads in each thread block to the shared memory variable **smem** inside each SM.

Shared memory is a valuable resource, so only the minimum amount is allocated. Based on the discussion of ILP in Chapter 4, the parallelism of only one warp of threads is used to perform the reduction from **N_THREADS** partial values on each SM to **WARP_SIZE** partial values. The register variable **myVal** already contains the correct values for the first warp. Thus, the shared memory **smem** variable needs only contain the contents of the **myVal** register variables in threads with a **threadIdx.x** greater than or equal to **WARP_SIZE**. As a result, **smem** can be allocated to contain **WARP_SIZE** fewer elements than **N_THREADS**.

Because the transfer from register to shared memory occurs in parallel, the CUDA **__syncthreads()** method must be called after the assignment to ensure that all the elements of **smem** have been written. All of this happens in the few lines of Example 6.5, "Part 5 of *functionReduce.h*":

Example 6.5

```
// 2) Use the second fastest memory (shared memory) in a warp
// synchronous fashion.
// Create shared memory for per-block reduction.
// Reuse the registers in the first warp.
volatile __shared__ T smem[N_THREADS-WARP_SIZE];

// put all the register values into a shared memory
if(threadIdx.x >= WARP_SIZE) smem[threadIdx.x - WARP_SIZE] = myVal;
__syncthreads(); // wait for all threads in the block to complete.
```

At this point in the kernel, there is no reason to use more than the number of threads in one warp because the SM can issue only a single instruction per warp. Because there are no unresolved data dependencies, a single warp is sufficient to keep the SM busy in reducing the contents of shared memory from (**N_THREADS** – **WARP_SIZE**) elements to **WARP_SIZE** partial values on each SM.[1] That is why a conditional is used to keep only threads with a **threadIdx.x** less than **WARP_SIZE** active. See Example 6.6, "Part 6 of *functionReduce.h*":

Example 6.6

```
if(threadIdx.x < WARP_SIZE) {
   // now using just one warp. The SM can only run one warp at a time
```

---

[1] Depending on the compute generation, the SM might be able to issue instructions on the half-warp.

```
#pragma unroll
    for(int i=threadIdx.x; i < (N_THREADS - WARP_SIZE); i += WARP_SIZE)
      myVal = fcn1(myVal,(T)smem[i]);
    smem[threadIdx.x] = myVal; // save myVal in this warp to the start of
    smem
}
```

What remains is to reduce the values in one warp to a single value on each SM. This equates to **N_BLOCKS** partial values, as **N_BLOCKS** was defined to use one block per SM. It is worth noting that the parallelism within the warp at this point does not contribute much to the performance, as only five calls to **fcn1()** are made in Example 6.7.

An alternative implementation can use a simple loop over **WARP_SIZE** running on a single thread (e.g., when **threadIdx.x == 0**) to create the single partial value per SM. If **fcn1()** were the **plus()** functor, this serial version would perform only 27 extra additions that would consume only a trivial amount of extra time—on the order of 100 nanoseconds. Thus, it is sometimes unnecessary to exploit all the parallelism in a system. Still, the parallel code was simple, and it might benefit us in a future compute generation, so we use the implementation in Example 6.7, "Part 7 of *functionReduce.h*":

Example 6.7

```
// reduce shared memory.
if (threadIdx.x < 16)
  smem[threadIdx.x] = fcn1((T)smem[threadIdx.x],(T)smem[threadIdx.
  x + 16]);
if (threadIdx.x < 8)
  smem[threadIdx.x] = fcn1((T)smem[threadIdx.x],(T)smem[threadIdx.
  x + 8]);
if (threadIdx.x < 4)
  smem[threadIdx.x] = fcn1((T)smem[threadIdx.x],(T)smem[threadIdx.
  x + 4]);
if (threadIdx.x < 2)
  smem[threadIdx.x] = fcn1((T)smem[threadIdx.x],(T)smem[threadIdx.x + 2]);
if (threadIdx.x < 1)
  smem[threadIdx.x] = fcn1((T)smem[threadIdx.x],(T)smem[threadIdx.x + 1]);
```

The final task requires reducing the remaining **N_BLOCKS** partial values into a single value that completes the reduction. At this point, the code can either:

- Transfer the **N_BLOCKS**, (14 for this example), partial values to the host, where the final reduction will occur.
- Utilize atomic operations as described in section B.5 of the *NVIDIA CUDA C Programming Guide* to ensure that all the partial values are written to global memory before completing the reduction.

Because both implementations require the allocation of scratch space for the
N_BLOCKS partial values, Example 6.8, "Part 8 of *functionReduce.h*," performs the transfer to the host because it demonstrates the use of the **fcn1()**
functor on both the host and device:

Example 6.8

```
// 3) Use global memory as a last resort to transfer results to
the host
// write result for each block to global mem
if (threadIdx.x == 0) g_odata[blockIdx.x] = smem[0];
// Can put the final reduction across SM here if desired.
}
```

The host method **partialReduce()** allocates the partial sums if needed and
calls the CUDA kernel, as in Example 6.9, "Part 8 of *functionReduce.h*":

Example 6.9

```
template<typename T, typename UnaryFunction, typename BinaryFunction>
  inline void partialReduce(const int n, T** d_partialVals, T initVal,
                     UnaryFunction const& fcn,
                     BinaryFunction const& fcn1)
{
  if(*d_partialVals == NULL)
    cudaMalloc(d_partialVals, (N_BLOCKS+1) * sizeof(T));

  _functionReduce<T><<< N_BLOCKS, N_THREADS>>>(*d_partialVals, n,
                                  initVal, fcn, fcn1);
}
```

As can be seen in Example 6.10, "Part 9 of *functionReduce.h*," the **N_BLOCK**
partial values are transferred from the GPU to the host, where a host-based
version of **fcn1()** is used to compete the reduction. An **#endif** completes
the preprocessor **#ifdef** statement to protect against compiler errors, should
the header file be included multiple times. See Example 6.10, "Part 9 of
functionReduce.h":

Example 6.10

```
template<typename T, typename UnaryFunction, typename BinaryFunction>
  inline T functionReduce(const int n, T** d_partialVals, T initVal,
                     UnaryFunction const& fcn,
                     BinaryFunction const& fcn1)
{
  T h_partialVals[N_BLOCKS];
  partialReduce(n, d_partialVals, initVal, fcn, fcn1);
```

```
  if(cudaMemcpy(h_partialVals, *d_partialVals, sizeof(T)*N_BLOCKS,
                cudaMemcpyDeviceToHost) != cudaSuccess) {
    cerr << "_functionReduce copy failed!" << endl;
    exit(1);
  }
  T val = h_partialVals[0];
  for(int i=1; i < N_BLOCKS; i++) val = fcn1(h_partialVals[i],val);
  return(val);
}
#endif
```

A Test Program for functionReduce.h

The test program for the *functionReduce.h* template creates a vector of sequential integers in memory similar to the examples in the first chapter. The size of the vector can be specified via the command line. The user can also provide a numerical option to run with a functor that utilizes the CUDA PTX **prefetch.global** assembly instruction, a functor that reads from memory (without any prefetching), and a **thrust::reduce()** call.

The **fcn1()** method can be specified at compile time. By default, the application performs a sum. Other functors such as **thrust::minimum()** or **thrust::maximum()** can be used by changing the definition of **FCN1** either in the code or via the **nvcc** command. The type of the run can be changed by changing the preprocessor variable **RUNTYPE**. Specifying the preprocessor variable **DO_CHECK** performs a verification test against the thrust reduction code.

Example 6.11, "Part 1 of *testPre.cu*," is a walkthrough of the test code. If desired, the individual code snippets can be combined to create a complete working test. The necessary preprocessors and namespace definitions occur at the beginning of the file:

Example 6.11

```
#include <iostream>
using namespace std;

#include <thrust/host_vector.h>
#include <thrust/device_vector.h>
#include <thrust/functional.h>
#include <thrust/random.h>

#include "functionReduce.h"

#ifndef RUNTYPE
#define RUNTYPE int
#endif
#ifndef FCN1
```

```
#define FCN1 plus
#endif
#include <iostream>
using namespace std;
```

The **prefetch** functor is a persistent functor that keeps a pointer to device memory. Each call to the functor returns the vector indexed by **i**. Prior to returning the vector element, the index is checked to see whether it is possible to prefetch the next grid of data values (e.g., **N_BLOCKS*N_THREADS** values) from global memory.

The prefetch index can be tested for validity because **_functionReduce()** traverses the vector in reverse order. Testing that the index is greater than or equal to zero ensures that only valid elements in the array will be prefetched. If the index is valid, the PTX **prefetch.global.L2** assembly instruction is used to perform the prefetch. This instruction is valid only for compute 2.0 devices. See Example 6.12, "Part 2 of *testPre.cu*":

Example 6.12

```
template<class T1, class T2>
  struct prefetch : public thrust::unary_function<T1,T2> {
  const T1* data;
prefetch(T1* _data) : data(_data) {};
  __device__
    // This method prefetchs the previous grid of data point into the L2.
  T1 operator()(T2 i) {
    if( (i-N_BLOCKS*N_THREADS) > 0) { //prefetch the previous grid
      const T1 *pt = &data[i - (N_BLOCKS*N_THREADS)];
      asm volatile ("prefetch.global.L2 [%0];"::"l"(pt) );
    }
    return data[i];
  }
};
```

The **memFetch()** functor is similar to the **prefetch()** functor except that it does not perform any prefetching. This functor can run on all compute devices. See Example 6.13, "Part 3 of *testPre.cu*":

Example 6.13

```
template<class T1, class T2>
  struct memFetch : public thrust::unary_function<T1,T2> {
  const T1* data;

memFetch(T1* _data) : data(_data) {};
  __host__ __device__
```

```
    T1 operator()(T2 i) {
    return data[i];
  }
};
```

This test utilizes a random sequence of zeros and ones based on the lowest bit of a random number. These numbers are created with the functor shown in the following code:

Example 6.14

```
// a parallel random number generator
// http://groups.google.com/group/thrust-users/browse_thread/
thread/dca23bfa678689a5
struct parallel_random_generator
{
  __host__ __device__
  unsigned int operator()(const unsigned int n) const
  {
    thrust::default_random_engine rng;
    // discard n numbers to avoid correlation
    rng.discard(n);
    // return a random number
    return rng() & 0x01;
  }
};
```

The **doTest()** routine is straightforward C++. The pointer to the scratch space, **d_partialVals**, is set to NULL, which means that the first call to **functionReduce()** will allocate the needed space. The device vector **d_data** is allocated via the thrust API according the size passed to this method in the variable **nData**.

The variable **op** selects the test that will be performed. A 0 specifies that no prefetching will be used; 1 selects the prefetching test. Any other value specifies that the thrust reduction method is called. See Example 6.15, "Part 4 of *testPre.cu*":

Example 6.15

```
/****************************************************************/
/* The test routine                                            */
/****************************************************************/

#define NTEST 100
template<typename T>
```

```
void doTest(const long nData, int op)
{
  T* d_partialVals=NULL;

  thrust::device_vector<T> d_data(nData);
  //fill d_data with random numbers (either zero or one)
  thrust::counting_iterator<int> index_sequence_begin(0);
  thrust::transform(index_sequence_begin,
                    index_sequence_begin + nData,
                    d_data.begin(), parallel_random_generator());
  cudaThreadSynchronize(); // wait for all the queued tasks to finish
  thrust::FCN1<T> fcn1;

  double startTime, endTime;
  T d_sum;
  T initVal = 0;
  switch(op) {
  case 0: {
    memFetch<T,int> fcn(thrust::raw_pointer_cast(&d_data[0]));
    startTime=omp_get_wtime();
    for(int loops=0; loops < NTEST; loops++)
        d_sum = functionReduce<T>(nData, &d_partialVals, initVal,
        fcn, fcn1);
    endTime=omp_get_wtime();
    cout << "NO prefetch ";
  } break;
  case 1: {
    prefetch<T,int> fcnPre(thrust::raw_pointer_cast(&d_data[0]));
    startTime=omp_get_wtime();
    for(int loops=0; loops < NTEST; loops++)
        d_sum = functionReduce<T>(nData, &d_partialVals, initVal,
        fcnPre, fcn1);
    endTime=omp_get_wtime();
    cout << "Using prefetch ";
  } break;
  default:
    startTime=omp_get_wtime();
    for(int loops=0; loops < NTEST; loops++)
        d_sum = thrust::reduce(d_data.begin(), d_data.end(), initVal,
        fcn1);
    endTime=omp_get_wtime();
    cout << "Thrust ";
  }

  cout << "Time for transform reduce " << (endTime-startTime)/NTEST
  << endl;
  cout << (sizeof(T)*nData/1e9) << " GB " << endl;
  cout << "d_sum    " << d_sum << endl;

  cudaFree(d_partialVals);
```

```
#ifdef DO_CHECK
  T testVal = thrust::reduce(d_data.begin(), d_data.end(), initVal,
  fcn1);
  cout << "testVal " << testVal << endl;
  if(testVal != (d_sum)) {cout << "ERROR " << endl;}
#endif
}
```

The **main()** routine simply parses the command line and runs the test. See Example 6.16, "Part 5 of *testPre.cu*":

Example 6.16

```
int main(int argc, char* argv[])
{
    if(argc < 3) {
      cerr << "Use: nData(K) op(0:no prefetch, 1:prefetch, 2:thrust)"
      << endl;
      return(1);
    }
  int nData=(atof(argv[1])*1000000);
  int op=atoi(argv[2]);

  doTest<RUNTYPE>(nData, op);
  return 0;
}
```

Results

The results in Table 6.1 were generated on an NVIDIA C2070. The time per reduction, averaged over 100 runs, is reported. For smaller vector sizes, **functionReduce()** clearly outperforms the thrust implementation with a maximum 8-times speedup. As noted in Chapter 3, much of this speedup can be attributed to the fact that the time to allocate scratch space occurs only once in the **functionReduce()** implementation. Care must be exercised when interpreting the timings of small runs because they finish very quickly. Even operating system daemon processes briefly waking up can affect performance, as noted in the paper "The Case of the Missing Supercomputer Performance" (Petrini, Kerbyson, & Pakin, 2003).

Use of the PTX prefetch instruction clearly benefits larger problems. The reason is that it makes better use of the available global memory bandwidth. Figure 6.2 is a comparison plot created with the visual profiler shows that the prefetch global memory read throughput (the top line) is 21.8 percent higher than the nonprefetch version of the code. The higher global memory

Table 6.1 Speedups over Thrust::Reduce for Several Problem Sizes

Number of Elements	No Prefetch (sec)	Prefetch (sec)	Thrust (sec)	No Prefetch Speedup over Thrust	Prefetch Speedup over Thrust
1,000 M	0.043434	0.033777	0.035986	0.8	1.1
100 M	0.004314	0.003387	0.003758	0.9	1.1
10 M	0.000447	0.000360	0.000536	1.2	1.5
1 M	0.000063	0.000055	0.000197	3.1	3.6
100 K	0.000021	0.000021	0.000160	7.8	7.7
10 K	0.000018	0.000018	0.000156	8.4	8.5

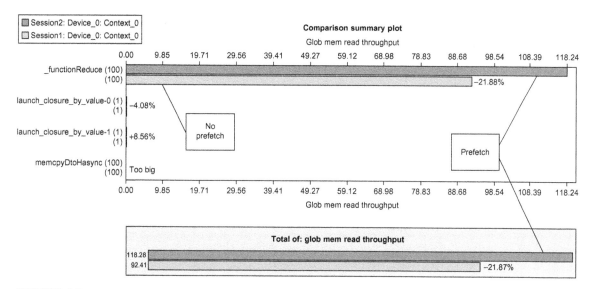

FIGURE 6.2

Visual profiler comparison showing that prefetch achieves higher global memory bandwidth.

read performance benefits larger vector problems, as the prefetch version is always faster than the nonprefetch version. Prefetching is also slightly faster than the thrust implementation, as shown in Table 6.1.

The cost of calculating the prefetch address does incur a slight performance penalty over the nonprefetch version for small vector length reductions. Prefetching data is beneficial only when the increased global memory bandwidth lets the kernel run fast enough to overcome the extra costs associated with the prefetch calculation. Keeping the cost of calculating the prefetch indexes is the reason why the example **prefetch()** functor used such a simple calculation.

UTILIZING IRREGULAR DATA STRUCTURES

The preceding examples utilize very regular access patterns that stream information from global memory.

A large body of computational problems, such as graph and tree algorithms, represents a worst-case scenario for coalescing parallel memory accesses on GPUs. Most of these algorithms exhibit irregular and even random memory access patterns.

Graph algorithms are common in social media analysis (Corley, Farber, & Reynolds, 2011) and, Biology (Jones and Pavel, 2004), and many other fields. Tree algorithms are commonly used for fast data storage and retrieval. Similarly, vector *gather* and *scatter* operations are commonly used in sparse matrix and numerical calculations.

A vector gather operation "gathers" data from arbitrary vector elements. See Example 6.17, "A Vector Gather Operation":

Example 6.17

```
for(int i = 0; i < n; i++) a[i] = b[index[i]];
```

A vector scatter operation is one that "scatters" data throughout a vector in memory, as in Example 6.18, "A Vector Scatter Operation":

Example 6.18

```
for(int i = 0; i < n; i++) a[index[i]] = b[i];
```

Irregular memory accesses are a challenge for massively parallel computers because increasing memory bandwidth does not necessarily increase performance. Coalesced memory accesses imply that memory accesses can be grouped together into a single memory transaction that works on a number of consecutive bytes of information. Tables 5.10 and 5.11 show the coalesced memory efficiencies for various use cases with caching enabled and disabled on compute 2.0 GPUs.

Irregular memory accesses break the assumption that memory transactions can be coalesced into one or a few large memory transactions. For example, the **index** vector in Example 6.16 can contain random index values that will cause each thread accessing **b[index[i]]** to generate a separate global memory transaction. This is a worst-case scenario for the SM (along with the GPU memory subsystem), as each warp will have to wait for all 32 memory accesses to complete before the warp can issue an instruction.

In the absolute worst case, all the warps and SM will issue memory transactions that fall on a single memory partition in global memory, which will decrease the available memory bandwidth to that of a single memory subsystem.

The L2 cache in compute 2.0 and later devices provides the best single solution to accelerate algorithms that perform irregular memory accesses. Though not a general solution, the L2 cache will transparently speed most applications just because it provides a high-speed region of memory where the threads on each SM can request small, irregular memory accesses.

Localizing memory accesses can make a tremendous difference in application performance because it allows the L2 cache to work more effectively on behalf of the application threads. Sorting the index array is a reasonable method to use for random data assuming some reordering of the indices is allowed. Of course, much better performance can be achieved when the programmer works to exploit the locality of reference within the algorithm.

The following program, *testGather.cu*, implements Example 6.16 in a CUDA test code. The thrust API was used to conveniently transfer data to and from the host as well as fill and sort the index array. The first part of the program—Example 6.19, "Part 1 of *testGather.cu*"—defines a gather functor:

Example 6.19

```
#include <omp.h>
#include <iostream>
using namespace std;

#include <thrust/host_vector.h>
#include <thrust/device_vector.h>
#include <thrust/sort.h>
#include <thrust/sequence.h>
#include <thrust/functional.h>

struct gather_functor {
  const int* index;
  const int* data;

gather_functor(int* _data, int* _index) : data(_data), index(_index) {};
  __host__ __device__
  int operator()(int i) {
    return data[index[i]];
  }
};
```

Example 6.20, "Part 2 of *testGather.cu*," parses the command-line arguments and performs the test:

Example 6.20

```
int main(int argc, char *argv[])
{
  if(argc < 3) {
    cerr << "Use: size (k) nLoops sequential" << endl;
    return(1);
  }
  int n = atof(argv[1])*1e3;
  int nLoops = atof(argv[2]);
  int op = atoi(argv[3]);
  cout << "Using " << (n/1.e6) << "M elements and averaging over "
      << nLoops << " tests" << endl;

  thrust::device_vector<int> d_a(n), d_b(n), d_index(n);
  thrust::sequence(d_a.begin(), d_a.end());
  thrust::fill(d_b.begin(), d_b.end(),-1);
  thrust::host_vector<int> h_index(n);

  switch(op) {
  case 0:
    // Best case: sequential indicies
    thrust::sequence(d_index.begin(), d_index.end());
    cout << "Sequential data " << endl;
    break;
  case 1:
    // Mid-performance case: random indices
    for(int i=0; i < n; i++) h_index[i]=rand()%(n-1);
    d_index = h_index; // transfer to device
    thrust::sort(d_index.begin(), d_index.end());
    cout << "Sorted random data " << endl;
    break;
  default:
    // Worst case: random indices
    for(int i=0; i < n; i++) h_index[i]=rand()%(n-1);
    d_index = h_index; // transfer to device
    cout << "Random data " << endl;
    break;
  }

  double startTime = omp_get_wtime();
  for(int i=0; i < nLoops; i++)
    thrust::transform(thrust::counting_iterator<unsigned int>(0),
                  thrust::counting_iterator<unsigned int>(n),
                  d_b.begin(),
                  gather_functor(thrust::raw_pointer_cast(&d_a[0]),
                            thrust::raw_pointer_cast(&d_index[0])));
  cudaDeviceSynchronize();
```

```
double endTime = omp_get_wtime();

// Double check the results
thrust::host_vector<int> h_b = d_b;
thrust::host_vector<int> h_a = d_a;
h_index = d_index;
for(int i=0; i < n; i++) {
  if(h_b[i] != h_a[h_index[i]]) {
    cout << "Error!" << endl; return(1);
  }
}
cout << "Success!" << endl;
cout << "Average time " << (endTime-startTime)/nLoops << endl;
}
```

This program requires the user specify:

- The size of the vector in millions of elements.
- The number of tests to perform in calculating the average runtime.
- An integer value that specifies what type of test *testGather.cu* should perform. The program understands the following values:
  - A 0 value fills the index vector with sequential values. All memory accesses are sequential and coalesced.
  - A 1 specifies that **index** contains a sorted list of random index values. This option shows the performance that can be achieved by regularizing the index values to exploit any locality.
  - The default is to fill **index** with random values. This is a worst-case scenario for the GPU memory system.

Running *testGather.cu* on an NVIDIA C2070 GPU shows that the L2 cache does a remarkably good job when handling small problems. It can provide an order of magnitude of increased performance when the random accesses are localized by sorting. Of course, sorting is good only in the average case. Worst-case performance will not be any different from the random case. This test assumes that index will be reused, so the time to perform the sort was not included in the runtimes reported in Table 6.2.

SPARSE MATRICES AND THE CUSP LIBRARY

Sparse matrix structures arise in numerous computational disciplines. For many applications, sparse matrix methods are often the rate-limiting methods that dictate application performance. In particular, sparse matrix-vector multiplication (SpMV) represents the dominant cost in many iterative methods for solving large linear systems and eigenvalue

Table 6.2 Performance of *testGather.cu* on Various Problem Sizes

Size	Op	nTests	Time	Slowdown Relative to Sequential Performance
0.01 M	Sequential	1000	3.37E-06	
0.01 M	Sorted	1000	3.44E-06	1.0
0.01 M	Random	1000	7.46E-06	2.2
0.1 M	Sequential	1000	1.39E-05	
0.1 M	Sorted	1000	1.42E-05	1.0
0.1 M	Random	1000	6.94E-05	5.0
1 M	Sequential	1000	0.000107	
1 M	Sorted	1000	0.000106	1.0
1 M	Random	1000	0.000972	9.1
10 M	Sequential	1000	0.001077	
10 M	Sorted	1000	0.00105	1.0
10 M	Random	1000	0.011418	10.6
100 M	Sequential	1000	0.011553	
100 M	Sorted	1000	0.013233	1.1
100 M	Random	1000	0.132465	11.5

problems that arise in a wide variety of scientific and engineering applications.

The CUSP library (Generic Parallel Algorithms for Sparse Matrix and Graph Computations) is a thrust-based project for running sparse matrix and graph computations on the GPU. It provides a flexible, high-level interface for manipulating sparse matrices and solving sparse linear systems. The source code for the library can be downloaded from Google Code, where the project is hosted (http://code.google.com/p/cusp-library/). This library uses a variety of common sparse matrix formats with various advantages, as described in the documentation.

Results in the literature show a compute 1.x GPU can deliver an order of magnitude increased performance over an Intel quad-core Clovertown system (Bell & Garland, 2009). This is an active area of research where people are investigating optimal use of the hardware (El Zein & Rendell, 2011) and sparse matrix representations (Cao, Yao, Li, Wang, & Wang, 2010).

CUSP provides a straightforward interface for sparse matrix operations, as can be seen in Example 6.21, to determine the maximal independent set, which is an independent set that is not a subset of any other independent set. It is an important metric used in social network analysis to identify groups or cliques of people.

Example 6.21

```cpp
#include <cusp/graph/maximal_independent_set.h>
#include <cusp/gallery/poisson.h>
#include <cusp/coo_matrix.h>

// This example computes a maximal independent set (MIS)
// for a 10x10 grid. The graph for the 10x10 grid is
// described by the sparsity pattern of a sparse matrix
// corresponding to a 10x10 Poisson problem.
//
// [1] http://en.wikipedia.org/wiki/Maximal_independent_set

int main(void)
{
  size_t N = 10;

  // initialize matrix representing 10x10 grid
  cusp::coo_matrix<int, float, cusp::device_memory> G;
  cusp::gallery::poisson5pt(G, N, N);

  // allocate storage for the MIS
  cusp::array1d<int, cusp::device_memory> stencil(G.num_rows);

  // compute the MIS
  cusp::graph::maximal_independent_set(G, stencil);

  // print MIS as a 2d grid
  std::cout << "maximal independent set (marked with Xs)\n";
  for (size_t i = 0; i < N; i++)
  {
    std::cout << " ";
    for (size_t j = 0; j < N; j++)
    {
      std::cout << ((stencil[N * i + j]) ? "X" : "0");
    }
    std::cout << "\n";
  }

  return 0;
}
```

GRAPH ALGORITHMS

Research on efficient graph algorithm implementations is also an active area
of research on GPUs and for parallel computing in general. Instead of using
the sparse matrix approach taken by CUSP, these efforts implement a graph
data structure composed of nodes and edges. Figure 6.3 shows an example
of a labeled graph containing six vertices and edges.

FIGURE 6.3

An example of a graph.

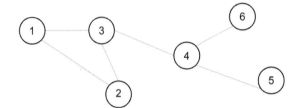

Typical higher-level operations performed on a graph include finding a path between two nodes via either depth-first or breadth-first search and finding the shortest path between two nodes. Graph similarity is an important problem in pattern recognition. For example, chemical compounds can be represented as a graph. In searching chemical databases, it is frequently necessary to compare two graphs to see if they are equal. This leads to interesting computational problems such as how to canonically label a graph for exact search. With a canonical label, it is possible to find graph structures via a string search. Alternatively, graph isomorphism is an important method used to find graphs that have the same or similar structure.

Centrality in a graph is a measure of the relative importance of a vertex within the graph. Examples include: how important a person is within a social network and how critical a road is within a traffic network. The principle centrality metrics are as follows (Corley, Farber, & Reynolds, 2011):

- Degree centrality: A metric of the connectedness of a node. It is simply a count of the number of edges that attach to a node. For a graph G with n vertices, edges e and vertices v, the degree centrality $C_D(v)$ for vertex v is:

$$C_D(v) = \frac{\deg(v)}{n-1} \tag{6.1}$$

- Closeness centrality: A metric that counts the average distance of a node to all other nodes. Closeness can be productive in communicating information among the nodes or actors in a graph. It is defined in Equation 6.2 as the average shortest path or geodesic distance from node v and all reachable nodes (t in V/v):

$$C_{C_v}(v) = \frac{\sum_{t \in V/v} d_G(v, t)}{n-1} \tag{6.2}$$

- Betweenness centrality: A metric that measures how often paths between nodes must traverse a given node. Betweenness centrality (Equation 6.3) measures internode influence. In social media analysis, for example, an individual or blog is central if it lies between other individuals or blogs on their geodesics – the blog is "between" many others, where g_{jk} is the number of geodesics linking blog j and blog k (Wasserman and Faust, 1994):

$$C_{B_v} = \sum_{j<k} \frac{g_{jk}(n_i v, t)}{g_{jk}}$$ (6.3)

- Page rank: Page rank (Example 6.4) is an example of eigenvector centrality that measures the importance of a node by assuming links from more central nodes contribute more to its ranking than less central nodes (Brin & Page, 1998). Let d be a damping factor (usually 0.85), n be the index to the node of interest, p_n be the node, $M(p_i)$ be the set of nodes linking to p_n and $L(p_j)$ be the out-link counts on page p_j:

$$R_{p_n} = \frac{1-d}{N} + d \sum_{p_j \in M(p_n)} \frac{PR(p_j)}{L(p_j)}$$ (6.4)

Certain complex metrics (e.g., betweenness, eigenvector centrality) can become intractable when presented with large volumes of data unless appropriate machines and algorithms are utilized. Developers and users must understand the runtime performance, accuracy, and problem size trade-offs between exact and approximate centrality algorithms (Ediger et al., 2010).

It is possible for a GPU to deliver an order of magnitude or more of increased performance on graph centrality metrics. The **gpu-fan** (GPU-based Fast Analysis of Networks) project at Vanderbilt provides a working software package that includes methods for computing four shortest path-based centrality metrics. This project reports that the GPU speeds up the application by 10 to 50 times on real-world protein interaction and gene co-expression networks as well as simulated scale-free networks (Shi & Zhang, 2011). The nascent thrust-graph library that is hosted on Google Code is attempting to create a common graph API and set of algorithms for CUDA-enabled GPUs.

Programming graph algorithms on GPUs is in a particularly early stage of development. The paper "Exploring the Limits of GPUs with Parallel Graph Algorithms" (Dehne & Yogaratnam, 2010) is a recent survey of the field. A more dated but still relevant paper is "Accelerating Large Graph Algorithms on the GPU Using CUDA" (Harish & Narayanan, 2007).

SoA, AoS, AND OTHER STRUCTURES

Many legacy applications store data as arrays of structures (AoS) that can lead to coalescing issues. From a GPU performance perspective, it is preferable to store data as a structure of arrays (SoA). Example 6.22, "An AoS Example," creates an AoS:

Example 6.22
```
struct S {
    float x;
    float y;
};
struct S myData[N];
```

Arranging data in this fashion leads to coalescing issues as the data are interleaved. Performing an operation that only requires the variable x will result in a 50 percent loss of bandwidth and waste of L2 cache memory.

Example 6.23, "An SoA Example," shows how to allocate an SoA:

Example 6.23
```
struct S {
    float x[N];
    float y[N];
};
struct S myData;
```

Arranging data as an SoA makes full use of the memory bandwidth even when individual elements of the structure are utilized. There is no data interleaving; this data structure should provide coalesced memory accesses and achieve high global memory performance.

The CUDA program *sorting_aos_vs_soa.cu* is included in the thrust teaching examples that are available for free download from Google Code. It demonstrates how to sort SoA and AoS structures with thrust. The comments in the code note that a 5-times speedup can be achieved by using a SoA data structure.

TILES AND STENCILS

The computational grid defined in the kernel execution configuration can be used to break a computation into subproblems that execute in parallel. *Tiles* and *stencils* are an abstraction used in the creation of these multidimensional grids. In particular, these abstractions help the programmer group data accesses into common patterns plus define shared memory usage for interthread communications within a thread block.

Matrix multiplication provides the textbook example of the use of 2D regions, or *tiles*, on the GPU. The book *Programming Massively Parallel Processors: A Hands-on Approach* (Kirk & Hwu, 2010) has a detailed discussion of matrix multiplication and the use of tiles. However, tiles are a common design paradigm used in many problems aside from matrix multiplication. The CUDA N-body SDK example is another excellent demonstration of the use of tiles to solve a complicated problem on the GPU with high performance.

Stencils are a generalization of the concept of a tile to *n* dimensions. A stencil computation:

- Operates on each point in a discrete *n*-dimensional space.
- Uses neighboring points in computation.
- Are often surrounded by a time loop.
- Can have diverse boundary conditions.

Both tiles and stencils help the CUDA developer formulate problems to best utilize shared memory and register in the SM as well as exploit parallelism across all the SM. The paper "3D Finite Difference Computation on GPUs using CUDA" (Micikevicius, 2010) provides a detailed discussion of stencils that can be freely downloaded from the NVIDIA website. Volkov demonstrates how to use ILP to accelerate stencil problems in "Programming Inverse Memory Hierarchy: Case of Stencils on GPUs" (Volkov, 2010).

Tiles and stencils are also important in performing GPU computations with *quadtrees* and *octrees*. A quadtree is a tree-based structure in which each internal node has four children. It is used to partition a two-dimensional space by recursively dividing it into quadrants. An octree has eight children per internal node and is used to recursively divide a 3D space into regions. Both of these data structures can exhibit irregular global memory accesses. The book *GPU Computing Gems* (Hwu, 2011) contains several detailed examples of how experts in the field have used these and other irregular data structures in CUDA to solve complex scientific problems.

SUMMARY

This chapter introduced techniques and examples to efficiently use GPU memory. The three-orders-of-magnitude performance difference between the slowest and fastest GPU memory systems means that GPU programmers have the opportunity to capitalize on the extreme performance that GPU hardware offers.

What makes CUDA so special is that it exposes the features of the underlying hardware so that the full potential of the hardware can be realized. As the reduction example in this chapter showed, it is possible to delve down into the lowest levels of the hardware execution model to attain high performance.

Thrust, on the other hand, bundled this complexity into a simple API call that was used in the very first program in this book. As demonstrated in this chapter, generic programming lets CUDA programmers create simple, generic methods that fully exploit the capability of the GPU.

Much of the future in CUDA development lies in creating generic libraries and APIs like thrust and CUSP. As these interfaces mature, CUDA programmers will be able to do more in less time. The concept is simple:

- Make your life easy and write your code with the highest-level API that you feel comfortable using.
- Profile and see where the bottlenecks occur. In most cases, the efficient use of global memory will likely dominate the application performance.
- Drop down to a lower-level API to get the performance needed.
- When possible, write generic methods that can potentially be combined into a generic library for others to use.

## CHAPTER 7

Techniques to Increase Parallelism

CUDA was designed to exploit the massive parallelism inside the GPU as well as through the use of concurrent streams of execution to utilize multiple GPUs, asynchronous data transfers, and simultaneous kernel execution on a single device. By default, CUDA creates a single stream of execution on a one GPU, which is usually device 0.[1] All data transfers and kernel invocations are queued on this single stream and processed sequentially in the order they were queued. By explicitly creating and using multiple streams of execution, a CUDA programmer can perform more work per unit time to make applications run faster. For example, multiple GPUs can be utilized by simply changing the device with **cudaSetDevice()**. Work can then be queued on each device, which can potentially increase application performance by the number of GPUs in the system. CUDA programmers can overlap computation and data transfers to reduce application runtime plus enable real-time data processing on both single and multi-GPU systems. Under special circumstances, greater efficiency per device can be achieved when running multiple streams on a single device to exploit concurrent kernel execution. The addition of UVA in CUDA 4.0 simplifies data management to facilitate the use of these techniques to increase parallelism and application performance.

At the end of this chapter, the reader will have a basic understanding of:

- How to run on multiple GPUs in a system.
- UVA and how it makes multi-GPU applications simpler.
- How to use asynchronous data transfers to speed application performance.
- The use and performance implications of using mapped memory.

---

[1] As will be discussed, the default GPU device can be changed by either the programmer or the systems administrator.

- How to use asynchronous kernel execution; plus, how it can benefit application performance and potentially decrease kernel performance.
- The use of the profiler to understand performance and identify bottlenecks in multi-GPU systems.

CUDA CONTEXTS EXTEND PARALLELISM

A CUDA application interacts with the GPU hardware through the device driver as shown in Figure 7.1.

The driver supports multiple concurrent applications by creating a separate *context* for each GPU-based application that runs on the system. The context contains all of the driver state information required by the application such as the virtual address space, streams, events, allocated blocks of memory, and other data necessary to run a GPU-based application. By switching between contexts, the device driver acts like a small operating system that can multitask multiple GPU applications. For example, a user can run multiple OpenGL rendering applications plus multiple CUDA computational applications at the same time. In a similar fashion, the GPU device driver lets individual CUDA applications utilize multiple devices simply by giving the application access to multiple contexts in the device driver.

Only one context can be active at a time, which is why the CUDA driver incorporates a timer to detect GPU applications that hang while performing some operation on the GPU. Mistakenly running a CUDA kernel that contains an infinite loop is one example of an application that will cause a time out. The good news is that control eventually reverts to the user so that he or she can correct the problem without rebooting the system.

By default, CUDA creates a context during the first call to a function that changes the state of the driver. Calling **cudaMalloc()** is one such call that changes the context state. Many CUDA programmers rely on this default behavior to transparently utilize a single GPU. Note that a context is usually created

FIGURE 7.1

GPUs and the host communicate via the device driver.

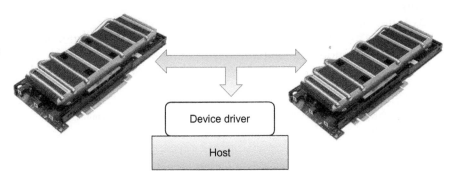

on GPU zero by default unless another GPU is selected by the programmer prior to context creation with **cudaSetDevice()**. The context is destroyed either by calling **cudaDeviceReset()** or when the controlling host process exits.

Starting with CUDA 2.2, a Linux administrator can select *exclusive mode* via the SMI (System Management Interface) tool. In exclusive mode, a context is no longer created by default on GPU 0, but rather on a GPU that does not have an active context. If there are no available GPUs, or if **cudaSetDevice()** specifies a GPU that already has an active context, the first CUDA call that attempts to change the device state will fail and return an error. This capability can be used to run compute or memory intensive applications on unused GPUs in a system.

STREAMS AND CONTEXTS

CUDA applications manage work and concurrency by queuing operations onto a stream. CUDA implicitly creates a stream when it creates a context so commands can be queued for execution on the device. For example, calling **cudaMemcpy()** queues a blocking data transfer on the current stream. Similarly, calling a CUDA kernel queues the kernel invocation on the stream associated with the current device. If desired, the programmer can specify the stream in the execution configuration as shown in Example 7.1, "An Execution Configuration Including a Stream Specification":

Example 7.1
```
Kernel<<<nBlocks, nThreadsPerBlock, 0, stream[i]>>>(parameters)
```

All operations queued on a stream execute *in order*, which means that each operation is pulled off the queue in the order it was placed on the queue. In other words, the queue acts as a FIFO (first-in, first-out) buffer whereby operations are sequentially pulled off the queue in the order they appeared for execution on the device.

Multiple streams are required for concurrent execution across devices or to run multiple kernels concurrently on a single device.

Multiple GPUs

The simplest way to use multiple GPUs in a single application is to implicitly create a single stream per context per device as shown in the following example. The method **cudaGetDeviceCount()** is used to determine the number of devices in the system. Calling **cudaSetDevice()** sets the device. In this code snippet, **cudaMalloc()** was used to induce the creation of the context by causing a change of context state. If desired, additional device properties can be enumerated via the **cudaDeviceProp** variable passed to **cudaGetDeviceProperties()**. See Example 7.2, "Creating Contexts on Multiple Devices":

Example 7.2

```
cudaGetDeviceCount(&nGPU);

int *d_A[nGPU];
for(int i=0; i < nGPU; i++) {
  cudaSetDevice(i);
  cudaMalloc(&d_A[i],n*sizeof(int));
}
```

Work can then be queued on the default stream associated with each device. Again, **cudaSetDevice()** is used to select the device context. All GPU operations queued after a **cudaSetDevice()** are implicitly queued on the stream associated with the device unless a stream is explicitly specified in the API call or kernel execution.

Explicit Synchronization

There are various ways to explicitly synchronize streams with each other.

Events are a way for the programmer to create a placeholder in a stream. The event can then be monitored to determine when a group of tasks have completed. Note that:

- CUDA 4.0 also allows events to be shared across contexts, which gives events the ability to coordinate tasks across multiple devices in a system.
- Events in stream 0 complete after all tasks in all streams have completed.
- For profiling purposes, the elapsed time between two events can be determined with **cudaEventElapsedTime()**.

The following example shows how to create two events in variables **stop** and **start**. The **start** event is placed on the queue after which one or more tasks are queued. The **stop** event is then pushed on the queue. The host then stops at the call to **cudaEventSynchronize()**. Execution will not continue on the host until after the stop event has been marked complete.

Meanwhile, the driver asynchronously works through the queue in order. This means that it processes and marks the **start** event as complete. Work proceeds through the rest of the tasks on the queue. Eventually the driver processes the **stop** event and marks that it is completed. This wakes up the host thread, which continues on to process the code after the call to **cudaEventSynchronize()**.

As shown in this example, time is a property associated with an event. The difference between the time when the **start** and **stop** events were marked complete is retrieved with the call to **cudaEventElapsedTime()**. Thus, Example 7.3, "Timing Tasks with Events," demonstrates how to time a group of tasks:

Example 7.3
```
// create two events
cudaEvent_t start, stop;
cudaEventCreate(&start); cudaEventCreate(&stop);

cudaEventRecord(start, 0)
// Queue some tasks
...
cudaEventRecord(stop, 0);
cudaEventSynchronize(stop);

// get the elapsed time
float elapsedTime;
cudaEventElapsedTime(&elapsedTime, start, stop);

// destroy the events

cudaEventDestroy(start);
cudaEventDestroy(stop)
```

Following are runtime methods for explicitly synchronizing streams and events:

- **cudaDeviceSynchronize()** waits until all preceding commands in all streams of all host threads have completed.
- **cudaStreamSynchronize()** takes a stream as a parameter and waits until all preceding commands in the given stream have completed. It can be used to synchronize the host with a specific stream, allowing other streams to continue executing on a device.
- **cudaStreamWaitEvent()** takes a stream and an event as parameters and makes all the commands added to the given stream after the call to **cudaStreamWaitEvent()** delay their execution until the given event has completed. The stream can be 0, in which case all the commands added to any stream after the call to **cudaStreamWaitEvent()** wait on the event.
- **cudaStreamQuery()** checks whether all preceding commands in a stream have completed.

Implicit Synchronization

Tasks queued on different streams generally run concurrently. Some host-based operations force all streams to pause until the host operation completes. Care must be taken when performing the following host operations, as they will stop all concurrent operations and negatively impact application performance:

- A page-locked host memory allocation.
- A device memory allocation.

- A device memory set.
- A device–device memory copy.
- A switch between the L1/shared memory configurations.

The Unified Virtual Address Space

UVA space provides a single address space for all host and GPU devices in a system. UVA is available to all 64-bit applications on Windows Vista/7 running in TCC mode, on Windows XP, and on Linux. UVA does not work on 32-bit systems.

On supported systems, the pointer returned from any allocation made with **cudaHostAlloc()** or any of the **cudaMalloc*()** methods (**cudaMalloc()**, **cudaMallocPitch()**, and others) uniquely identifies both the region of memory and the device upon which the memory resides. If desired, the CUDA programmer can determine where the memory resides with **cudaPointerGetAttributes()**.

As a consequence of UVA:

- The **cudaMemcpy()** method no longer pays attention to the **cudaMemcpyKind** parameter. For compatibility with non-UVA environments, the direction of the transfer (host to device or device to host) can still be specified. If portability is not a concern, **cudaMemcpyDefault** can be used for convenience.
- High-performance GPU to GPU transfers are now possible by simply specifying pointers to memory on the two devices.
- On UVA systems, host memory pointers returned by **cudaHostAlloc()** can be used directly by device kernels. There is no need to obtain a device pointer via **cudaHostGetDevicePointer()**. This includes mapped memory created by passing the flag **cudaHostAllocMapped** to **cudaHostAlloc()** or **cudaHostRegisterMapped** to **cudaHostRegister()**. For compatibility with compute 1.x devices and 32-bit applications, **cudaHostGetDevicePointer()** can still be used. Thrust-based applications will need to cast the pointer with **thrust::device_pointer_cast()**.

Applications may query whether the unified address space is used for a particular device by checking that the **unifiedAddressing** device property is set.

A Simple Example

The following example demonstrates how to concurrently run one or more GPUs. It:

1. Allocates space for **n** integers on each GPU. In this example, **n** is one million.
2. Concurrently fills the vectors on each GPU to create a single large vector of consecutive integers.

3. Asynchronously transfers the GPU memory to the host memory.
4. Checks the result for correctness.

The following walkthrough discusses the multi-GPU and concurrent aspects of the code. All the code segments can be combined into a single source file that can be compiled and executed.

The CUDA kernel, **fillKernel()**, writes the sequential integers **offset**+0 to **offset**+n to the vector on the device. Each integer is written 100 times to global memory to increase the runtime of **fillKernel()** to better illustrate the concurrent execution of this kernel on two GPUs, as shown in Figure 7.2. See Example 7.4, "Part 1 of *multiGPU.cu*":

Example 7.4
```
#include <stdio.h>

__global__ void fillKernel(int *a, int n, int offset)
{
  int tid = blockIdx.x*blockDim.x + threadIdx.x ;
  if (tid < n)
     for(int i=0 ; i < 100 ; i++)
    a[tid] = offset+tid ;
}
```

The **main()** routine starts by calling **cudaGetDeviceCount()** to determine the number of GPUs in the system. The value is saved in the variable **nGPU**. See Example 7.5, "Part 2 of *multiGPU.cu*":

Example 7.5
```
int main(int argc, char* argv[])
{
  int nGPU ;
  int n = 1000000 ;
  int size=n*sizeof(int) ;

  cudaGetDeviceCount(&nGPU) ;
```

Memory is allocated on the host with **cudaHostAlloc()**. The flag **cuda-HostAllocPortable** specifies that the host memory will be page-locked. The page-locked memory permits the following:

- Copies between page-locked host memory and device memory can be performed concurrently with kernel execution.
- On systems with a front-side bus, bandwidth between host memory and device memory is higher if host memory is allocated as page-locked.

The method **cudaSetDevice()** is then used to change the context to each GPU device. The context is actually created with the call to **cudaMalloc()**, which changes the state of the context and implicitly creates a stream per device, as in Example 7.6, "Part 3 of *multiGPU.cu*":

Example 7.6

```
int *d_A[nGPU];
for(int i=0; i < nGPU; i++) {
  cudaSetDevice(i);
  cudaMalloc(&d_A[i],size);
}
```

The **fillKernel()** kernel is then queued on each device along with a call to **cudaMemcpyAsync()** to transfer the values back to the host. The method **cudaDeviceSynchronize()** is used to ensure that the work on all devices has completed. See Example 7.7, "Part 4 of *multiGPU.cu*":

Example 7.7

```
int *h_A;
cudaHostAlloc(&h_A, nGPU*n*sizeof(int), cudaHostAllocPortable);

for(int i=0; i < nGPU; i++) {
  int nThreadsPerBlock= 512;
  int nBlocks= n/nThreadsPerBlock + ((n%nThreadsPerBlock)?1:0);
  cudaSetDevice(i);
  fillKernel<<<nBlocks, nThreadsPerBlock>>>(d_A[i], n, i*n);
  cudaMemcpyAsync(&h_A[i*n], d_A[i], size, cudaMemcpyDeviceToHost);
}
cudaDeviceSynchronize();
```

The host then checks the vector for correctness, as in Example 7.8, "Part 5 of *multiGPU.cu*":

Example 7.8

```
for(int i=0; i < nGPU*n; i++)
  if(h_A[i] != i) {
    printf("Error h_A[%d] = %d\n",i,h_A[i]); exit(1);
  }
printf("Success!\n");
```

All the device resources are freed, as in Example 7.9, "Part 6 of *multiGPU.cu*":

Example 7.9

```
cudaFreeHost(h_A);
for(int i=0; i < nGPU; i++) {
  cudaSetDevice(i); // to be same, set the context for the free
  cudaFree(d_A[i]);
}
return(0);
}
```

This source code can be saved to a file *multiGPU.cu*. The application can be compiled and executed with the following **nvcc** command. Note the use of the **-run** command-line option. The application reports that multiple GPUs were used to successfully fill the vector with consecutive integers.

Example 7.10

```
$ nvcc multiGPU.cu -run
Success!
```

Profiling Results

Figure 7.2, a width plot from the Visual Profiler, clearly shows that **fillKernel()** runs concurrently on both device 0 and device 1. Further, the asynchronous memory transfers also run concurrently. Due to variations in when operations start on each queue, one of the data transfers finishes slightly later that the other.

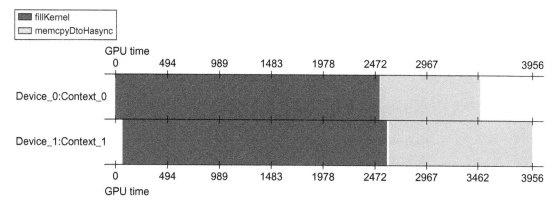

FIGURE 7.2
Visual Profiler width plot showing concurrent device execution.

OUT-OF-ORDER EXECUTION WITH MULTIPLE STREAMS

CUDA developers can also explicitly create streams with **cudaStreamCreate()**. As shown in Example 7.11, "Example Showing the Creation of Multiple Streams," **cudaSetDevice()** can be called to set the device (and context) in which the stream will be created.

Example 7.11

```
for(int i=0; i < nGPU; i++) {
    cudaSetDevice(i)
    if(cudaStreamCreate(&streams[i]) != 0) {
      fprintf(stderr,"Stream create failed!\n"); exit(1);
    }
  }
```

A kernel launch or memory copy will fail if it is issued to a stream that is not associated to the current device as illustrated in Example 7.12, "Example Showing that the Correct Context Must Be Used," taken from the *NVIDIA CUDA C Programming Guide*:

Example 7.12

```
cudaSetDevice(0);                    // Set device 0 as current
cudaStream_t s0;
cudaStreamCreate(&s0);               // Create stream s0 on device 0
MyKernel<<<100, 64, 0, s0>>>();      // Launch kernel on device 0 in s0
cudaSetDevice(1);                    // Set device 1 as current
cudaStream_t s1;
cudaStreamCreate(&s1);               // Create stream s1 on device 1
MyKernel<<<100, 64, 0, s1>>>();      // Launch kernel on device 1 in s1
// This kernel launch will fail:
MyKernel<<<100, 64, 0, s0>>>();      // Launch kernel on device 1 in s0
```

As demonstrated in *multGPU.cu*, multiple streams can be created in different contexts to perform *out-of-order execution* to support multiple GPUs in a single host thread. In other words, there is no guarantee that the commands on different streams will run in the same order relative to each other. Similarly, multiple streams can be created within a single context to support out-of-order execution within a single context. Asynchronous kernel execution is one example of out-of-order execution within a single context, where multiple kernels run concurrently on the same device.

The following source code (Example 7.13) modifies *multiGPU.cu* to demonstrate concurrent kernel execution on a single GPU. Changes are highlighted in the source code:

- The number of loops in **fillKernel()** was increased to better highlight the difference between synchronous versus concurrent kernel runtime.
- The value of **n** was decreased to 1024, so only two blocks are utilized by **fillKernel()** to process each vector.
- Five streams are created that run concurrent **fillKernel()** instances.
- For timing comparison, all the kernels will run sequentially on **stream[0]** when the C processor variable **USE_SINGLE_STREAM** is defined.

Example 7.13

```
__global__ void fillKernel(int *a, int n, int offset)
{
  int tid = blockIdx.x*blockDim.x + threadIdx.x;
  if (tid < n) {
    register int delay=1000000;
    while(delay > 0) delay--;
    a[tid] = delay + offset+tid;
  }
}

int main(int argc, char* argv[])
{
  int nStreams=5;
  int n = 1024;
  int size = n * sizeof(int);
  cudaStream_t streams[nStreams];
  int *d_A[nStreams];

  for(int i=0; i < nStreams; i++) {
    cudaMalloc(&d_A[i],size);
    if(cudaStreamCreate(&streams[i]) != 0) {
      fprintf(stderr,"Stream create failed!\n"); exit(1);
    }
  }

  int *h_A;
  cudaHostAlloc(&h_A, nStreams*size, cudaHostAllocPortable);

  int nThreadsPerBlock= 512;
  int nBlocks= n/nThreadsPerBlock + ((n%nThreadsPerBlock)?1:0);
  double startTime = omp_get_wtime();
  for(int i=0; i < nStreams; i++) {
#ifdef USE_SINGLE_STREAM
    fillKernel<<<nBlocks, nThreadsPerBlock>>>(d_A[i], n, i*n);
```

```
#else
    fillKernel<<<nBlocks, nThreadsPerBlock, 0, streams[i]>>>(d_A[i],
    n, i*n);
#endif
  }
  cudaDeviceSynchronize();
  double endTime= omp_get_wtime();
  printf("runtime %f\n",endTime-startTime);
  for(int i=0; i < nStreams; i++) {
    cudaMemcpyAsync(&h_A[i*n], d_A[i], size, cudaMemcpyDefault,
    streams[i]);
  }
  cudaDeviceSynchronize();

  for(int i=0; i < nStreams*n; i++)
    if(h_A[i] != i) {
      printf("Error h_A[%d] = %d\n",i,h_A[i]); exit(1);
    }
  printf("Success!\n");

  for(int i=0; i < nStreams; i++) {
    cudaFree(d_A[i]);
  }
  return(0);
}
```

Example 7.13 can be saved to a file called *asyncGPU.cu*. The following commands demonstrate how to build and run the code. A comparison of the runtime between the sequential and parallel version shows that asynchronous kernel execution does speed this application according to the number of concurrent kernels. See Example 7.14, *"asyncGPU.cu Results"*:

Example 7.14

```
$ nvcc -D USE_SINGLE_STREAM -arch sm_20 -O3 -Xcompiler -fopenmp
asyncGPU.cu -run
runtime 4.182832
Success!

$ nvcc -arch sm_20 -O3 -Xcompiler -fopenmp asyncGPU.cu -run
runtime 0.836606
Success!
```

In CUDA 4.0, the visual profiler cannot profile concurrent kernel execution. For this reason, wallclock time as reported by **omp_get_wtime()** is utilized to detect a speedup. This example demonstrates nearly perfect speedup by a factor of 5 as the runtime decreased according to the number of concurrent streams that ran on the GPU.

Tip for Concurrent Kernel Execution on the Same GPU

The linear speedup according to the number of kernels exhibited by *asyncGPU.cu* demonstrates that concurrent kernel execution can be an important tool to increase performance when running small compute-bound kernels. It is important to consider how the multiple kernels will interact with global memory. For example, a single kernel may access global memory in a cache friendly high-performance coalesced manner. Running multiple kernels may change the locality of reference, increase L2 cache misses, and reduce or eliminate the effectiveness of this cache. Concurrently running different kernels can exacerbate this problem and introduce additional problems with bank conflicts and memory partition camping, as discussed in Chapter 5. As a result, performance will degrade. Although the overall speedup when running multiple concurrent kernels will likely be better than running each kernel sequentially, a linear speedup may not always be possible.

The following guidelines should improve the potential for concurrent kernel execution on devices that support concurrent kernel execution:

- All independent operations should be issued before dependent operations.
- Synchronization of any kind should be delayed as long as possible.

Atomic Operations for Implicitly Concurrent Kernels

CUDA is designed to let each SM run independently of each other. In this way, the CUDA model does not impose any scalability limit on the number of devices. The gating factor for kernel scalability in a kernel is the number of thread blocks. With concurrent kernel execution, the scalability of an application is limited by the number of blocks of all the independent tasks that can run at one time.

The **functionReduce()** example from Chapter 6 demonstrates that the CUDA model does introduce some complexity for reduction types of operations. By definition, a reduction operation must provide a single value that is based on computations performed by all the SM on the GPU, which requires that some form of synchronization happen between computational units. This is antithetical to the CUDA programming model. The simple solution used by the **functionReduce()** example was to move the data to the host, where the final step of the reduction is performed.

This approach works but presents challenges when programming with multiple devices or streams because host-side operations are not queued on a CUDA stream.

There are two options that allow the complete reduction to a single value to happen via a CUDA stream:

1. Write a separate kernel that runs after **functionReduce()**. CUDA guarantees that all global memory transactions will be completed prior to the start of the next kernel. Because global memory has the lifetime of the application, the partial sums stored in global memory can be used by the second kernel to complete the reduction operation.
2. Utilize atomic operations to synchronize operations within a kernel. Basically, an atomically incremented counter is used to determine which SM is the last to finish. An atomic operation performed on a memory location is guaranteed to complete before any other processing element can access the result of the operation. The atomic increment lets the CUDA programmer determine when all the SM on the GPU have finished performing their part of the reduction. Atomic operations force each SM to serially access a single memory location, which imposes obvious scaling limitations. However, atomic operations do allow kernels such as **functionReduce()** to perform a reduction to one value in a single kernel call.

The NVIDIA SDK includes *threadFenceReduction*, a well-documented example that utilizes atomic operations to synchronize all the SM on a GPU. This SDK example is rather long and complicated. Example 7.15, "Using Atomics to Complete a Reduction Inside a Kernel," is a concise and highly abbreviated example that utilizes an **atomicInc()** in the same fashion as the SDK example:

Example 7.15

```
#include <iostream>
using namespace std;

__global__ void gmem_add(int *a, int n, unsigned int *counter, int
*result)
{
  bool finishSum;

  if(threadIdx.x == 0) {
    // introduce some variable delay based on threadIdx.x
    register int delay=blockIdx.x * 1000000;
    while(delay >0) delay--;
    // write blockIdx.x to global memory
```

```
    a[blockIdx.x] = blockIdx.x;
    __threadfence();
  }

  // Use an atomic increment to find the last SM to finish.
  // The counter must start at zero!
  if(threadIdx.x == 0) {
    unsigned int ticket = atomicInc(counter, gridDim.x);
    finishSum = (ticket == gridDim.x-1);
  }
  if(finishSum) {
    register int sum = a[0];
  #pragma unroll
    for(int i=1; i < n; i++) sum += a[i];
    result[0] = sum;
  }
  counter=0; // reset the counter
}

#define N_BLOCKS 1400
int main(int argc, char *argv[])
{
  int *d_a, *d_result;
  unsigned int *d_counter;
  cudaMalloc(&d_a, sizeof(int)*N_BLOCKS);
  cudaMalloc(&d_result, sizeof(int));
  cudaMalloc(&d_counter, sizeof(unsigned int));

  int zero=0;
  cudaMemcpy(d_counter, &zero, sizeof(int), cudaMemcpyHostToDevice);

  gmem_add<<<N_BLOCKS, 64>>>(d_a, N_BLOCKS, d_counter, d_result);

  int h_a[N_BLOCKS], h_result;
  cudaMemcpy(h_a, d_a, sizeof(int)*N_BLOCKS, cudaMemcpyDeviceToHost);
  cudaMemcpy(&h_result, d_result, sizeof(int), cudaMemcpyDeviceToHost);
  int sum=0;
  for(int i=0; i< N_BLOCKS; i++) sum += h_a[i];
  cout << "should be " << sum << " got " << h_result << endl;
}
```

In Example 7.15:

1. The first thread in each thread block is delayed by a variable amount.
2. The first thread in each thread block atomically increments a counter to show that the thread block has completed all prior work.
3. Only the first thread in the last thread block will see that the counter equals the number of thread blocks. That indicates it is safe for it to perform the final sum.

TYING DATA TO COMPUTATION

Tying data to computation is essential to attaining program correctness and performance in a distributed multi-GPU environment. CUDA programmers have the following options to make data available to kernels running on multiple GPUs:

- Map the memory into the memory space of all the GPUs. In this case, data will be transparently transferred between the host and GPUs.
- Manually allocate space and transfer the data.
- For applications that will run in a distributed MPI (Message Passing Interface) environment, space can be allocated on each device and transferred directly to the GPU via MPI send and receive calls. This is discussed further in Chapter 10.

Manually Partitioning Data

The most flexible, scalable, and highest-performance method to tie data to computation is manually partitioning and transfering data amongst devices. With this technique, the programmer can control and optimize all aspects of the computation. Unlike mapped memory, the programmer assumes the responsibility of ensuring that all data is on the GPU when it is needed. The *multiGPU.cu* example (starting with Example 7.4) provided a simple demonstration that manually partitioned data.

Effectively partitioning data across many devices is a hard problem. The decision-making process of how to distribute data across devices does create a very deep and detailed insight into the computational problem being solved. Most important from a performance perspective, this design process highlights how asynchronous data transfers and overlapped kernel execution can speed performance. The good news is that the technical and scientific literature contains numerous examples of excellent parallelization schemes that have been created by very bright people. Look to these sources early in your design process to see how others have addressed parallelism in problems similar to the one to be solved.

The discussion in Chapter 6 concerning tiles, stencils, and quad- and octrees provides some good starting points for research. Data-parallel APIs such as Thrust implement common parallel design patterns that can be used to simplify and implement many high-performance applications. Again, the good news is that these general libraries are rapidly expanding and improving.

For all applications, the three rules of high-performance GPU programming discussed in this book should be used as a basic starting point in all your design efforts:

1. Get the data on the GPGPU and keep it there.
2. Give the GPGPU enough work to do.
3. Focus on data reuse within the GPGPU to avoid memory bandwidth limitations.

Mapped Memory

Simplicity is the advantage of mapping memory among the devices in a system:

- There is no need to partition data. All devices see the complete memory image.
- There is no need to allocate space in device memory or to manually copy data. All data transfers are implicitly performed by the kernel as needed.
- There is no need to use streams to overlap data transfers with kernel execution. All data transfers originate from the kernel and are asynchronous.

Application performance is the cost associated with this simplicity. Using mapped memory does mean that the programmer gives up control over the data movement between the host and devices. From the forums and experience, it is not unusual for kernel performance to drop when using mapped memory because there are no guarantees when or how often data will need to be transferred across the PCIe bus. Other considerations to using mapped memory include:

- If the contents of the mapped memory are modified, the application must synchronize memory accesses using streams or events to avoid any potential read-after-write, write-after-read, or write-after write hazards.
- The host memory needs to be page aligned. The simplest and most portable way to enforce this is to use **cudaAllocHost()** when allocating mapped host memory.

The simplicity of using mapped memory is illustrated by the following example (Example 7.16), which fills a mapped memory vector using one or more GPUs in the system. The highlighted command **cudaHostAlloc()** creates a mapped region of memory when passed the **cudaHostAllocMapped** flag. This region is freed at the end of the program with **cudaFreeHost()**.

Thrust was used to make this code concise and easy to read. The **device_pointer_cast()** method was used to correctly cast the mapped host memory for the thrust **sequence()** method.

The highlighted call to **cudaDeviceSynchronize()** ensures that the mapped data is synchronized between the host and devices prior to checking the results on the host. All data transfers occur transparently and asynchronously. Finally, the contents of the mapped region of memory are checked for correctness on the host and the mapped region is freed.

Example 7.16

```
#include <iostream>
using namespace std;

#include <thrust/device_vector.h>
#include <thrust/sequence.h>

int main(int argc, char* argv[])
{
  int nGPU;

  if(argc < 2) {
    cerr << "Use: number of integers" << endl;
    return(1);
  }

  cudaGetDeviceCount(&nGPU);

  int n = atoi(argv[1]);
  int size = nGPU * n * sizeof(int);

  cout << "nGPU " << nGPU << " " << (n*nGPU*sizeof(int)/1e6) << "MB" << endl;

  int *h_A;
  cudaHostAlloc(&h_A, size, cudaHostAllocMapped);

  for(int i=0; i < nGPU; i++) {
    cudaSetDevice(i);
    thrust::sequence(thrust::device_pointer_cast(h_A + i*n),
              thrust::device_pointer_cast(h_A + (i+1)*n),
                 i*n);
  }
  cudaDeviceSynchronize(); // synchronize the writes

  for(int i=0; i < nGPU*n; i++)
    if(h_A[i] != i) { cout << "Error " << h_A[i] << endl; exit(1); }

  cout << "Success!\n" << endl;
  cudaFreeHost(h_A);
  return(0);
}
```

Compiling and running this example on a system containing two GPUs shows that the vector **h_A** is correctly initialized for both very small and large problems (Example 7.17, "Sample Output from the Mapped Memory Example"):

Example 7.17

```
$ ./mappedGPUsthrust 2
nGPU 2 1.6e-05MB
Success!

$ ./mappedGPUsthrust 200000000
nGPU 2 1600MB
Success!
```

The result when using two integers per GPU illustrates a very important characteristic of mapped memory: it allows multiple devices to correctly update adjacent, nonoverlapping locations in memory! This makes mapped memory a very valuable tool, as programmers need to ensure only that their codes write to nonoverlapping addresses in memory. Of course, concurrent writes to the same memory location are undefined. Also, writes will become visible across devices only after synchronization.

How Mapped Memory Works

All CUDA threads operate in a virtual address space. This means that every address generated by a CUDA kernel is translated by the MMU (Memory Management Unit) into a physical address that is used by the hardware to actually read data from the physical memory. Virtual memory makes life simple for application programmers, as they can use a single virtual memory address to correctly access data within a kernel or across devices – even when that same data resides at a different physical address on each separate device.

When presented with a virtual address, the MMU consults an internal cache (called a TLB or Translation Lookaside Buffer) to find the correct value needed to translate the virtual address into a physical address. The MMU views memory in terms of fixed-sized blocks of memory called pages. If the MMU does not find the page offset for a given virtual address, it will load the correct offset into the TLB from a data structure in physical memory called a page table. No address translation is required for page table access by the MMU. Once the MMU has the correct offset in the TLB, the address translation completes, which lets the application memory transaction proceed at the correct location in physical memory.

Microbenchmarks indicate that the size of a page of memory in a GPU can vary according to the hardware and the CUDA driver. Generally, 4 KB is the accepted size of a GPU page, but 64 KB pages have also been observed (Wong, Papadopoulou, Sadooghi-Alvandi, & Moshovos, 2010). The lesson learned is that the page size can vary even across device driver updates.

In addition to translating virtual addresses to physical memory, the MMU also keeps track of other information in the page table. For example, each page in the page table contains a bit that specifies whether the page is resident in memory. When the MMU is asked to translate an address for a page that is not resident, it generates a page fault that informs the device driver that it needs to fetch some data on behalf of the GPU. Address translation resumes only once the page has been loaded into the GPU memory.

When a region of memory is mapped, none of the pages are marked as resident. As a result, the first access to each page of mapped memory will be slow, as the GPU must wait while the GPU and device driver interact to transfer the required page of memory. Later accesses will be very fast, as the page will already be resident on the GPU. Of course, the GPU can decide at any time to free memory for other purposes, in which case a follow-on page access will again be slow.

The successful two-integer test case using the code in Example 7.16 tell us that the device driver has implemented a mechanism that correctly modifies adjacent, nonoverlapping regions of mapped memory *even when multiple devices modify addresses that reside in the same page*. The implication for the CUDA programmer is that data can be modified in mapped memory as long as the programmer:

- Takes care not to modify the same memory location on different devices.
- Synchronizes as needed to make updates visible to all devices.

SUMMARY

This chapter introduced multi-GPU programming, which is one of the most exciting areas of research and application development in GPU computing. Current technology allows up to 16 GPUs devices to be installed in a single workstation or computational node. Such a workstation has a potential computational capability that is three times greater than the $30 million supercomputer at Pacific Northwest National Laboratory that was replaced in 2006.

Data partitioning and scalability are key challenges for multi-GPU application development. Ideally, CUDA programmers should be able to achieve a linear speedup according to the number of devices in the system. This is where understanding the computational problem and creative thinking can really make a difference in application performance.

Still to be discussed is MPI programming for distributed GPU clusters. With this technology, CUDA programmers can scale to literally thousands of GPU devices to address big computational problems. It also creates opportunities to perform "leadership"-class computations on some of the largest supercomputers in the world. To accelerate performance for distributed applications, NVIDIA has introduced GPUdirect technology, which allows GPUs to communicate directly with each other across a distributed network. Chapter 10 discusses this technology and the use of GPUs for distributed computing and supercomputers.

## CHAPTER 8

CUDA for All GPU and CPU Applications

Software development takes time and costs money. CUDA has evolved from a solid platform to accelerate numerical computation into a platform that is appropriate for *all* application development. What this means is that a single source tree of CUDA code can support applications that run exclusively on conventional x86 processors, exclusively on GPU hardware, or as hybrid applications that simultaneously use all the CPU and GPU devices in a system to achieve maximal performance. The Portland Group, Inc. (PGI)[1] native CUDA-x86 compiler is one realization of this maturation process that has made CUDA C/C++ a viable source platform for generic application development, just like C++ and Java. Unlike Java and other popular application languages, CUDA can efficiently support tens of thousands of concurrent threads of execution. CUDA also supports the conventional approach to cross-language development that uses language bindings to interface with existing languages. As with other languages, libraries simplify application development and handle commonly used methods such as linear algebra, matrix operations, and the Fast Fourier Transform (FFT). Dynamic compilation is also blurring the distinction between CUDA and other languages, as exemplified by the Copperhead project (discussed shortly), which lets Python programmers write their code entirely in Python. The Copperhead runtime then dynamically compiles the Python methods to run on CUDA-enabled hardware.

At the end of this chapter, the reader will have a basic understanding of:

- Tools to transparently build and run CUDA applications on non-GPU systems and GPUs manufactured by any vendor.
- The Copperhead project, which dynamically compiles Python for CUDA execution.

---

[1] http://www.pgroup.com/.

- How to incorporate CUDA with most languages, including Python, FORTRAN, R, Java, and others.
- Important numerical libraries such as CUBLAS, CUFFT, and MAGMA.
- How to use CUFFT concurrently on multiple GPUs.
- CURAND and problems with naïve approaches to random number generation.
- The effect of PCIe hardware on multi-GPU applications.

PATHWAYS FROM CUDA TO MULTIPLE HARDWARE BACKENDS

Example 8.1 illustrates the paths that are currently available to run CUDA C/C++ on x86 and GPU hardware. These are capabilities that give CUDA programmers the ability—with a single source tree—to create applications that can reach both those customers who own the third of a billion CUDA-enabled GPUs sold to date as well as the massive base of customers who already own x86-based systems. Example 8.1, "Pathway to use CUDA source code on CPUs, GPUs, and other vendor GPUs."

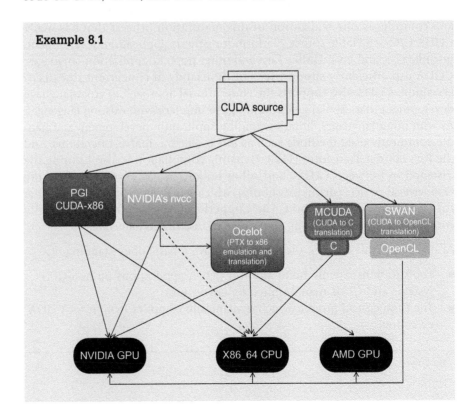

Example 8.1

The PGI CUDA x86 Compiler

The concept behind native x86 compilation is to give CUDA programmers the ability—with a single source tree—to create applications that can reach most customers with a computer. When released, the PGI unified binary will greatly simplify product support and delivery as a single application binary can be shipped to customers. At runtime, the PGI unified binary will query the hardware and selectively run on any CUDA-enabled GPUs or the host multicore processor.

What distinguishes the PGI effort from source translators such as the Swan[2] CUDA to OpenCL translator; the MCUDA[3] CUDA to C translator; the Ocelot[4] open source emulator and PTX translation project; and the ability of the NVIDIA **nvcc** compiler to generate both x86 and GPU based code is:

- **Speed:** The PGI CUDA C/C++ compiler is a native compiler that transparently compiles CUDA to run on x86 systems even when a GPU is not present in the system. This gives the compiler the opportunity to perform x86 specific optimization to best use the multiple cores of the x86 processor as well as the SIMD parallelism in the AVX or SSE instructions within each core. (AVX is an extension of SSE to 256-bit operation.)
- **Transparency:** Both NVIDIA and PGI state that even CUDA applications utilizing proprietary features of the GPU texture units will exhibit identical behavior on both x86 and GPU hardware.
- **Convenience:** In 2012, the PGI compiler will be able to create a unified binary, which will simplify the software distribution process tremendously as mentioned previously. The simplicity of shipping a single binary to customers reflects the completeness of the thought behind the PGI CUDA C/C++ project.

From a planning perspective, CUDA for x86 dramatically impacts the software development decision-making process. Rather than CUDA filling the role of a niche development platform for GPU-based products, CUDA is now a platform for all product development—even for applications that are not intended to be accelerated by GPUs!

The motivation is clearly exemplified by the variety and number of projects on the NVIDIA showcase that have achieved 100 times or greater performance over commodity processors, as summarized in Figure 8.1.

---

[2] http://www.multiscalelab.org/swan.
[3] http://impact.crhc.illinois.edu/mcuda.php.
[4] http://code.google.com/p/gpuocelot/.

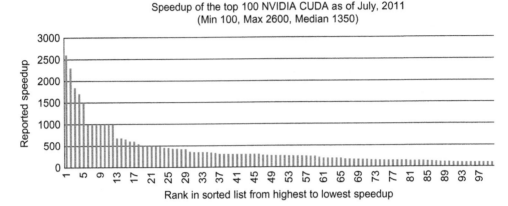

FIGURE 8.1

NVIDIA's top 100 fastest reported speedups over conventional processors.

In short, the performance of applications that fail to capitalize on the parallel performance capabilities of multicore and GPU devices will plateau at or near current levels and not increase with future hardware generations. Such applications risk stagnation and a loss of competitiveness (Farber, 2010).

From a software development point of view, prudence dictates the selection of a platform that works well right now. Foresight requires picking a software framework that keeps the application running competitively on future hardware platforms without requiring a substantial rewrite or additional software investment.

Following are the top reasons to use CUDA for all application development:

- CUDA is based on standard C and C++. Both of these languages have a solid history of application development spanning decades.
- Applications written in CUDA and compiled with CUDA-x86 can potentially run faster on x86 platforms than code written in traditional languages through better use of parallelism and the multicore SIMD units.
- Multicore CUDA codes will contain fewer bugs because the CUDA execution model precludes many common parallel programming errors including race conditions and deadlock.
- CUDA will future-proof the application because CUDA was designed to scale effectively to tens of thousands of concurrent threads of execution. This benefit can save future software development dollars and allow fast penetration into new markets.
- GPU acceleration comes for free, which opens the door for order of magnitude application acceleration on the third of a billion CUDA-enabled GPUs that have already been sold worldwide.

- CUDA has a large base of educated developers; plus, this developer base is rapidly expanding. CUDA is currently taught at more than 450 universities and colleges worldwide. The number of institutions teaching CUDA is also rapidly expanding.

In other words, the future looks bright for literate CUDA programmers!

The PGI CUDA x86 Compiler

Using the PGI CUDA-x86 compiler is straightforward. Currently, PGI offers the compiler a free evaluation period. Just download and install it per the instructions on the PGI website.[5]

Setup is straightforward and well described in the installation guide. Example 8.2, "Setting the Environment for the PGI Compilor," contains the commands to set the environment using bash under Linux:

Example 8.2

```
PGI=/opt/pgi; export PGI
MANPATH=$MANPATH:$PGI/linux86-64/11.5/man; export MANPATH
LM_LICENSE_FILE=$PGI/license.dat; export LM_LICENSE_FILE
PATH=$PGI/linux86-64/11.5/bin:$PATH; export PATH
```

It is quite easy to use the software. For example, copy the PGI NVIDIA SDK samples to a convenient location and build them, as in Example 8.3, "Building the PGI SDK":

Example 8.3

```
cp -r /opt/pgi/linux86-64/2011/cuda/cudaX86SDK .
cd cudaX86SDK ;
make
```

Example 8.4, "Output of deviceQuery When Running on a Quad-CoreCPU," shows the output of **deviceQuery** on an Intel Xeon e5560:

Example 8.4

```
CUDA Device Query (Runtime API) version (CUDART static linking)

There is 1 device supporting CUDA
```

---

[5] http://pgroup.com.

```
Device 0: "DEVICE EMULATION MODE"
  CUDA Driver Version:                        99.99
  CUDA Runtime Version:                       99.99
  CUDA Capability Major revision number:      9998
  CUDA Capability Minor revision number:      9998
  Total amount of global memory:              128000000 bytes
  Number of multiprocessors:                  1
  Number of cores:                            0
  Total amount of constant memory:            1021585952 bytes
  Total amount of shared memory per block:    1021586048 bytes
  Total number of registers available per block: 1021585904
  Warp size:                                  1
  Maximum number of threads per block:        1021585920
  Maximum sizes of each dimension of a block: 32767 × 2 × 0
  Maximum sizes of each dimension of a grid:  1021586032 × 32767 ×
                                              1021586048
  Maximum memory pitch:                       4206313 bytes
  Texture alignment:                          1021585952 bytes
  Clock rate:                                 0.00 GHz
  Concurrent copy and execution:              Yes
  Run time limit on kernels:.                 Yes
  Integrated:                                 No
  Support host page-locked memory mapping:    Yes
  Compute mode:                               Unknown
  Concurrent kernel execution:                Yes
  Device has ECC support enabled:             Yes

deviceQuery, CUDA Driver = CUDART, CUDA Driver Version = 99.99, CUDA
Runtime Version = 99.99, NumDevs = 1, Device = DEVICE EMULATION MODE

PASSED

Press <Enter> to Quit...
------------------------------------------------------------
```

Similarly, the output of **bandwidthTest** shows that device transfers work as expected (Example 8.5, "Output of bandwidthTest When Running on a Quad-Core CPU):

Example 8.5

```
Running on...

Device 0: DEVICE EMULATION MODE
Quick Mode

Host to Device Bandwidth, 1 Device(s), Paged memory
  Transfer Size (Bytes)    Bandwidth(MB/s)
  33554432                 4152.5
```

```
Device to Host Bandwidth, 1 Device(s), Paged memory
  Transfer Size (Bytes)      Bandwidth(MB/s)
  33554432                   4257.0

Device to Device Bandwidth, 1 Device(s)
  Transfer Size (Bytes)      Bandwidth(MB/s)
  33554432                   8459.2

[bandwidthTest] - Test results:
PASSED

Press <Enter> to Quit...
- - - - - - - - - - - - - - - - - - - - - - - - - - - - - - - - - - - - - - - - -
```

Just as with NVIDIA's **nvcc** compiler, it is easy to use the PGI **pgCC** compiler to build an executable from a CUDA source file. For example, the *arrayReversal_multiblock_fast.cu* code from part 3 of my Doctor Dobb's article series just compiles and runs.[6]

To compile and run it under Linux, type the code in Example 8.6, "Output of *arrayReversal_multiblock_fast.cu* When Running on a Quad-Core CPU":

Example 8.6

```
pgCC arrayReversal_multiblock_fast.cu
./a.out
Correct!
```

An x86 core as an SM

In CUDA-x86, thread blocks are efficiently mapped to the processor cores. Thread-level parallelism is mapped to the SSE (Streaming SIMD Extensions) or AVX SIMD units, as shown in Figure 8.2.

CUDA programmers should note:

- The size of a warp will be different from the expected 32 threads per warp for a GPU. For x86 computing, a warp might be the size of the SIMD units on the x86 core (either four or eight) or one thread per warp when SIMD execution is not utilized.
- In many cases, the PGI CUDA C compiler will remove explicit synchronization of the thread processors when the compiler can determine that it is safe to split loops where the synchronization calls occur.

---

[6] http://drdobbs.com/high-performance-computing/207603131.

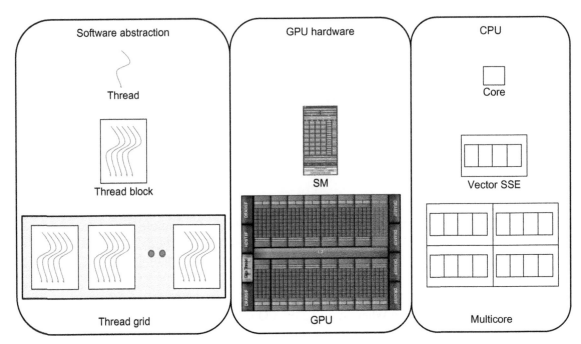

FIGURE 8.2
Mapping GPU computing onto a CPU.

- CUDA programmers must consider data transfer times, as explicit movement of data between host and device memory and global to shared memory will still happen in CUDA-x86.

The NVIDIA NVCC Compiler

The NVIDIA **nvcc** compiler can generate both host- and device-based kernels. Chapter 2 utilized this capability for testing and performance analysis purposes. Though very useful, this approach requires manual effort on the part of the CUDA programmer to set up memory correctly and to call the functor appropriately.

Thrust can also transparently generate code for different backends such as x86 processors just by passing some additional command-line options to nvcc. No source code modification is required.

The following **nvcc** command-line demonstrated building the NVIDIA SDK Monte Carlo example to run on the host processor:

Example 8.7

```
nvcc -O2 -o monte_carlo monte_carlo.cu -Xcompiler -fopenmp \
    -DTHRUST_DEVICE_BACKEND=THRUST_DEVICE_BACKEND_OMP -lcudart -lgomp
```

Table 8.1 Reported Time When Running a Thrust Example Using OpenMP

Device	Seconds
GPU	0.222
4 OpenMP threads	2.090
2 OpenMP threads	4.168
1 OpenMP thread	8.333

Timing reported on the Thrust website shows that the performance is acceptable (see Table 8.1). Be aware that Thrust is not optimized to produce the best x86 runtimes.

Ocelot

Ocelot is a popular, actively maintained package with a large user base. The website notes that Ocelot can run CUDA binaries on NVIDIA GPUS, AMD GPUs, and x86 processors at full speed without recompilation. It can be freely downloaded and is licensed under a new BSD license. A paper by Gregory Diamos, "The Design and Implementation Ocelot's[7] Dynamic Binary Translator from PTX to Multi-Core x86," is recommended reading (Diamos, 2009), as is his chapter in *GPU Computing Gems* (Hwu, 2011).

Ocelot's core capabilities consist of:

- An implementation of the CUDA Runtime API.
- A complete internal representation of PTX kernels coupled to control- and data-flow analysis procedures for analysis.
- A functional emulator for PTX.
- A PTX translator to multicore x86-based CPUs for efficient execution.
- A backend to NVIDIA GPUs via the CUDA driver API.
- Support for an extensible trace generation framework in which application behavior can be observed at instruction-level granularity.

Ocelot has three backend execution targets:

- A PTX emulator.
- A translator from PTX to multicore instructions.
- A CUDA-enabled GPU.

Ocelot has been validated against more than 130 applications taken from the CUDA SDK, the UIUC Parboil benchmark, the Virginia Rodinia benchmarks (Che et al., 2009, 2010), the GPU-VSIPL signal and image processing library,[8] the thrust library, and several domain-specific applications. It is an exemplary

---

[7] http://code.google.com/p/gpuocelot/.
[8] http://gpu-vsipl.gtri.gatech.edu/.

tool to use in profiling and analyzing the behavior of CUDA applications that can also be used as a platform for CUDA application portability.

Swan

Swan is a freely available source-to-source translation tool that converts an existing CUDA code to use the OpenCL model. Note that the conversion process requires human intervention and is not automatic.

The authors report that the performance of a CUDA application ported to OpenCL run about 50 percent slower (Harvey & De Fabritiis, 2010). The authors attribute the performance reduction to the immaturity of the OpenCL compilers. They conclude that OpenCL is a viable platform for developing portable GPU applications but also that the more mature CUDA tools continue to provide best performance.

It is not clear how active the development effort is on the Swan project, as the most recent update was in December 2010. The current version of Swan does not support:

- CUDA C++ templates in kernel code.
- OpenCL Images/Samplers (analogous to Textures)—texture interpolation done in software.
- Multiple device management in a single process.
- Compiling kernels for the CPU.
- CUDA device-emulation mode.

MCUDA

MCUDA is an academic effort by the IMPACT Research Group at the University of Illinois. It is available for free download. This project does not appear to be actively maintained.

The paper "MCUDA: An Efficient Implementation of CUDA Kernels for Multi-Core CPUs" is interesting reading (Stratton, Stone, & Hwu, 2008). A related paper, "FCUDA: Enabling Efficient Compilation of CUDA Kernels onto FPGAs," discusses translating CUDA to FPGAs (Field Programmable Gate Arrays) (Papakonstantinou et al., 2009).

ACCESSING CUDA FROM OTHER LANGUAGES

CUDA can be incorporated into any language that provides a mechanism for calling C or C++. To simplify this process, general-purpose interface generators have been created that will create most of the boilerplate code automatically. One of the most popular interface generators is SWIG. An alternative approach is to seamlessly integrate CUDA into the language, which is being investigated by the Copperhead Python project.

SWIG

SWIG (Simplified Wrapper and Interface Generator) is a software development tool that connects programs written in C and C++—including CUDA C/C++ applications—with a variety of high-level programming languages. SWIG is actively supported and widely used. It can be freely downloaded from the SWIG website.[9]

As of the current 2.0.4 release, SWIG generates interfaces for the following languages:

- AllegroCL
- C# – Mono
- C# – MS.NET
- CFFI
- CHICKEN
- CLISP
- D
- Go language
- Guile
- Java
- Lua
- MzScheme/Racket
- Ocaml
- Octave
- Perl
- PHP
- Python
- R
- Ruby
- Tcl/Tk

Part 9 of my *Doctor Dobb's Journal* "Supercomputing for the Masses" tutorial series[10] provides a complete working example that uses SWIG to interface a CUDA matrix operation with Python. This example can interface with other languages as well (Farber, 2008).

Copperhead

Copperhead is an early-stage research project to bring data parallelism to the Python language. It defines a small, data-parallel subset of Python that is dynamically compiled to run on parallel platforms. Right now, NVIDIA GPGPUs are the only parallel backend.

---

[9] http://swig.org.

[10] http://drdobbs.com/high-performance-computing/211800683.

Example 8.8, "Example Copperhead Python Code," is a simple example from the Copperhead website:

Example 8.8

```
from copperhead import *
import numpy as np

@cu
def axpy(a, x, y):
  return [a * xi + yi for xi, yi in zip(x, y)]

x = np.arange(100, dtype=np.float64)
y = np.arange(100, dtype=np.float64)

with places.gpu0:
  gpu = axpy(2.0, x, y)

with places.here:
  cpu = axpy(2.0, x, y)
```

Copperhead organizes computations around data parallel arrays. In this example, the Copperhead runtime intercepts the call to **axpy()** and compiles the function to CUDA. The runtime converts the input arguments to a type of parallel array, **CuArrays**, that are managed by the runtime.

The programmer specifies where the execution is to take place using the **with** construct shown in the previous example. Data is lazily copied to and from the execution location. Copperhead currently supports GPU execution and Python interpreter execution. Use of the Python interpreter is intended for algorithm prototyping.

EXCEL

Microsoft Excel is a widely adopted commercial spreadsheet application written and distributed by Microsoft for Windows and Mac OS. It features calculation, graphing tools, and a variety of other tools. Functionality can be programmed in Visual Basic. NVIDIA distributes the "Excel 2010 CUDA Integration Example"[11] on their website, which shows how to use CUDA in Excel. This SDK example is not included in the standard SDK samples.

MATLAB

MATLAB is a commercial application developed by MathWorks. The MATLAB software allows matrix manipulation, plotting of functions and data, and a wealth of other functionality. Developers can implement algorithms and user interfaces as well as integrate MATLAB into other

---

[11] http://developer.nvidia.com/cuda-cc-sdk-code-samples.

applications. MATLAB GPU support is available in the Parallel Computing Toolbox. It supports NVIDIA CUDA-enabled GPUs of compute 1.3 and higher. Third-party products such as those by Accelereyes provide both MATLAB access to GPU computing as well as matrix libraries for CUDA.[12]

LIBRARIES

The use of optimized libraries are often an easy way to improve the performance of an application. When porting large legacy projects, libraries may be the only real way to optimize for a new platform because code changes would require extensive validation efforts. Essentially, libraries are convenient and can greatly accelerate code development as well as application performance, but they cannot be blindly utilized. GPU-based libraries in particular require the developer to think carefully about data placement and how the library is used, or poor performance and excessive memory consumption will result.

CUBLAS

The Basic Linear Algebra Subprograms (BLAS) package is the de facto programming interface for basic linear algebra operations such as vector and matrix multiplication. NVIDIA supports this interface with their own library for the GPU called CUBLAS. The basic model by which applications use the CUBLAS library is to create matrix and vector objects in GPU memory space, fill these objects with data, call a sequence of CUBLAS functions, and return the result(s) to the host.

CUBLAS provides helper functions to create and destroy objects in GPU space and to utilize the data in these objects. CUDA programmers should note that CUBLAS uses column-major storage and 1-based indexing for maximum FORTRAN compatibility. C and C++ applications need to use macros or inline functions to facilitate access to CUBLAS created objects.

Chapter 1 contains a discussion of the BLAS runtime levels and the importance of minimizing or eliminating data movement. The simpleBLAS example, which can be downloaded from the NVIDIA website, provides a basic demonstration how to use CUBLAS.[13]

CUFFT

CUFFT is another NVIDIA supported library that provides a GPU based implementation of the FFT, a commonly used method in scientific and signal processing applications. CUFFT is modeled after FFTW, a very highly optimized and popular FFT package for general-purpose processors.

---

[12] http://www.accelereyes.com/.

[13] http://www.nvidia.com/object/cuda_sample_linear_algebra.html.

CUFFT utilizes a plan, which is a simple configuration mechanism that specifies the best "plan" of execution for a particular algorithm given a specified problem size, data type, and destination hardware platform. The advantage of this approach is that once a plan is created, it can be used for the remainder of the application lifetime. This is a commonly used programming pattern to perform runtime configuration in libraries and other high-performance portable codes. The NVIDIA CUFFT library uses this configuration model because different sizes and types of FFTs require different thread configurations and GPU resources. The simpleCUFFT example can be downloaded from the NVIDIA website.[14] It covers the basics of how to use the CUFFT library.

CUFFT also provides the method **cufftPlanMany()**, which creates a plan that will run multiple FFT operations at the same time. This can be both a performance boon and a memory hog.

The following test program demonstrates the use of CUFFT on one or more GPUs. It performs a 3D complex-to-complex forward and inverse in-place transform and calculates the error introduced by these transforms. Correct usage will result in a small error.

The user can specify the following runtime characteristics via the command line:

- The number of GPUs to use. This number must be less than or equal to the number of GPUs in the system.
- The size of each dimension.
- The total number of FFTs to perform.
- An optional value that specifies how many FFTs to perform on each call to CUFFT.

In addition, this test code makes use of C++ type defines. To create a double-precision executable, simply specify -**D REAL=double** on the **nvcc** command line.

General include files and constants are defined at the beginning of the example file. The preprocessor variable **REAL** is set to default to **float** if not otherwise defined during compilation. Example 8.9, "Part 1 of *fft3Dtest.cu*," contains a walkthrough of the test code:

Example 8.9

```
#include <iostream>
#include <cassert>
using namespace std;
#include <cuda.h>
```

---

[14] http://www.nvidia.com/object/cuda_sample_basic_topics.html.

```
#define CUFFT_FORWARD -1
#define CUFFT_INVERSE  1

#include "thrust/host_vector.h"
#include "thrust/device_vector.h"

#include <cufft.h>

#ifndef REAL
#define REAL float
#endif
```

The template class **DistFFT3D** is defined and a number of variables are created in Example 8.10, "Part 2 of *fft3Dtest.cu*":

Example 8.10
```
template <typename Real>
class DistFFT3D {
  protected:
    int nGPU;
    cudaStream_t *streams;
    int nPerCall;
    vector<cufftHandle> fftPlanMany;
    int dim[3];
    Real *h_data;
    long h_data_elements;
    long nfft, n2ft3d, h_memsize, nelements;
    long totalFFT;
    vector<Real *> d_data;
    long bytesPerGPU;
```

The public constructor takes a vector of host data and partitions it equally across the user defined number of GPUs. These vectors are kept in the variable **d_data**.

For generality, an array of streams is passed to the constructor, which allows the user to queue work before and after the test. This capability is not used but is provided, in case the reader wishes to use this example in another code. It is assumed that one stream is associated with each GPU.

A vector of CUFFT handles is created in **fftPlanMany()** where one plan is associated with each stream. This setup implies that there will be one plan per GPU, as each stream is associated with a different GPU.

The number of multiplan FFTs is defined in the call to **NperCall()**. The method **initFFTs()** creates the handles. Similarly, a vector of device vectors

is created per GPU. The pointers to device memory are held in the vector
d_data. See Example 8.11, "Part 3 of *fft3Dtest.cu*":

Example 8.11

```
public:
  DistFFT3D(int _nGPU, Real* _h_data, long _h_data_elements,
            int *_dim, int _nPerCall, cudaStream_t *_streams) {
    nGPU= _nGPU;
    h_data = _h_data;
    h_data_elements = _h_data_elements;
    dim[0] = _dim[0]; dim[1] = _dim[1]; dim[2] = _dim[2];
    nfft = dim[0]*dim[1]*dim[2];
    n2ft3d = 2*dim[0]*dim[1]*dim[2];
    totalFFT = h_data_elements/n2ft3d;

    set_NperCall(_nPerCall);
    bytesPerGPU = nPerCall*n2ft3d*sizeof(Real);
    h_memsize = h_data_elements*sizeof(Real);
    assert( (totalFFT/nPerCall*bytesPerGPU) == h_memsize);

    streams = _streams;
    fftPlanMany = vector<cufftHandle>(nGPU);

    initFFTs();

    for(int i=0; i<nGPU; i++) {
      Real* tmp;
      cudaSetDevice(i);
      if(cudaMalloc(&tmp,bytesPerGPU)) {
        cerr << "Cannot allocate space on device!" << endl;
        exit(1);
      }
      d_data.push_back(tmp);
    }

  }
  void set_NperCall(int n) {
    cerr << "Setting nPerCall " << n << endl;
    nPerCall = n;
    if( (nGPU * nPerCall) > totalFFT) {
      cerr << "Too many nPerCall specified! max " << (totalFFT/nGPU) <<
      endl;
      exit(1);
    }
  }
```

The destructor frees the data allocated on the devices in Example 8.12, "Part 4 of *fft3Dtest.cu*":

Example 8.12

```
~DistFFT3D() {
  for(int i=0; i < nGPU; i++){
    cudaSetDevice(i);
    cudaFree(d_data[i]);
    }
  }
```

Example 8.13, "Part 5 of *fft3Dtest.cu*," initializes the multiplan FFTs and provides the template wrappers to correctly call the CUFFT method for **float** and **double** variable types. Note that the stream is set with **cufftSetStream()**:

Example 8.13

```
void inline initFFTs()
{
  if((nPerCall*nGPU) > totalFFT) {
    cerr << "nPerCall must be a multiple of totalFFT" << endl;
    exit(1);
  }
  // Create a batched 3D plan
  for(int sid=0; sid < nGPU; sid++) {
    cudaSetDevice(sid);
    if(sizeof(Real) == sizeof(float) ) {
      cufftPlanMany(&fftPlanMany[sid], 3, dim, NULL, 1, 0, NULL, 1, 0,
                  CUFFT_C2C,nPerCall);
    } else {
      cufftPlanMany(&fftPlanMany[sid], 3, dim, NULL, 1, 0, NULL, 1, 0,
                  CUFFT_Z2Z,nPerCall);
    }
    if(cufftSetStream(fftPlanMany[sid],streams[sid])) {
      cerr << "cufftSetStream failed!" << endl;
    }
  }
  cudaSetDevice(0);
}

inline void _FFTerror(int ret) {
  switch(ret) {
  case CUFFT_SETUP_FAILED: cerr << "SETUP_FAILED" << endl; break;
  case CUFFT_INVALID_PLAN: cerr << "INVALID_PLAN" << endl; break;
```

```
    case CUFFT_INVALID_VALUE: cerr << "INVALID_VALUE" << endl; break;
    case CUFFT_EXEC_FAILED: cerr << "EXEC_FAILED" << endl; break;
    default: cerr << "UNKNOWN ret code " << ret << endl;
    }
}

//template specialization to handle different data types (float,
double)
inline void cinverseFFT_(cufftHandle myFFTplan, float* A, float* B ) {
  int ret=cufftExecC2C(myFFTplan, (cufftComplex*)A,
                       (cufftComplex*) B, CUFFT_INVERSE);
  if(ret != CUFFT_SUCCESS) {
    cerr << "C2C FFT failed! ret code " << ret << endl;
    _FFTerror(ret); exit(1);
  }
}

 inline void cinverseFFT_(cufftHandle myFFTplan, double *A, double *B)
 {
  int ret = cufftExecZ2Z(myFFTplan, (cufftDoubleComplex*)A,
                       (cufftDoubleComplex*) B, CUFFT_INVERSE);

  if(ret != CUFFT_SUCCESS) {
    cerr << "Z2Z FFT failed! ret code " << ret << endl;
    _FFTerror(ret); exit(1);
  }
 }

 inline void cforwardFFT_(cufftHandle myFFTplan, float* A, float* B )
 {
    int ret = cufftExecC2C(myFFTplan, (cufftComplex*)A,
                       (cufftComplex*) B, CUFFT_FORWARD);

    if(ret != CUFFT_SUCCESS) {
      cerr << "C C2C FFT failed!" << endl; _FFTerror(ret); exit(1);
    }
 }

 inline void cforwardFFT_(cufftHandle myFFTplan, double *A, double *B)
 {
    int ret = cufftExecZ2Z(myFFTplan, (cufftDoubleComplex*)A,
                       (cufftDoubleComplex*) B, CUFFT_FORWARD);

    if(ret != CUFFT_SUCCESS) {
      cerr << "Z2Z FFT failed!" << endl; _FFTerror(ret); exit(1);
    }
 }
```

Calculate the error on the host using scaled values of the FFT results and the original host vector, as in Example 8.14, "Part 6 of *fft3Dtest.cu*":

Example 8.14

```
double showError(Real* h_A1)
{
  double error=0.;
#pragma omp parallel for reduction (+ : error)
  for(int i=0; i < h_data_elements; i++) {
    h_data[i] /= (Real)nfft;
    error += abs(h_data[i] - h_A1[i]);
  }
  return error;
}
```

Example 8.15, "Part 7 of *fft3Dtest.cu*," performs the actual test:

Example 8.15

```
void doit()
{
  double startTime = omp_get_wtime();
  long h_offset=0;
  for(int i=0; i < totalFFT; i += nGPU*nPerCall) {
    for(int j=0; j < nGPU; j++) {
      cudaSetDevice(j);
      cudaMemcpyAsync(d_data[j], ((char*)h_data)+h_offset,
                 bytesPerGPU, cudaMemcpyDefault,streams[j]);
      cforwardFFT_(fftPlanMany[j],d_data[j], d_data[j]);
      cinverseFFT_(fftPlanMany[j],d_data[j], d_data[j]);
      cudaMemcpyAsync(((char*)h_data)+h_offset, d_data[j],
                 bytesPerGPU, cudaMemcpyDefault,streams[j]);
      h_offset += bytesPerGPU;
    }
  }
  cudaDeviceSynchronize();
  cudaSetDevice(0);

  double endTime = omp_get_wtime();

  cout << dim[0] << " " << dim[1] << " " << dim[2]
     << " nFFT/s " << 1./(0.5*(endTime-startTime)/totalFFT)
     << " average 3D fft time " << (0.5*(endTime-startTime)/totalFFT)
```

```
       << " total " << (endTime-startTime) << endl;
    }
};
```

The outer loop ensures that all the FFTs are performed by iterating from zero to **totalFFT** in steps of the number of multiplan FFT performed by all the GPUs.

The inner loop sets the device and queues:

- The transfer of data to the device from the host. Note that the transfer with **cudamemcpyAsync()** is asynchronous to the host but not to the other tasks in the queue.
- The forward and inverse FFT transforms.
- The asynchronous transfer of data from the device back to the host.

The increment of **h_offset** at the end of the inner loop ensures that each GPU (and queued FFT operation) operates on different, nonoverlapping regions of host memory, so no synchronization between GPUs is required. Finally, the overall performance of this method is measured and the average number of FFTs performed per second is reported.

The **main()** routine parses the command line and performs some basic checks. It also creates the streams array and associates one stream per GPU.

Of particular interest is the use of pinned memory on the host for fast asynchronous data transfers between the host and devices. This memory is created with **cudaHostAlloc()**, using the flag **cudaHostAllocPortable**. The host vector is filled with recurring sequential values. See Example 8.16, "Part 8 of *fft3Dtest.cu*":

Example 8.16

```
main(int argc, char *argv[])
{
  if(argc < 6) {
    cerr << "Use nGPU dim[0] dim[1] dim[2] numberFFT [nFFT per call]" <<
    endl;
    exit(1);
  }

  int nPerCall = 1;
  int nGPU = atoi(argv[1]);
  int dim[] = { atoi(argv[2]), atoi(argv[3]), atoi(argv[4])};
  int totalFFT=atoi(argv[5]);
  nPerCall = totalFFT;
  if( argc > 6) {
```

```
    nPerCall = atoi(argv[6]);
    if(totalFFT % nPerCall != 0) {
      cerr << "nPerCall must be a multiple of totalFFT!" << endl;
      return(1);
    }
  }

  int systemGPUcount;
  cudaGetDeviceCount(&systemGPUcount);
  if(nGPU > systemGPUcount) {
    cerr << "Attempting to use too many GPUs!" << endl;
    return(1);
  }

  cerr << "nGPU = " << nGPU << endl;
  cerr << "dim[0] = " << dim[0] << endl;
  cerr << "dim[1] = " << dim[1] << endl;
  cerr << "dim[2] = " << dim[2] << endl;
  cerr << "totalFFT = " << totalFFT << endl;
  cerr << "sizeof(REAL) is " << sizeof(REAL) << " bytes" << endl;

  cudaStream_t streams[nGPU];
  for(int sid=0; sid < nGPU; sid++) {
    cudaSetDevice(sid);
    if(cudaStreamCreate(&streams[sid]) != 0) {
      cerr << "Stream create failed!" << endl;
    }
  }
  cudaSetDevice(0);

  long nfft = dim[0]*dim[1]*dim[2];
  long n2ft3d = 2*dim[0]*dim[1]*dim[2];
  long nelements = n2ft3d*totalFFT;

  REAL *h_A, *h_A1;
  if(cudaHostAlloc(&h_A, nelements*sizeof(REAL), cudaHostAllocPortable)
      != cudaSuccess) {
    cerr << "cudaHostAlloc failed!" << endl; exit(1);
  }
  h_A1 = (REAL*) malloc(nelements*sizeof(REAL));
  if(!h_A1) {
    cerr << "malloc failed!" << endl; exit(1);
  }

  // fill the test data
#pragma omp parallel for
  for(long i=0; i < nelements; i++) h_A1[i] = h_A[i] = i%n2ft3d;

  DistFFT3D<REAL> dfft3d(nGPU, h_A, nelements, dim, nPerCall,
  streams);
  dfft3d.doit();
```

```
double error = dfft3d.showError(h_A1);
cout << "average error per fft " << (error/nfft/totalFFT) << endl;
cudaFreeHost(h_A1);
}
```

This source code can be compiled with the command-line Example 8.17, "command-line to compile *fft3dtest.cu*", which assumes that the file is saved in *fft3dtest.cu*:

Example 8.17

```
nvcc -Xcompiler -fopenmp -O3 -arch sm_20 fft3Dtest.cu -lcufft \
    -o fft3Dtest_float
nvcc -Xcompiler -fopenmp -O3 -arch sm_20 -D REAL=double fft3Dtest.cu \
    -lcufft -o fft3Dtest_double
```

Running the test shows that the test program correctly utilizes CUFFT, as the error is small even when using single precision. For example, a 32^3 run that performs 128 FFT tests generates an error of 0.00225.

Further, there is a speedup benefit when running on two GPUs, as seen in Figure 8.3, which shows plotted results for both single- and double-precision FFTs. The second GPU appears to provide limited additional performance in the double-precision runs, probably due to doubling the amount of data that must be transferred across the PCIe bus. Performing more than a few FFTs per CUFFT call also appears to have a minimal impact on performance.

A **computeprof** width plot shows that the application is concurrently running on both GPUs. The following width plot was captured on a Dell

FIGURE 8.3

Single- and double-precision 32x32x32 FFT performance.

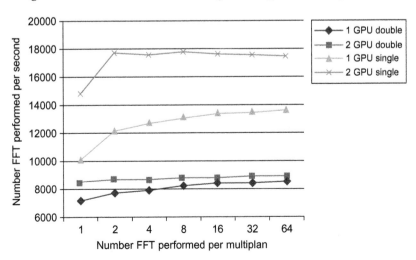

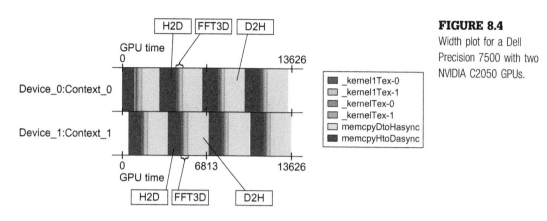

FIGURE 8.4
Width plot for a Dell
Precision 7500 with two
NVIDIA C2050 GPUs.

Precision 7500 with two NVIDIA C2050 GPUs.[15] The original color screen-shot was converted to grayscale for this book. The H2D (Host to Device) and D2H (Device to Host) transfers are noted as well as the computational kernels that implement the 3D FFT.

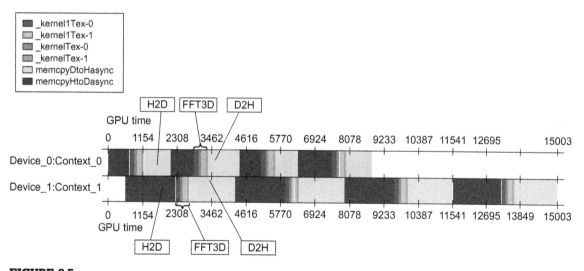

FIGURE 8.5
Width plot for an HP Z800 with two GPUs.

Results from the same run on an HP Z800 illustrate the importance of the PCIe hardware. Slow performance in the asynchronous transfer of data to one of the GPUs can dramatically decrease performance.

---

[15] Access to this machine was provided by the ICHEC (Irish Center for High-End Computing) NVIDIA CUDA Research Center.

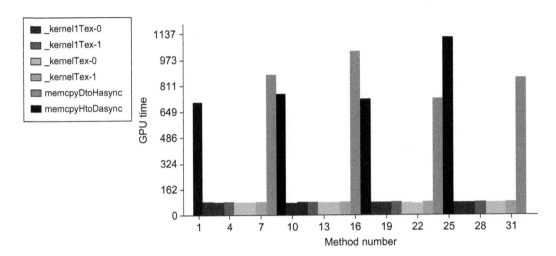

FIGURE 8.6

Height plot for device 0 on an HP Z800.

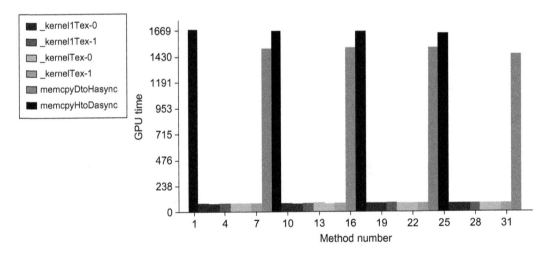

FIGURE 8.7

Height plot for device 1 on an HP Z800.

This observation is confirmed via the **computeprof** height plot for each GPU on the HP Z800, as there are clear differences between the two GPU devices as well as variations in the transfers performed on the device.

MAGMA

The MAGMA project aims to develop a dense linear algebra library similar to LAPACK but for heterogeneous/hybrid architectures. The initial focus is to provide a package that will concurrently run on multicore processors and a single GPU to deliver the combined performance of this hybrid environment. Later efforts will combine multiple GPUs with multiple cores.

The MAGMA team has made the conclusion that dense linear algebra (DLA), "has become a better fit for the new GPU architectures, to the point where DLA can run more efficiently on GPUs than on current, high-end homogeneous multicore-based systems" (Nath, Stanimire, & Dongerra, 2010, p. 1). According to Volkov, the current MAGMA BLAS libraries achieve up to 838 GF/s (Volkov, 2010).

The MAGMA software is freely downloadable from the University of Tennessee Innovative Computing Laboratory website.[16]

phiGEMM Library

The phiGEMM library is a freely available open source library that was written by Ivan Girotto and Filippo Spiga at ICHEC.[17] It performs matrix–matrix multiplication (e.g., GEMM operations) on heterogeneous systems containing multiple GPUs and multicore processors.

The phiGEMM library extends the mapping of Fatica (Fatica, 2009) to support single-precision, double-precision, and complex matrices. The LINPACK TOP 500 benchmark HPL benchmark suite uses this mapping for a heterogeneous matrix multiply as one of the core methods to evaluate the fastest supercomputers in the world.[18] The phiGEMM library is able to deliver comparable performance to the LINPACK benchmark using a single GPU and multicore processor. As can be seen in Figure 8.8, even greater performance can be achieved using two or more GPUs.

The phiGEMM library transparently manages memory and the asynchronous data transfers amongst all the devices in the system (i.e., multiple GPUs and multicore processors). It can process matrices that are much larger than the memory capacity of a single GPU by recursively multiplying smaller submatrices. Again, the library makes this process transparent to the user. Figure 8.9 shows performance using up to four GPUs for a 15 GB matrix. The phiGEMM library is being considered for inclusion in the MAGMA library discussed earlier.

CURAND

Generating random numbers on parallel computers is challenging. The naïve approach is to have each thread supply a different seed to a common

---

[16] http://icl.cs.utk.edu/.

[17] http://qe-forge.org/projects/phigemm/.

[18] http://www.nvidia.com/content/GTC-2010/pdfs/2057_GTC2010.pdf.

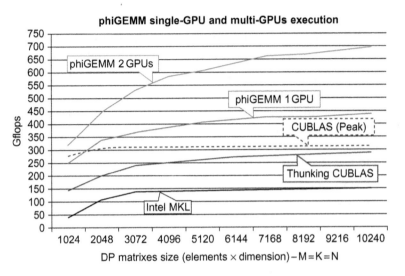

FIGURE 8.8

phiGEMM performance using one and two GPUs (data obtained on two Intel Xeon X5680 3.33 GHz and two Tesla NVIDIA C2050 GPUs).

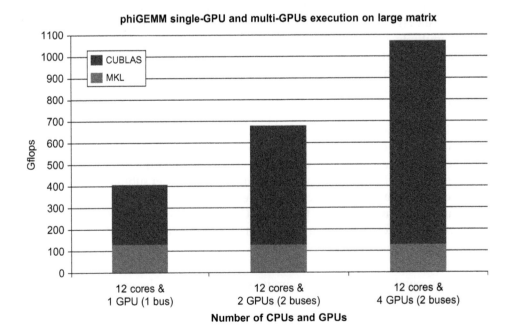

FIGURE 8.9

Performance of phiGEMM for a 15 GB matrix, M = K = N = 25000(DP) (data obtained on two Intel Xeon X5670 2.93 GHz and four Tesla NVIDIA C2050 GPUs).

random number generation method. This approach is not guaranteed to be independent and can inadvertently introduce correlations into the "random" data (Coddington, 1997).

The CURAND library provides a simple and efficient API to generate high-quality *pseudorandom* and *quasirandom* numbers. A pseudorandom sequence of numbers satisfies most of the statistical properties of a truly random sequence but is generated by a deterministic algorithm. A quasirandom sequence of n-dimensional points is generated by a deterministic algorithm designed to fill an n-dimensional space evenly.

Application areas include:

- **Simulation:** Random numbers are required to make things realistic. In the movies, computer-generated characters start and move in slightly different ways. People also arrive a airports at random intervals.
- **Sampling:** For many interesting problems, it is impractical to examine all possible cases. However, random sampling can provide insight into what constitutes "typical" behavior.
- **Computer programming:** Testing an algorithm with random numbers is an effective way to find problems and programmer biases.

SUMMARY

Commercial and research projects must now have parallel applications to compete for customer and research dollars. This need translates into pressure on software development efforts to control costs while supporting a range of rapidly evolving parallel hardware platforms. CUDA has been rapidly evolving to meet this need. Unlike current programming languages, CUDA was designed to create applications that run on hundreds of parallel processing elements and manage many thousands of threads. This design makes CUDA an attractive choice compared with current development languages like C++ and Java. It also creates a demand for CUDA developers.

Projects like Copperhead are expanding the boundaries of what can be done with dynamic compilation and CUDA. Solid library support makes CUDA attractive for numerical and signal-processing applications. General interface packages like SWIG create the opportunity to add massively parallel CUDA support to many existing languages.

## CHAPTER 9

Mixing CUDA and Rendering

With the focus on the use of CUDA to accelerate computational tasks, it is easy to forget that GPU technology is also a splendid platform for visualization. In combination with the Open Graphics Library (OpenGL), CUDA-enabled GPUs become visualization supercomputers. Even highly experienced OpenGL programmers will find this chapter both new and informative, as the examples use **primitive restart**—a feature recently added to the OpenGL 3.1 standard— to render high-performance, high-quality graphics even when the images require irregular meshes. Example kernels demonstrate data sharing between CUDA and OpenGL through buffer sharing. Profiling will show that primitive restart is 60 times faster than the optimized OpenGL **multiDraw()** method because it avoids performance robbing transfers across the PCIe bus. This chapter will also discuss how primitive restart can produce images of higher quality than other OpenGL methods and optimize texture rendering as well. Readers should note that this chapter is intended only to teach how to mix CUDA and OpenGL in the same application and demonstrate the speed of the methods used. The provided software framework is quite general and can be used for experimentation merely by changing the CUDA kernel. For example, Chapter 12 will use this framework with live video streams from a webcam. Those who wish a more detailed discussion of OpenGL should look to the many other, far more detailed books and Internet tutorials that teach OpenGL and computer graphics.

At the end of this chapter, the reader will have a basic understanding of:

- Mixing OpenGL and CUDA in the same application.
- How to use primitive restart and why it can generate images of higher quality than other methods.
- The performance implications of primitive restart for CUDA and in comparison to other OpenGL rendering techniques.

- How to use the simple general OpenGL framework in this chapter for your own kernels.
- The use of Perlin noise to generate artificial terrain.
- The difference between a PBO and VBO.

OPENGL

OpenGL is one of the most common programming interfaces used in visual applications from games to HPC (high-performance computing). OpenGL is standards-based and gives developers the ability to create graphics and special effects that appear nearly identical on any operating system running OpenGL-compliant hardware, making it possible for developers of 3D games and programs to port their software to multiple platforms.

OpenGL is controlled by an Architectural Review Board (ARB) composed of members from many institutions, including NVIDIA, SGI, Microsoft, AMD, HP, and others. The intention of the board is to:

- Keep the API stable.
- Ensure that the standard evolves to reflect new hardware capabilities.
- Allow for platform-specific features through extensions.

There are two very clear benefits of the separation (yet efficient interoperability) between CUDA and OpenGL:

- **From a programming view:** When not mapped into the CUDA memory space, OpenGL gurus are free to exploit existing legacy code bases, their expertise, and the full power of all the tools available to them, such as GLSL (the OpenGL Shading Language) and Cg. CUDA programmers can demonstrate their computational prowess when the buffer is mapped into the CUDA memory space.
- **From an investment view:** The mapped approach allows efficient exploitation of existing legacy OpenGL software investments. Essentially, CUDA code can be gradually added into existing legacy libraries and applications just by mapping the buffer into the CUDA memory space. This feature allows organizations to test CUDA code without significant risk and then enjoy the benefits of CUDA once they are confident of the performance and productivity rewards delivered by this programming model.

GLUT

The OpenGL Utility Toolkit (GLUT) is a programming interface for writing window system–independent OpenGL programs. Applications that utilize GLUT can be compiled on many platforms. NVIDIA uses GLUT in the CUDA SDK examples.

The GLUT toolkit provides various functionalities, but only a small subset will be used in this chapter:

- Windows for OpenGL rendering.
- Callback-driven event processing.
- Mouse and keyboard input devices.

Mapping GPU Memory with OpenGL

From a CUDA programmer's point of view, OpenGL creates and manages regions of memory on the GPU in generic buffers called buffer objects. The CUDA/OpenGL interoperability happens when a CUDA kernel maps a buffer into CUDA memory space. Control of the buffer is returned to OpenGL when the buffer is released, or unmapped. Mapping is a low-overhead operation that happens quickly and provides high-speed interoperability with CUDA without requiring any memory copies.

Interoperability with OpenGL requires that the CUDA device be specified by **cudaGLSetGLDevice()** before any other runtime calls. Note that **cudaSet-Device()** and **cudaGLSetGLDevice()** are mutually exclusive.[1] Interoperability with OpenGL requires that the CUDA device be specified by **cudaGLSet-GLDevice()** before any other runtime calls. Once a resource is registered to CUDA, it can be mapped and unmapped as many times as necessary using **cudaGraphicsMapResources()** and **cudaGraphicsUnmapResources()**. The method **cudaGraphicsResourceSetMapFlags()** can be called to provide hints (e.g., read-only, write-only) that the CUDA driver can use to optimize resource management.

There are two principal OpenGL memory objects that CUDA programmers will manipulate:

1. **Pixel buffer objects (PBOs):** A region of memory used by OpenGL to store *pixels*. A 2D image is composed of multiple pixels, or dots of color. CUDA applications map a PBO to create or modify images on a pixel-by-pixel basis and display them using OpenGL.
2. **Vertex buffer objects (VBOs):** A region of memory that OpenGL uses for 3D vertices. CUDA applications map a VBO to generate or modify 3D information that OpenGL can render meshes as a colored surface, wireframe image, or set of 3D points.

The following is an outline of the key OpenGL calls associated with VBO usage (excerpted from the OpenGL VBO whitepaper on http://spec.org):

- **glBindBuffer():** This function allows client-state functions to use binding buffers instead of working in absolute memory on the client side. Buffer object names are unsigned integers. The value zero is reserved. Setting

---

[1] Please see section 3.2.7.1 of the NVIDIA C Programming Guide, May 2011, p. 38).

the buffer name to zero effectively unbinds any buffer object previously bound, and restores client memory usage for that buffer object target.

- **glBufferData(), glBufferSubData(), and glGetBufferSubData():** These functions control the size of the buffer data, provide usage hints, and allow copying to a buffer.
- **glMapBuffer() and glUnmapBuffer():** These functions lock and unlock buffers, allowing data to be loaded into them or relinquishing control to the server. A temporary pointer is returned as an entry to the beginning of the buffer, which also maps the buffer into client memory. OpenGL is responsible for how this mapping into the client's absolute memory occurs. Because of this responsibility, mapping must be done for a short operation, and the pointer is not persistent and should be stored for further use.

More detailed information about the CUDA API and OpenGL calls used when mixing CUDA with OpenGL can be found in parts 15[2] and 18[3] of my *Doctor Dobb's* tutorial series. Another excellent source of information is Joe Stam's 2009 NVIDIA GTC conference presentation, "What Every CUDA Programmer Should Know about OpenGL," (Stam, 2009) which is available in both PDF and video formats.[4]

Using Primitive Restart for 3D Performance

As mentioned in the introduction to this chapter, the examples herein utilize an OpenGL extension called *primitive restart* to minimize communications across the PCIe bus and to speed rendering. Primitive restart gives the programmer the ability to specify a data value that is interpreted by the OpenGL state machine as a token indicating that the current graphics primitive has completed. The next data item is assumed to be at the start of another graphics primitive of the same type. Valid graphics primitives include **GL_TRIANGLE_STRIP**, **GL_TRIANGLE_FAN**, **GL_LINE_STRIP**, and others.

Figure 9.1 illustrates this process for two lines containing different numbers of vertices. The figure shows that **glPrimitiveRestartIndexNV()** is first called to specify the value of **TAG** to be the primitive restart token. The routine **glEnableClientState()** is then called to tell the OpenGL state machine to start using primitive restart. The lines are then drawn with **glDrawElements()**.

The advantages of the primitive restart approach include:

- All control tokens and data for viewing can be generated and kept on the GPU.

---

[2] http://drdobbs.com/cpp/222600097.
[3] http://drdobbs.com/open-source/225200412.
[4] http://www.nvidia.com/content/GTC/documents/1055_GTC09.pdf.

```
         glPrimitiveRestartIndexNV(TAG);
Code     glEnableClientState(GL_PRIMITIVE_RESTART_NV);
         glDrawElements(GL_LINE_STRIP, qIndexSize, GL_UNSIGNED_INT, qIndices);
```

FIGURE 9.1

Drawing two lines with primitive restart.

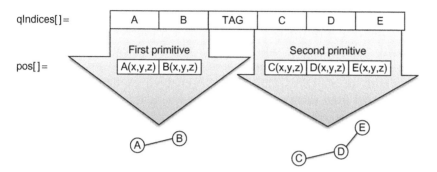

- Variable numbers of items can be specified between the primitive restart tokens. This allows irregular grids and surfaces to be drawn, as arbitrary numbers of line segments, triangle strips, triangle fans, and so on, can be specified depending on the drawing mode passed to **glDrawElements()**.
- Rendering performance can be optimized by arranging the indices to achieve the highest reuse of data cache in the texture units.
- Higher-quality images can be created by alternating the direction of tessellation as noted in the primitive restart specification and illustrated in Figures 9.2 and 9.3. The centers of the triangle fan are marked with dots in Figure 9.3.

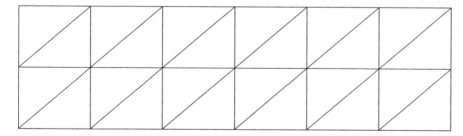

FIGURE 9.2

Two triangle strips showing aliasing artifacts.

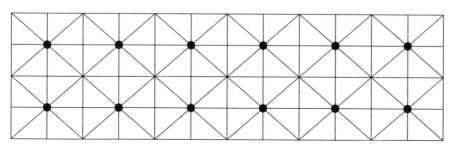

FIGURE 9.3

Triangle fans (center marked with filled circle).

OpenGL offers other optimized rendering methods aside from primitive restart, such as **multiDraw()**. However, these methods, as the primitive restart specification notes, "still remain more expensive than one would like" (Craighead, 2002).

Following is a performance comparison of primitive restart against other OpenGL rendering methods. Primitive restart is clearly faster. These tests were performed using an Intel 2.3 GHz Core 2 Duo processor running Linux with an NVIDIA GTX 280 CUDA-enabled gaming GPU running the Perlin kernel from this chapter to generate a virtual terrain map.

When interpreting these numbers, it is important to understand that these frame rates include the time required to recompute the 3D position and color for every vertex and color in the image. This represents a worst-case frame-rate scenario that demonstrates the power and speed possible with hybrid CUDA/OpenGL applications. Real applications will undoubtedly deliver much higher performance by recalculating only the minimum data necessary to render the scene.

Table 9.1 Approximate Performance Number on GTX 280

Method	Observed FPS	Rough Average (FPS)
Simple one by one	470–500	500
MultiDraw	490–510	508
Primitive Restart	550–590	560

More details can be found in parts 18[5] and 20[6] of my freely available "Supercomputing for the Masses" CUDA tutorials on the *Doctor Dobb's Journal* website.

The timeline in Figure 9.4 from Parallel Nsight shows that the Perlin kernel consumes very little time compared to the OpenGL buffer swapping.

The OpenGL API Call Summary in Parallel Nsight reports the following time for each rendering method.

- Primitive restart: around 60 µs (microseconds).
- Multidraw: around 3,900 µs.
- Iteratively drawing each triangle fan: approximately 1,100,000 µs.

---

[5] http://drdobbs.com/open-source/225200412.
[6] http://drdobbs.com/tools/227400145.

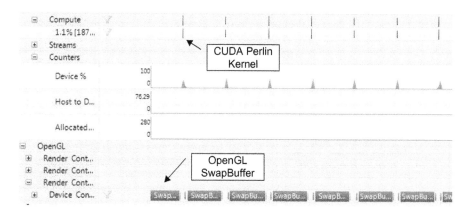

FIGURE 9.4
Parallel Nsight showing computation versus rendering time when using primitive restart.

INTRODUCTION TO THE FILES IN THE FRAMEWORK

Readers should note that care was taken in the design of the software framework so that it could be adapted to new applications. For example, this same framework was used in chapter twelve to display and modify live video streams. To compartmentalize operations, the framework was broken into four separate files. Merely by changing the CUDA kernel, this example code can be used to render an animated sinusoidal surface or an artificial terrain that the user can explore and fly around in. The examples are known to compile and run on Linux and Windows.

For clarity and flexibility, separate 3D vertex and color arrays are used within the example code. This helps speed understanding and makes data visualization as easy as writing a new kernel or loading data from disk to alter the 3D vertex array, color array, or both. Those readers who choose to create their own CUDA kernels should gain a strong practical sense of how easy and flexible visualization can be with a combined CUDA/OpenGL approach.

The relationship between the four files used in the framework discussed in this chapter is illustrated in Figure 9.5. Each of the files is discussed in more detail below.

The Demo and Perlin Example Kernels

Two example kernels are provided in this chapter, demo and Perlin. Each kernel generates both 3D vertices and colors.

FIGURE 9.5

Organization of files and activities.

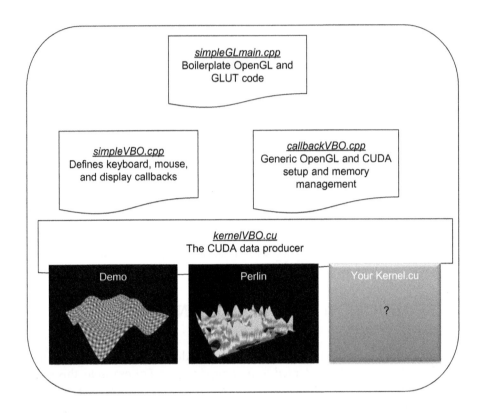

The Demo Kernel

The demo kernel creates an animated sinusoidal surface very similar to the NVIDIA simpleGL SDK example. It is a good test case to confirm that the code is working and to evaluate the speed of a GPU.

Figure 9.6 shows a grayscale screenshot of the highly colorful surface generated with the demo kernel. Also, note that the colors will evolve with time. Keyboard input allows selecting between rendering the surface with triangles (shown in Figure 9.6), lines (not shown), or dots (shown in Figure 9.7).

The Demo Kernel to Generate a Colored Sinusoidal Surface

The demo kernel draws a time-varying sinusoidal surface by calculating a height value for each location in a 2D mesh. The height value varies by time. See Example 9.1, "Calculating the Heights of the Sinusoidal Surface":

Example 9.1

```
// calculate simple sine wave pattern
float freq = 4.0f;
float w = sinf(u*freq + time) * cosf(v*freq + time) * 0.5f;
```

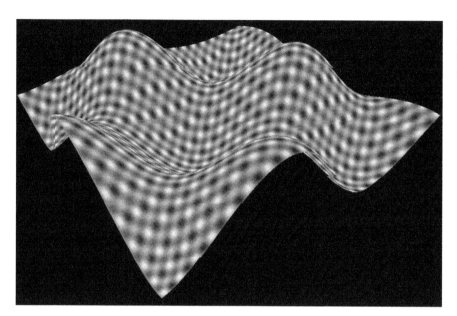

FIGURE 9.6
Grayscale example of a surface created with the sinusoidal-surface VBO.

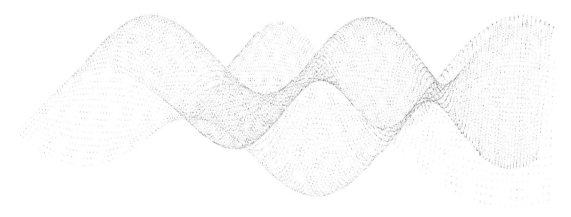

FIGURE 9.7
Grayscale of a sinusoid of points (the image colors were inverted to increase visibility).

The position and height information is stored in the float4 position, or **pos**, array, as shown in Example 9.2

Example 9.2

```
// write output vertex
pos[y*width+x] = make_float4(u, w, v, 1.0f);
```

Similarly, the colors are calculated based on position in the mesh and the animation time, as shown in Example 9.3, "Calculating the Colors of the Sinusoidal Surface":

Example 9.3

```
// write the color
colorPos[y*width+x].w = 0;
colorPos[y*width+x].x = 255.f *0.5*(1.f+sinf(w+x));
colorPos[y*width+x].y = 255.f *0.5*(1.f+sinf(x)*cosf(y));
colorPos[y*width+x].z = 255.f *0.5*(1.f+sinf(w+time/10.f));
```

The complete listing for **kernelVBO** is as shown in Example 9.4, "The Complete Source for the demo Kernel":

Example 9.4

```
// sinusoidal kernel (Rob Farber)
// Simple kernel to modify vertex positions in sine wave pattern
__global__ void kernel(float4* pos, uchar4 *colorPos,
                       unsigned int width, unsigned int height, float time)
{
    unsigned int x = blockIdx.x*blockDim.x + threadIdx.x;
    unsigned int y = blockIdx.y*blockDim.y + threadIdx.y;

    // calculate uv coordinates
    float u = x / (float) width;
    float v = y / (float) height;
    u = u*2.0f - 1.0f;
    v = v*2.0f - 1.0f;

    // calculate simple sine wave pattern
    float freq = 4.0f;
    float w = sinf(u*freq + time) * cosf(v*freq + time) * 0.5f;

    // write output vertex
    pos[y*width+x] = make_float4(u, w, v, 1.0f);
    colorPos[y*width+x].w = 0;
    colorPos[y*width+x].x = 255.f *0.5*(1.f+sinf(w+x));
    colorPos[y*width+x].y = 255.f *0.5*(1.f+sinf(x)*cosf(y));
    colorPos[y*width+x].z = 255.f *0.5*(1.f+sinf(w+time/10.f));
}
```

The **launch_kernel()** method calculates the execution configuration and queues the launch of the demo kernel with the appropriate parameters, as shown in Example 9.5, "The Source Showing the Logic to Launch the demo Kernel":

Example 9.5

```
// Wrapper for the __global__ call that sets up the kernel call
extern "C" void launch_kernel(float4* pos, uchar4* colorPos,
                        unsigned int mesh_width, unsigned int
                        mesh_height,
                        float time)
{
    // execute the kernel
    dim3 block(8, 8, 1);
    dim3 grid(mesh_width / block.x, mesh_height / block.y, 1);
    kernel<<< grid, block>>>(pos, colorPos, mesh_width, mesh_height,
    time);
}
```

Perlin Noise

Many people use random number generators to add variation and unpredictability to their applications. Landscapes exhibit both variation and seeming unpredictability, but not purely at random. Instead they vary at different scales, meaning that they have various levels of detail. A mountain range demonstrates this variation in scale:

- **Large scale:** the outline of the mountain range.
- **Medium scale:** various hills, valleys, and other features.
- **Small variation:** boulders and rock outcroppings are common examples.
- **Tiny variations:** stones and the bumps you see when hiking on a trail.

Perlin noise is function for generating *coherent noise* over a space. Coherent noise means that for any two points in the space, the value of the noise function changes smoothly as you move from one point to the other; that is, there are no discontinuities. Natural phenomena tend to exhibit the same pattern of large and small variations. The Perlin noise function recreates this natural effect by simply adding up noisy functions at a range of different scales.

In 1997, Ken Perlin received an academy award for developing the Perlin noise generator. Perlin noise has a multitude of uses ranging from the creation of natural textures to artificial terrain and even worlds! Numerous websites discuss Perlin noise. Ken Perlin's homepage is an excellent place to start.[7]

---

[7] http://cs.nyu.edu/~perlin/.

The Perlin noise kernel will be used to create a height map of virtual terrain shown in Figures 9.8 through 9.10. The user can fly around this virtual world and dynamically alter it with the keyboard commands defined in *callbacksVBO.cu*. Figure 9.8 shows the virtual terrain rendered as a surface with triangles. Figure 9.9 show the surface rendered as a wireframe with lines, and Figure 9.10 shows a pilot's-eye view of the artificial terrain during a virtual "flight."

FIGURE 9.8

Grayscale example of a 3D surface created with the Perlin noise kernel.

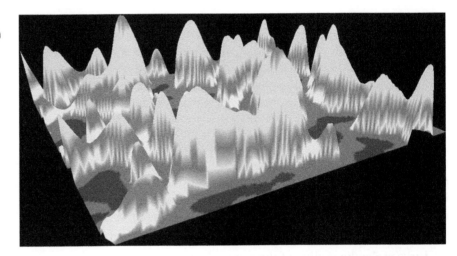

FIGURE 9.9

Grayscale of a terrain wireframe.

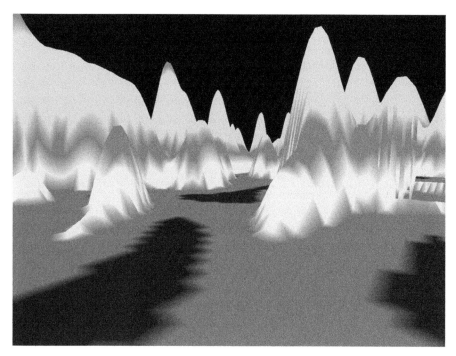

FIGURE 9.10
Grayscale version of a pilot's-eye view.

Using the Perlin Noise Kernel to Generate Artificial Terrain

The following example uses the Improved Perlin Noise generator from parts 15[8] and 18[9] of my "Supercomputing for the Masses" tutorial series on the *Doctor Dobb's Journal* website. For implementation simplicity, fBm (Fractal Brownian Motion) was chosen to generate the fractal terrain, which is simply a weighted sum of multiple scales of an arbitrary basis function, such as noise. Better methods exist to create more realistic landscapes, as noted in "Fractal Landscape and Texture Generation" on the Max Plank Institute website (Max Planck Institute, 2004).[10]

The kernel starting in Example 9.6 is slightly more complicated than the demo kernel. The first part of the kernel specifies the include files, variables, and methods used in the Perlin noise calculation. A discussion and link to the reference paper is found on the NYU Media Research Lab website.[11]

---

[8] http://drdobbs.com/cpp/222600097.
[9] http://drdobbs.com/open-source/225200412.
[10] http://www.mpi-inf.mpg.de/departments/irg3/ws0405/cg/rcomp/29/x173.html.
[11] http://vlg.cs.nyu.edu/.

Example 9.6

```
//Perlin kernel (Rob Farber)
#include <cutil_math.h>
#include <cutil_inline.h>
#include <cutil_gl_inline.h>
#include <cuda_gl_interop.h>

extern float gain, xStart, yStart, zOffset, octaves, lacunarity;
#define Z_PLANE 50.f

__constant__ unsigned char c_perm[256];
__shared__ unsigned char s_perm[256]; // shared memory copy of
permuation array
unsigned char* d_perm=NULL; // global memory copy of permutation array
// host version of permutation array
const static unsigned char h_perm[] = {151,160,137,91,90,15,
    131,13,201,95,96,53,194,233,7,225,140,36,103,30,69,142,8,99,
    37,240,21,10,23,190, 6,148,247,120,234,75,0,26,197,62,94,252,
    219,203,117,35,11,32,57,177,33,88,237,149,56,87,174,20,125,
    136,171,168, 68,175,74,165,71,134,139,48,27,166,77,146,158,
    231,83,111,229,122,60,211,133,230,220,105,92,41,55,46,245,
    40,244,102,143,54, 65,25,63,161, 1,216,80,73,209,76,132,187,
    208, 89,18,169,200,196,135,130,116,188,159,86,164,100,109,198,
    173,186, 3,64,52,217,226,250,124,123,5,202,38,147,118,126,255,
    82,85,212,207,206,59,227,47,16,58,17,182,189,28,42,223,183,
    170,213,119,248,152,2,44,154,163, 70,221,153,101,155,167, 43,
    172,9,129,22,39,253, 19,98,108,110,79,113,224,232,178,185,
    112,104,218,246,97,228,251,34,242,193,238,210,144,12,191,179,
    162,241, 81,51,145,235,249,14,239,107,49,192,214, 31,181,199,
    106,157,184,84,204,176,115,121,50,45,127, 4,150,254,138,236,
    205,93,222,114,67,29,24,72,243,141,128,195,78,66,215,61,156,180
    };

__device__ inline int perm(int i) { return(s_perm[i&0xff]); }
__device__ inline float fade(float t) { return t * t * t * (t * (t * 6.f
- 15.f) + 10.f); }
__device__ inline float lerpP(float t, float a, float b) { return a +
t * (b - a); }
__device__ inline float grad(int hash, float x, float y, float z) {
   int h = hash & 15;              // CONVERT LO 4 BITS OF HASH CODE
   float u = h<8 ? x : y,          // INTO 12 GRADIENT DIRECTIONS.
     v = h<4 ? y : h==12||h==14 ? x : z;
   return ((h&1) == 0 ? u : -u) + ((h&2) == 0 ? v : -v);
}

__device__ float inoise(float x, float y, float z) {
   int X = ((int)floorf(x)) & 255,  // FIND UNIT CUBE THAT
     Y = ((int)floorf(y)) & 255,    // CONTAINS POINT.
     Z = ((int)floorf(z)) & 255;
```

```
  x -= floorf(x);        // FIND RELATIVE X,Y,Z
  y -= floorf(y);        // OF POINT IN CUBE.
  z -= floorf(z);
  float u = fade(x),     // COMPUTE FADE CURVES
    v = fade(y),         // FOR EACH OF X,Y,Z.
    w = fade(z);
  int A = perm(X)+Y, AA = perm(A)+Z, AB = perm(A+1)+Z, // HASH
  COORDINATES OF
    B = perm(X+1)+Y, BA = perm(B)+Z, BB = perm(B+1)+Z; // THE 8 CUBE
    CORNERS,

  return lerpP(w, lerpP(v, lerpP(u, grad(perm(AA), x , y , z ),
  // AND ADD
                              grad(perm(BA), x-1.f, y , z )),    // BLENDED
                   lerpP(u, grad(perm(AB), x , y-1.f, z ),    // RESULTS
                         grad(perm(BB), x-1.f, y-1.f, z ))),    // FROM 8
          lerpP(v, lerpP(u, grad(perm(AA+1), x , y , z-1.f ), // CORNERS
                      grad(perm(BA+1), x-1.f, y , z-1.f )),    // OF CUBE
              lerpP(u, grad(perm(AB+1), x , y-1.f, z-1.f ),
                   grad(perm(BB+1), x-1.f, y-1.f, z-1.f ))));
}

__device__ float fBm(float x, float y, int octaves,
                float lacunarity = 2.0f, float gain = 0.5f)
{
  float freq = 1.0f, amp = 0.5f;
  float sum = 0.f;
  for(int i=0; i<octaves; i++) {
    sum += inoise(x*freq, y*freq, Z_PLANE)*amp;
    freq *= lacunarity;
    amp *= gain;
  }
  return sum;
}
```

The **colorElevation()** method returns a pixel color based on the elevation in the terrain. The colors were chosen to give the user a sense of looking at a map. See Example 9.7, "Part 2 of the Improved Perlin Noise Kernel":

Example 9.7

```
__device__ inline uchar4 colorElevation(float texHeight)
{
  uchar4 pos;

  // color textel (r,g,b,a)
        if (texHeight < -1.000f) pos = make_uchar4(000, 000, 128, 255);
        //deeps
```

```
  else if (texHeight < -.2500f) pos = make_uchar4(000, 000, 255, 255);
  //shallow
  else if (texHeight < 0.0000f) pos = make_uchar4(000, 128, 255, 255);
  //shore
  else if (texHeight < 0.0125f) pos = make_uchar4(240, 240, 064, 255);
  //sand
  else if (texHeight < 0.1250f) pos = make_uchar4(032, 160, 000, 255);
  //grass
  else if (texHeight < 0.3750f) pos = make_uchar4(224, 224, 000, 255);
  //dirt
  else if (texHeight < 0.7500f) pos = make_uchar4(128, 128, 128, 255);
  //rock
  else                          pos = make_uchar4(255, 255, 255, 255);
                                //snow

  return(pos);
}
```

A method to check for errors is shown in Example 9.8, "Part 3 of the Improved Perlin Noise Kernel":

Example 9.8

```
void checkCUDAError(const char *msg) {
  cudaError_t err = cudaGetLastError();
  if( cudaSuccess != err) {
    fprintf(stderr, "Cuda error: %s: %s.\n", msg, cudaGetErrorString(
    err) );
    exit(EXIT_FAILURE);
  }
}
```

The **k_perlin()** kernel calls the Perlin noise to generate the terrain map. Regions that are below sea level are set to zero. The call to **cudaThreadSynchronize()** is important because it causes the host to wait until after the kernel has completed updating the OpenGL buffers. See Example 9.9, "Part 4 of the Improved Perlin Noise Kernel":

Example 9.9

```
//Simple kernel fills an array with perlin noise
__global__ void k_perlin(float4* pos, uchar4 *colorPos,
                  unsigned int width, unsigned int height,
                  float2 start, float2 delta, float gain, float
                  zOffset,
```

```
                        unsigned char* d_perm, float octaves, float
                        lacunarity)
{
  int idx = blockIdx.x * blockDim.x + threadIdx.x;
  float xCur = start.x + ((float) (idx%width)) * delta.x;
  float yCur = start.y + ((float) (idx/width)) * delta.y;

  if(threadIdx.x < 256)
    // Optimization: this causes bank conflicts
    s_perm[threadIdx.x] = d_perm[threadIdx.x];
  // this synchronization can be important if there are more than 256
  threads
  __syncthreads();

  // Each thread creates one pixel location in the texture (textel)
  if(idx < width*height) {
    float w = fBm(xCur, yCur, octaves, lacunarity, gain) + zOffset;

    colorPos[idx] = colorElevation(w);
    float u = ((float) (idx%width))/(float) width;
    float v = ((float) (idx/width))/(float) height;
    u = u*2.f - 1.f;
    v = v*2.f - 1.f;
    w = (w>0.f)?w:0.f; // don't show regions underwater
    pos[idx] = make_float4( u, w, v, 1.0f);
  }
}

uchar4 *eColor=NULL;
// Wrapper for the __global__ call that sets up the kernel call
extern "C" void launch_kernel(float4 *pos, uchar4* posColor,
                              unsigned int image_width, unsigned int
                              image_height, float time)
{
  int nThreads=256; // must be equal or larger than 256! (see s_perm)
  int totalThreads = image_height * image_width;
  int nBlocks = totalThreads/nThreads;
  nBlocks += ((totalThreads%nThreads)>0)?1:0;

  float xExtent = 10.f;
  float yExtent = 10.f;
  float xDelta = xExtent/(float)image_width;
  float yDelta = yExtent/(float)image_height;

  if(!d_perm) { // for convenience allocate and copy d_perm here
    cudaMalloc((void**) &d_perm,sizeof(h_perm));
    cudaMemcpy(d_perm,h_perm,sizeof(h_perm),
    cudaMemcpyHostToDevice);
    checkCUDAError("d_perm malloc or copy failed!");
  }
```

```
k_perlin<<< nBlocks, nThreads>>>(pos, posColor, image_width,
image_height,
                            make_float2(xStart, yStart),
                            make_float2(xDelta, yDelta),
                            gain, zOffset, d_perm,
                            octaves, lacunarity);

// make certain the kernel has completed
cudaThreadSynchronize();
checkCUDAError("kernel failed!");
}
```

The simpleGLmain.cpp File

The *simplGLmain.cpp* file opens a window on the screen and sets some basic viewing transforms. The call to **gluPerspective()** places a camera in a three-dimensional location from which to view the data generated with CUDA.

Three-dimensional rendering occurs in OpenGL when the programmer:

- Specifies objects in 3D space using simple triangles, vertices, and lines.
- Defines a virtual camera position and viewing angle.

OpenGL can then identify and update the display pixels as the data and/or viewing position changes.

Rendering requires the following 3D transform:

1. Position and point the camera at the scene (a view transformation).
2. Arrange the scene composition (a model transform).
3. Adjust the camera zoom (a projection transform).
4. Choose the final size (a viewport transform).

OpenGL view, model, projection, and viewport transforms plus specification of the coordinate system require very detailed thinking and explanation. Song Ho Ann[12] has an excellent set of tutorials, including visual aids to help understand the details of OpenGL transforms and the OpenGL rendering pipeline, the differences between pixel and geometry rendering, the OpenGL projection matrix, and much more. Numerous other excellent sources are also available, including the online version of the OpenGL Red Book.

---

[12] http://songho.ca/opengl.

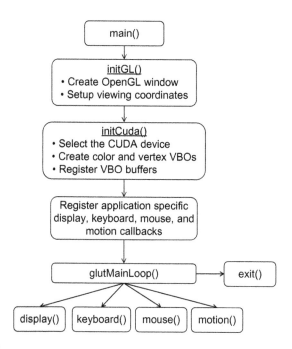

FIGURE 9.11
Schematic of GLUT VBO code interactions.

The schematic in Figure 9.11 summarizes how the VBO example code interacts with GLUT.[13]

The following example is the complete source code for the VBO version of *simpleGLmain.cpp*. This is fairly generic code that should not require modification. The start of the file specifies the needed include files and prototypes for the external methods. The **main()** routine initializes a timer to calculate frame rates, calls a user-defined method to initialize the CUDA kernel(s), registers the user-defined callbacks, and calls the GLUT main loop, as shown in Example 9.10, "Part 1 of *simpleGLmain.cpp*":

Example 9.10

```
// simpleGLmain (Rob Farber)
#include <GL/glew.h>
#include <cutil_inline.h>
#include <cutil_gl_inline.h>
#include <cutil_gl_error.h>
```

---

[13] http://www.opengl.org/documentation/red_book/.

```
#include <cuda_gl_interop.h>
#include <rendercheck_gl.h>

// GLUT specific contants
const unsigned int window_width = 512;
const unsigned int window_height = 512;

// The user must create the following routines:
void initCuda(int argc, char** argv);
CUTBoolean initGL(int argc, char** argv);
void fpsDisplay(), display();
void keyboard(unsigned char key, int x, int y);
void mouse(int button, int state, int x, int y);
void motion(int x, int y);

unsigned int timer = 0; // a timer for FPS calculations
int sleepTime=0, sleepInc=100;

// Main program
int main(int argc, char** argv)
{
  // Create the CUTIL timer
  cutilCheckError( cutCreateTimer( &timer));
  if (CUTFalse == initGL(argc, argv)) { return CUTFalse; }

  initCuda(argc, argv);
  CUT_CHECK_ERROR_GL();

  // register callbacks
  glutDisplayFunc(fpsDisplay);
  glutKeyboardFunc(keyboard);
  glutMouseFunc(mouse);
  glutMotionFunc(motion);

  // start rendering mainloop
  glutMainLoop();

  // clean up
  cudaThreadExit();
  cutilExit(argc, argv);
}
```

Example 9.11, "Part 2 of *simpleGLmain.cpp*," computes the frame rate and displays it in the window title.

Example 9.11

```
// Simple method to display the frames per second in the window title
void computeFPS()
```

```
{
  static int fpsCount=0;
  static int fpsLimit=100;

  fpsCount++;

  if (fpsCount == fpsLimit) {
    char fps[256];
    float ifps = 1.f / (cutGetAverageTimerValue(timer) / 1000.f);
    if(sleepTime)
      sprintf(fps, "CUDA Interop (Rob Farber): %3.1f fps sleepTime %
      3.1f ms ",
            ifps, sleepTime/1000.);
    else
      sprintf(fps, "CUDA Interop (Rob Farber): %3.1f fps ", ifps);

    glutSetWindowTitle(fps);
    fpsCount = 0;

    cutilCheckError(cutResetTimer(timer));
  }
}

void fpsDisplay()
{
  cutilCheckError(cutStartTimer(timer));
  display();
  cutilCheckError(cutStopTimer(timer));
  computeFPS();
}
```

The GLUT and OpenGL initialization creates a window and specifies a viewing location in the 3D space, as shown in Example 9.12, "Part 3 of *simpleGLmain.cpp*":

Example 9.12

```
float animTime = 0.0;       // time the animation has been running

// Initialize OpenGL window
CUTBoolean initGL(int argc, char **argv)
{
  glutInit(&argc, argv);
  glutInitDisplayMode(GLUT_RGBA | GLUT_DOUBLE);
  glutInitWindowSize(window_width, window_height);
  glutCreateWindow("CUDA GL Interop Demo (adapted from NVIDIA's
  simpleGL)");
  glutDisplayFunc(fpsDisplay);
  glutKeyboardFunc(keyboard);
  glutMotionFunc(motion);
```

```
// initialize necessary OpenGL extensions
glewInit();
if (! glewIsSupported("GL_VERSION_2_0 ")) {
  fprintf(stderr, "ERROR: Support for necessary OpenGL extensions
  missing.");
  return CUTFalse;
}

// default initialization
glClearColor(0.0, 0.0, 0.0, 1.0);
glDisable(GL_DEPTH_TEST);

// viewport
glViewport(0, 0, window_width, window_height);

// set view matrix
glMatrixMode(GL_MODELVIEW);
glLoadIdentity();

// projection
glMatrixMode(GL_PROJECTION);
glLoadIdentity();
gluPerspective(60.0, (GLfloat)window_width/(GLfloat) window_
height,0.10, 10.0);

return CUTTrue;
}
```

The simpleVBO.cpp File

The *simpleVBO.cpp* file contains the logic that creates and maps both the color PBO and the vertex VBO. The start of the file specifies the include files and the variables used in the file. The variables **mesh_width** and **mesh_height** specify the size of the mesh calculated on the GPU. The variable **RestartIndex** specifies the integer value used by the OpenGL state machine to restart the user-defined graphics primitive. See Example 9.13, "Part 1 of *simpleVBO.cpp*":

Example 9.13

```
//simpleVBO (Rob Farber)
#include <GL/glew.h>
#include <GL/gl.h>
#include <GL/glext.h>
#include <cutil_inline.h>
#include <cutil_gl_inline.h>
#include <cuda_gl_interop.h>
#include <rendercheck_gl.h>

extern float animTime;
```

```
//////////////////////////////////////////////////////////////////////
// VBO specific code
#include <cutil_inline.h>

// constants
const unsigned int mesh_width = 256;
const unsigned int mesh_height = 256;
const unsigned int RestartIndex = 0xffffffff;

typedef struct {
  GLuint vbo;
  GLuint typeSize;
  struct cudaGraphicsResource *cudaResource;
} mappedBuffer_t;

extern "C"
void launch_kernel(float4* pos, uchar4* posColor,
                   unsigned int mesh_width, unsigned int mesh_height,
                   float time);

// vbo variables
mappedBuffer_t vertexVBO = {NULL, sizeof(float4), NULL};
mappedBuffer_t colorVBO = {NULL, sizeof(uchar4), NULL};
GLuint* qIndices=NULL; // index values for primitive restart
int qIndexSize=0;
```

The **createVBO()** method performs the actual allocation of the graphics buffer on the GPU through the call to **glBufferData()**. The **GL_DYNAMIC_DRAW** flag lets OpenGL know that this data store will be repeatedly modified and used. The buffer object is registered for access with CUDA with the call to **cudaGraphicsGLRegisterBuffer()**. The **deleteVBO()** method unregisters and frees the memory held by the OpenGL buffer object. See Example 9.14, "Part 2 of *simpleVBO.cpp*":

Example 9.14

```
//////////////////////////////////////////////////////////////////////
//! Create VBO
//////////////////////////////////////////////////////////////////////
void createVBO(mappedBuffer_t* mbuf)
{
  // create buffer object
  glGenBuffers(1, &(mbuf->vbo) );
  glBindBuffer(GL_ARRAY_BUFFER, mbuf->vbo);

  // initialize buffer object
  unsigned int size = mesh_width * mesh_height * mbuf->typeSize;
  glBufferData(GL_ARRAY_BUFFER, size, 0, GL_DYNAMIC_DRAW);
```

```
  glBindBuffer(GL_ARRAY_BUFFER, 0);

  cudaGraphicsGLRegisterBuffer( &(mbuf->cudaResource), mbuf->vbo,
                                cudaGraphicsMapFlagsNone );
}
////////////////////////////////////////////////////////////////////
//! Delete VBO
////////////////////////////////////////////////////////////////////
void deleteVBO(mappedBuffer_t* mbuf)
{
  glBindBuffer(1, mbuf->vbo );
  glDeleteBuffers(1, &(mbuf->vbo) );

  cudaGraphicsUnregisterResource( mbuf->cudaResource );
  mbuf->cudaResource = NULL;
  mbuf->vbo = NULL;
}

void cleanupCuda()
{
  if(qIndices) free(qIndices);
  deleteVBO(&vertexVBO);
  deleteVBO(&colorVBO);
}
```

The **runCUDA()** method performs all the work of mapping and retrieving the pointer to both the color PBO and the vertex VBO. These addresses are passed to the **launch_kernel()** method for use by the user-defined kernel. Note that **launch_kernel()** waits for the kernel to complete before returning, which is why it is safe to return the OpenGL resources after this method returns. See Example 9.15, "Part 3 of *simpleVBO.cpp*":

Example 9.15

```
////////////////////////////////////////////////////////////////////
//! Run the CUDA part of the computation
////////////////////////////////////////////////////////////////////
void runCuda()
{
    // map OpenGL buffer object for writing from CUDA
    float4 *dptr;
    uchar4 *cptr;
    uint *iptr;
    size_t start;
    cudaGraphicsMapResources( 1, &vertexVBO.cudaResource, NULL );
    cudaGraphicsResourceGetMappedPointer( ( void ** )&dptr, &start,
                                    vertexVBO.cudaResource );
```

```
      cudaGraphicsMapResources( 1, &colorVBO.cudaResource, NULL );
      cudaGraphicsResourceGetMappedPointer( ( void ** )&cptr, &start,
                                    colorVBO.cudaResource );
      // execute the kernel
      launch_kernel(dptr, cptr, mesh_width, mesh_height, animTime);

      // unmap buffer object
      cudaGraphicsUnmapResources( 1, &vertexVBO.cudaResource, NULL );
      cudaGraphicsUnmapResources( 1, &colorVBO.cudaResource, NULL );
  }
```

The **initCuda()** method chooses the fastest device according to the NVIDIA documentation. It makes the appropriate calls to allocate the OpenGL buffers. The **qIndices** array needed for rendering with primitive restart is allocated and initialized. See Example 9.16, "Part 4 of *simpleVBO.cpp*":

Example 9.16

```
void initCuda(int argc, char** argv)
{
  // First initialize OpenGL context, so we can properly set the GL
  // for CUDA. NVIDIA notes this is necessary in order to achieve
  // optimal performance with OpenGL/CUDA interop. Use the command-line
  // specified CUDA device ; otherwise use device with highest Gflops/s
  if( cutCheckCmdLineFlag(argc, (const char**)argv, "device") ) {
    cutilGLDeviceInit(argc, argv);
  } else {
    cudaGLSetGLDevice( cutGetMaxGflopsDeviceId() );
  }

  createVBO(&vertexVBO);
  createVBO(&colorVBO);

  // allocate and assign trianglefan indices
  qIndexSize = 5*(mesh_height-1)*(mesh_width-1);
  qIndices = (GLuint *) malloc(qIndexSize*sizeof(GLint));
  int index=0;
  for(int i=1; i < mesh_height; i++) {
    for(int j=1; j < mesh_width; j++) {
      qIndices[index++] = (i)*mesh_width + j;
      qIndices[index++] = (i)*mesh_width + j-1;
      qIndices[index++] = (i-1)*mesh_width + j-1;
      qIndices[index++] = (i-1)*mesh_width + j;
      qIndices[index++] = RestartIndex;
    }
  }
}
```

```
// make certain the VBO gets cleaned up on program exit
atexit(cleanupCuda);

runCuda();
}
```

The **renderCuda()** method binds the buffers with the appropriate type and size information for use in rendering. Rendering is performed as defined by **drawMode**.

Note the simplicity of the call when rendering triangles with primitive restart. The OpenGL state machine is informed of the value of the restart index via the **glPrimitiveRestartIndexNV()** method, after which primitive restart is enabled in the OpenGL client state machine. The call to **glDrawElements()** causes data to be rendered. Once completed, primitive restart is disabled in the OpenGL state machine. See Example 9.17, "Part 5 of *simpleVBO.cpp*":

Example 9.17

```
void renderCuda(int drawMode)
{
  glBindBuffer(GL_ARRAY_BUFFER, vertexVBO.vbo);
  glVertexPointer(4, GL_FLOAT, 0, 0);
  glEnableClientState(GL_VERTEX_ARRAY);

  glBindBuffer(GL_ARRAY_BUFFER, colorVBO.vbo);
  glColorPointer(4, GL_UNSIGNED_BYTE, 0, 0);
  glEnableClientState(GL_COLOR_ARRAY);

  switch(drawMode) {
  case GL_LINE_STRIP:
    for(int i=0 ; i < mesh_width*mesh_height; i+= mesh_width)
      glDrawArrays(GL_LINE_STRIP, i, mesh_width);
    break;
  case GL_TRIANGLE_FAN: {
    glPrimitiveRestartIndexNV(RestartIndex);
    glEnableClientState(GL_PRIMITIVE_RESTART_NV);
    glDrawElements(GL_TRIANGLE_FAN, qIndexSize, GL_UNSIGNED_INT,
    qIndices);
    glDisableClientState(GL_PRIMITIVE_RESTART_NV);
  } break;
  default:
    glDrawArrays(GL_POINTS, 0, mesh_width * mesh_height);
    break;
  }
}
```

```
  glDisableClientState(GL_VERTEX_ARRAY);
  glDisableClientState(GL_COLOR_ARRAY);
}
```

The callbacksVBO.cpp File

The keyboard routine is very simple. Basically, it allows the user to toggle through the display modes (point, line, surface) by pressing the "d" or "D" key.

The mouse and motion routines work in concert with each other to modify the values of the **rotate_x** and **rotate_y** variables based on user mouse movements and the state of the mouse buttons.

Most of the work occurs in the display routine that defines the view transforms, as shown in Example 9.18, "Code Snippet Showing Where Most of the Work Occurs in the callbacksVBO.cu":

Example 9.18

```
// set view matrix
glMatrixMode(GL_MODELVIEW);
glLoadIdentity();
glTranslatef(0.0, 0.0, translate_z);
glRotatef(rotate_x, 1.0, 0.0, 0.0);
glRotatef(rotate_y, 0.0, 1.0, 0.0);

// run CUDA kernel to generate vertex positions
runCuda();

// render the data
renderCuda(drawMode);
```

The CUDA kernel is then called to create the data with **runCuda()** and render it with **renderCuda()**.

The buffers are swapped so that the latest version can be made visible and GLUT is informed that the display needs to be updated. The animation time is also incremented. See Example 9.19, "Logic to Swap the OpenGL Buffers and Post a Redisplay Event to OpenGL":

Example 9.19

```
glutSwapBuffers();
glutPostRedisplay();

animTime += 0.01;
```

Table 9.2 lists the keyboard commands and the applicable kernels.

Table 9.2 Keyboard Commands for the Demo and Perlin Examples

Key	Applicable Kernel	Action
+	Perlin	Lower the ocean level
−	Perlin	Raise the ocean level
k	Perlin	Vi-type key command to move terrain up
J	Perlin	Vi-type command to move terrain down
h	Perlin	Vi-type command to move terrain left
l	Perlin	Vi-type command to move terrain right
d	Perlin/Demo	Toggle draw mode
D	Perlin/Demo	Toggle draw mode
I	Perlin	Increase gain by 0.25
i	Perlin	Decrease gain by 0.25
O	Perlin	Increase octaves (number of frequencies in the fBm) by 1
o	Perlin	Decrease octaves (number of frequencies in the fBm) by 1
P	Perlin	Increase lacunarity (the gap between successive frequencies) by 0.25
p	Perlin	Decrease lacunarity (the gap between successive frequencies) by 0.25
S	Perlin/Demo	Slow down rendering by 100 microseconds per frame
s	Perlin/Demo	Speed rendering by 100 microseconds per frame

The complete source code is provided in Example 9.20, "Part 1 of *callbacksVBO. cpp.*" The start of the file defines the include files and required variables:

Example 9.20

```
//callbacksVBO (Rob Farber)
#include <GL/glew.h>
#include <cutil_inline.h>
#include <cutil_gl_inline.h>
#include <cuda_gl_interop.h>
#include <rendercheck_gl.h>

// The user must create the following routines:
void initCuda(int argc, char** argv);
void runCuda();
void renderCuda(int);

// Callback variables
extern float animTime;
extern int sleepTime, sleepInc;
int drawMode=GL_TRIANGLE_FAN; // the default draw mode
int mouse_old_x, mouse_old_y;
int mouse_buttons = 0;
float rotate_x = 0.0, rotate_y = 0.0;
float translate_z = -3.0;
```

```
// break the file modularity so that both Perlin and demo kernels build
// some initial values for Perlin
float gain=0.75f, xStart=2.f, yStart=1.f;
float zOffset = 0.0f, octaves = 2.f, lacunarity = 2.0f;
```

The GLUT display callback is called whenever there is a need to draw the screen. The OpenGL calls define the 3D transformation and rotation operations. The **runCuda()** method is called to generate the data and **renderCuda()** is called to render the data. The OpenGL buffers are then swapped to utilize the latest update. This use of double buffering allows the screen to be updated causing visual artifacts such as screen flicker. See Example 9.21, "Part 2 of *callbacksVBO.cpp*":

Example 9.21

```
// GLUT callbacks display, keyboard, mouse
void display()
{
  glClear(GL_COLOR_BUFFER_BIT | GL_DEPTH_BUFFER_BIT);

  // set view matrix
  glMatrixMode(GL_MODELVIEW);
  glLoadIdentity();
  glTranslatef(0.0, 0.0, translate_z);
  glRotatef(rotate_x, 1.0, 0.0, 0.0);
  glRotatef(rotate_y, 0.0, 1.0, 0.0);

  runCuda(); // run CUDA kernel to generate vertex positions

  renderCuda(drawMode); // render the data
  glutSwapBuffers();
  glutPostRedisplay();

  animTime += 0.01;
}
```

The keyboard callback is a very straightforward code that implements the logic to be performed on each keystroke, as shown in Example 9.22, "Part 3 of *callbacksVBO.cpp*":

Example 9.22

```
void keyboard(unsigned char key, int x, int y)
{
  switch(key) {
  case('q') : case(27) : // exit
    exit(0);
    break;
```

```
case 'd': case 'D': // Drawmode
  switch(drawMode) {
  case GL_POINTS: drawMode = GL_LINE_STRIP; break;
  case GL_LINE_STRIP: drawMode = GL_TRIANGLE_FAN; break;
  default: drawMode=GL_POINTS;
  } break;
case '+': // Perlin: lower the ocean level
  zOffset += 0.01;
  zOffset = (zOffset > 1.0)? 1.0:zOffset; // guard input
  break;
case '-': // Perlin: raise the ocean level
  zOffset -= 0.01;
  zOffset = (zOffset < -1.0)? -1.0:zOffset; // guard input
  break;
case 'k': // move within the Perlin function
  yStart -= 0.1;
  break;
case 'j': // move within the Perlin function
  yStart += 0.1;
  break;
case 'l': // move within the Perlin function
  xStart += 0.1;
  break;
case 'h': // move within the Perlin function
  xStart -= 0.1;
  break;
case 'I': // Perlin: change gain
  gain += 0.25;
  break;
case 'i': // Perlin: change gain
  gain -= 0.25;
  gain = (gain < 0.25)?0.25:gain; // guard input
  break;
case 'O': // Perlin: change octaves
  octaves += 1.0f;
  octaves = (octaves > 8)?8:octaves; // guard input
  break;
case 'o': // Perlin: change octaves
  octaves -= 1.0f;
  octaves = (octaves<2)?2:octaves; // guard input
  break;
case 'P': // Perlin: change lacunarity
  lacunarity += 0.25;
  break;
case 'p': // Perlin: change lacunarity
  lacunarity -= 0.25;
  lacunarity = (lacunarity<0.2)?0.2:lacunarity; // guard input
  break;
```

```
case 'S': // Slow the simulation down
  sleepTime += 100;
  break;
case 's': // Speed the simulation up
  sleepTime = (sleepTime > 0)?sleepTime -= sleepInc:0;
  break;
}
glutPostRedisplay();
}
```

The mouse and motion callbacks handle mouse events to enable rotation and scaling. The motion callback for a window is called when the mouse moves within the window while one or more mouse buttons are pressed, as seen in Example 9.23, "Part 4 of *callbacksVBO.cpp*":

Example 9.23

```
void mouse(int button, int state, int x, int y)
{
  if (state == GLUT_DOWN) {
    mouse_buttons |= 1<<button;
  } else if (state == GLUT_UP) {
    mouse_buttons = 0;
  }

  mouse_old_x = x;
  mouse_old_y = y;
  glutPostRedisplay();
}

void motion(int x, int y)
{
  float dx, dy;
  dx = x - mouse_old_x;
  dy = y - mouse_old_y;

  if (mouse_buttons & 1) {
    rotate_x += dy * 0.2;
    rotate_y += dx * 0.2;
  } else if (mouse_buttons & 4) {
    translate_z += dy * 0.01;
  }
  rotate_x = (rotate_x < -60.)?-60.:(rotate_x > 60.)?60:rotate_x;
  rotate_y = (rotate_y < -60.)?-60.:(rotate_y > 60.)?60:rotate_y;

  mouse_old_x = x;
  mouse_old_y = y;
}
```

The **testDemo** example can be built with a variation of the bash script in Example 9.24, "An Example Script to Build testDemo." The bold items specify that this is a demo example that will create the **testDemo** executable. This script assumes that the callbacks and kernel are kept in the *demo* directory:

Example 9.24

```
#/bin/bash
DIR=demo
SDK_PATH … /cuda/4.0
SDK_LIB0=$SDK_PATH/C/lib
SDK_LIB1= … /4.0/CUDALibraries/common/lib/linux
echo $SDK_PATH
nvcc -O3 -L $SDK_LIB0 -L $SDK_LIB1 -I $SDK_PATH/C/common/inc
simpleGLmain.cpp simpleVBO.cpp $DIR/callbacksVBO.cpp $DIR/kernelVBO.
cu -lglut -lGLEW_x86_64 -lGLU -lcutil_x86_64 -o testDemo
```

The **testPerlin** example can be built with a variation of the bash script in Example 9.25, "An Example Script to Build testPerlin." The bold items specify that this is a demo example that will create the **testPerlin** executable. This script assumes that the callbacks and kernel are kept in the *perlin* directory:

Example 9.25

```
#/bin/bash
DIR=perlin
SDK_PATH=/ichec/packages/cuda/4.0
SDK_LIB0=$SDK_PATH/C/lib
SDK_LIB1=/ichec/packages/cuda/4.0/CUDALibraries/common/lib/linux
echo $SDK_PATH
nvcc -O3 -L $SDK_LIB0 -L $SDK_LIB1 -I $SDK_PATH/C/common/inc
simpleGLmain.cpp simpleVBO.cpp $DIR/callbacksVBO.cpp $DIR/kernelVBO.
cu -lglut -lGLEW_x86_64 -lGLU -lcutil_x86_64 -o testPerlin
```

SUMMARY

Mixing CUDA and visualization opens tremendous opportunities for commercial games and visual products as well as scientific applications. The examples in this article demonstrate that the current generation of CUDA-enabled graphics processors can both render and generate very complex data at hundreds of frames per second.

In particular, this article attempts to point the way to an extraordinarily simple and flexible way for CUDA developers to generate and render 3D images using the OpenGL standards compliant *primitive restart* capability so that minimal host processor interaction is required. As a result, PCIe bottlenecks and latencies can be avoided to deliver high-performance, high-quality graphics even when the images require irregular meshes and/or computationally expensive data generation. Of course, this issue is of interest when generating very realistic images on high-end GPUs, but do not forget that this same technique can enable product penetration into the mid- and lower-performance markets as well.

## CHAPTER 10

CUDA in a Cloud and Cluster Environments

Distributed GPUs are powering the fastest supercomputers as CUDA scales to thousands of nodes using MPI, the *de facto* standard for distributed computing. NVIDIA's GPUDirect has accelerated the key operations in MPI, send (MPI_Send) and receive (MPI_Recv), for communication over the network instead of the PCIe bus. As the name implies, GPUDirect moves data between GPUs without involving the processor on any of the host systems. This chapter focuses on the use of MPI and GPUDirect so that CUDA programmers can incorporate these APIs to create applications for cloud computing and computational clusters. The performance benefits of distributed GPU computing are very real but dependent on the bandwidth and latency characteristics of the distributed communications infrastructure. For example, the Chinese Nebulae supercomputer can deliver a peak 2.98 PFlops (or 2,980 trillion floating point per second) to run some of the most computationally intensive applications ever attempted. Meanwhile, commodity GPU clusters and cloud computing provide turn-key resources for users and organizations. To run effectively in a distributed environment, CUDA developers must develop applications and use algorithms that can scale given the limitations of the communications network. In particular, network bandwidth and latency are of paramount importance.

At the end of this chapter, the reader will have a basic understanding of:

- The Message Passing Interface (MPI).
- NVIDIA's GPUDirect 2.0 technology.
- How balance ratios act as an indicator of application performance on new platforms.
- The importance of latency and bandwidth to distributed and cloud computing.
- Strong scaling.

THE MESSAGE PASSING INTERFACE (MPI)

MPI is a standard library based on the consensus of the MPI Forum (http://www.mpi-forum.org/), which has more than 40 participating organizations, including vendors, researchers, software library developers, and users. The goal of the forum is to establish a portable, efficient, and flexible standard that will be widely used in a variety of languages. Wide adoption has made MPI the "industry standard" even though it is not an IEEE (Institute of Electrical and Electronics Engineers) or ISO (International Organization for Standardization) standard. It is safe to assume that some version of MPI will be available on most distributed computing platforms regardless of vendor or operating system.

Reasons for using MPI:

- **Standardization:** MPI is considered a standard. It is supported on virtually all HPC platforms.
- **Portability:** MPI library calls will not need to be changed when running on platforms that support a version of MPI that is compliant with the standard.
- **Performance:** Vendor implementations can exploit native hardware features to optimize performance. One example is the optimized data transport provided by GPUDirect.
- **Availability:** A variety of implementations are available from both vendors and public domain software.

The MPI Programming Model

MPI is an API that was originally designed to support distributed computing for C and FORTRAN applications. It was first implemented in 1992, with the first standard appearing in 1994. Since then, language bindings and wrappers have been created for most application languages, including Perl, Python, Ruby, and Java. C bindings use the format *MPI_Xxxx* in which "*Xxxx*" specifies the operation. The methods **MPI_Send()** and **MPI_Recv()** are two examples that use this binding.

Just as with a CUDA execution configuration, MPI defines a parallel computing topology to connect groups of processes in an MPI session. It is important to note that with MPI *the session size is fixed for the lifetime of the application*. This differs from *MapReduce* (discussed later in this chapter), which is a popular framework for cloud computing that was designed for fault-tolerant distributed computing. All parallelism is explicit with MPI, which means that the programmer is responsible for correctly identifying parallelism and implementing parallel algorithms with the MPI constructs.

The MPI Communicator

A fundamental concept in MPI is the *communicator*, a distributed object that supports both *collective* and *point-to-point* communication. As the name implies, collective communications refers to those MPI functions involving all the processors within the defined communicator group. Point-to-point communications are used by individual MPI processes to send messages to each other.

By default, MPI creates the **MPI_COMM_WORLD** communicator immediately after the call to **MPI_Init()**. **MPI_COMM_WORLD** includes all the MPI processes in the application An MPI application can create multiple, separate communicators to separate messages associated with one set of tasks or group of processes from those associated with another. This chapter uses only the default communicator. Look to the many MPI books and tutorials on the Internet for more information about the use of communicator groups.

MPI Rank

Within a communicator, every process has its own unique, integer identifier assigned by the system when the process initializes. A rank is sometimes also called a "task ID." Ranks are contiguous and begin at 0. They are often used in conditional operations to control execution of the MPI processes. A general paradigm in MPI applications is to use a master process, noted as rank 0, to control all other slave process of rank greater than 0.

MPI programs are generally structured as shown in Figure 10.1.

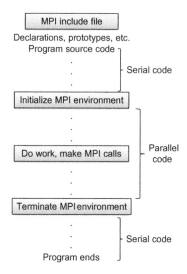

FIGURE 10.1
General structure of an MPI program.

Example 10.1, "A Basic MPI Program," illustrates a C implementation of this framework by having each MPI process print out its rank:

Example 10.1

```
#include "mpi.h"

#include <stdio.h>
int main(int argc, char *argv[])
{
  int numtasks, rank, ret;

  ret = MPI_Init(&argc,&argv);
  if (ret != MPI_SUCCESS) {
    printf ("Error in MPI_Init()!\n");
    MPI_Abort(MPI_COMM_WORLD, ret);
    }

  MPI_Comm_size(MPI_COMM_WORLD,&numtasks);
  MPI_Comm_rank(MPI_COMM_WORLD,&rank);
  printf ("Number of tasks= %d My rank= %d\n", numtasks,rank);

  /******* do some work *******/

  MPI_Finalize();
}
```

MPI is usually installed and configured by the systems administrator. See the documentation for your cluster on how to compile and run this application.

NVIDIA, for example, makes the suggestion shown in Example 10.2, "NVI-DIA Comment in the *simpleMPI* SDK Example," to build their *simpleMPI* SDK example:

Example 10.2

```
* simpleMPI.cpp: main program, compiled with mpicxx on linux/Mac
  platforms
*                on Windows, please download the Microsoft HPC Pack
                 SDK 2008
```

To build an application using CUDA and MPI in the same file, the **nvcc** command line in Example 10.3, "nvcc Command Line to Build *basicMPI* .cu," works under Linux. The method links to the MPI library:

Example 10.3

```
nvcc -I $MPI_INC_PATH basicMPI.cu -L $MPI_LIB_PATH -lmpich -o basicMPI
```

Usually **mpiexec** is used to start an MPI application. Some legacy implementations use **mpirun**. Example 10.4 shows the command and output when running the example with two MPI processes:

Example 10.4

```
$ mpiexec -np 2 ./basicMPI
Number of tasks= 2 My rank= 1
Number of tasks= 2 My rank= 0
```

Master-Slave

A common design pattern in MPI programs is a master-slave paradigm. Usually the process that is designated as rank 0 is defined as the master. This process then directs the activities of all the other processes. The code snippet in Example 10.5, "A Master-Slave MPI Snippet," illustrates how to structure master-slave MPI code:

Example 10.5

```
MPI_Comm_size(MPI_COMM_WORLD,&numtasks);
MPI_Comm_rank(MPI_COMM_WORLD,&rank);
if( rank == 0){
  // put master code here
} else {
  // put slave code here
}
```

This chapter uses the master-slave programming pattern. MPI supports many other design patterns. Consult the Internet or one of the many MPI books for more information. A good reference is *Using MPI* (Gropp, Lusk, & Skjellum, 1999).

Point-to-Point Basics

MPI point-to-point communication sends messages between two different MPI processes. One process performs a send operation while the other performs a matching read. MPI guarantees that every message will arrive intact without errors. Care must be exercised when using MPI, as *deadlock* will occur when the send and receive operations do not match. Deadlock means that neither the sending nor receiving process can proceed until the other completes its action, which will never happen when the send and receive operations do not match. CUDA avoids deadlock by sharing data between the threads of a thread block with shared memory. This frees the CUDA

Table 10.1 Data Types Required by the MPI Standard

C Data Types		Fortran Data Types	
MPI_CHAR	signed char	MPI_CHARACTER	character(1)
MPI_SHORT	signed short int		
MPI_INT	signed int	MPI_INTEGER	integer
MPI_LONG	signed long int		
MPI_UNSIGNED_CHAR	unsigned char		
MPI_UNSIGNED_SHORT	unsigned short int		
MPI_UNSIGNED	unsigned int		
MPI_UNSIGNED_LONG	unsigned long int		
MPI_FLOAT	float	MPI_REAL	real
MPI_DOUBLE	double	MPI_DOUBLE_PRECISION	double precision
MPI_LONG_DOUBLE	long double		
		MPI_COMPLEX	complex
		MPI_DOUBLE_COMPLEX	double complex
		MPI_LOGICAL	logical
MPI_BYTE	8 binary digits	MPI_BYTE	8 binary digits
MPI_PACKED	For data used with MPI_ Pack()/MPI_Unpack()	MPI_PACKED	For data used with MPI_ Pack()/MPI_Unpack()

programmer from having to explicitly match read and write operations but still requires the programmer to ensure that data is updated appropriately.

MPI_Send() and **MPI_Recv()** are commonly used *blocking* methods for sending messages between two MPI processes. Blocking means that the sending process will wait until the complete message has been correctly sent and the receiving process will block while waiting to correctly receive the complete message. More complex communications methods can be built upon these two methods.

Message size is determined by the **count** of an MPI data type and the type of the data. For portability, MPI defines the elementary data types. Table 10.1 lists data types required by the standard.

HOW MPI COMMUNICATES

MPI can use optimized data paths to send and receive messages depending on the network communications hardware. For example, MPI applications running within a computational node can communicate via fast shared memory rather than send data over a physical network interface card (NIC). Minimizing data movement is an overarching goal for MPI vendors and those who develop the libraries because moving data simply wastes precious time and degrades MPI performance.

In collaboration with vendors and software organizations, NVIDIA created GPUDirect to accelerate MPI for GPU computing. The idea is very simple: take the GPU data at the pointer passed to **MPI_Send()** and move it to the memory at the pointer to GPU memory used in the **MPI_Recv()** call. Don't perform any other data movements or rely on other processors. This process is illustrated in Figure 10.2. Although simple in concept, implementation requires collaboration between vendors, drivers, operating systems, and hardware.

InfiniBand (IB) is a commonly used high-speed, low-latency communications link in HPC. It is designed to be scalable and is used in many of the largest supercomputers in the world. Most small computational clusters also use InfiniBand for price and performance reasons. Mellanox is a well-known and respected vendor of InfiniBand products.

NVIDIA lists the following changes in the Linux kernel, the NVIDIA Linux CUDA driver, and the Mellanox InfiniBand driver:

- Linux kernel modifications:
  - Support for sharing pinned pages between different drivers.
  - The Linux Kernel Memory Manager (MM) allows NVIDIA and Mellanox drivers to share the host memory and provides direct access for the latter to the buffers allocated by the NVIDIA CUDA library, thus providing Zero Copy of data and better performance.
- NVIDIA driver:
  - Allocated buffers by the CUDA library are managed by the NVIDIA driver.
  - We have added the modifications to mark these pages to be shared so the Kernel MM will allow the Mellanox InfiniBand drivers to

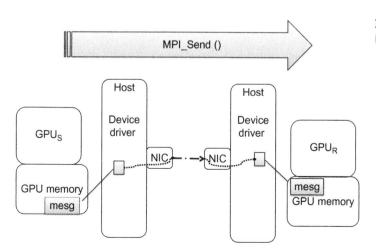

FIGURE 10.2
MPI GPUDirect data path.

access them and use them for transportation without the need for copying or repinning them.

- Mellanox OFED[1] drivers:
  - We have modified the Mellanox InfiniBand driver to query memory and to be able to share it with the NVIDIA Tesla drivers using the new Linux Kernel MM API.
  - In addition, the Mellanox driver registers special callbacks to allow other drivers sharing the memory to notify any changes performed during runtime in the shared buffers state in order for the Mellanox driver to use the memory accordingly and to avoid invalid access to any shared pinned buffers.

The result is the direct data transfer path between the send and receive buffers that provides a 30 percent increase in MPI performance.

Figure 10.2 shows that a registered region of memory can be directly transferred to a buffer in the device driver. Both the NIC and the device driver on the sending host know about this buffer, which lets the NIC send the data over the network interconnect without any host processor intervention. Similarly, the device driver and NIC on the receiving host know about a common receive buffer. When the GPU driver is notified that the data has arrived intact, it is transferred to the receiving GPU (GPU_R in Figure 10.2).

There are two ways for a CUDA developer to allocate memory in this model:

- Use cudaHostRegister().
- With the 4.0 driver, just set the environmental variable CUDA_NIC_INTEROP=1. This will tell the driver to use an alternate path for cudaMallocHost() that is compatible with the IB drivers. There is no need to use cudaHostRegister().

BANDWIDTH

Network bandwidth is a challenge in running distributed computations. The bandwidths listed in Table 10.2 show that most network interconnects transfer data significantly slower than the PCIe bus. (QDR stands for Quad Data Rate InfiniBand. DDR and SDR stand for double and single data rate, respectively.)

A poor InfiniBand network can introduce an order of magnitude slowdown relative to PCIe speeds, which emphasizes the first of the three rules of efficient GPU programming introduced in Chapter 1: "Get the data on the GPGPU and keep it there." It also raises portability issues for those who

---

[1] OpenFabrics Enterprise Distribution.

Table 10.2 Data Accessibility, Including InfiniBand Messages

Data Access	Memory Type	Bandwidth		
Internal to the SM	Register memory	≈8,000 GB/s		
Internal to the SM	Shared memory	≈1,600 GB/s		
GPU	Global memory	177 GB/s		
PCIe	Mapped memory	≈8 GB/s one-way		
MPI	12x InfiniBand	QDR	12 GB/s	
		DDR	6 GB/s	
		SDR	3 GB/s	
MPI	4x InfiniBand	QDR	4 GB/s	
		DDR	2 GB/s	
		SDR	1 GB/s	
MPI	1x InfiniBand	QDR	1 GB/s	
		DDR	0.5 GB/s	
		SDR	0.25 GB/s	

wish to ship distributed MPI applications. Unfortunately, users tend to blame the application first for poor performance rather than the hardware.

BALANCE RATIOS

Deciding whether an application or algorithm will run effectively across a network is a challenge. Of course, the most accurate approach is to port the code and benchmark it. This may be impossible due to lack of funding and time. It may also result in a lot of needless work.

Balance ratios are a commonsense approach that can provide a reasonable estimation about application or algorithm performance that does not require first porting the application. These metrics are also used to evaluate hardware systems as part of a procurement process (Farber, 2007).

Balance ratios define a system balance that is quantifiable and—with the right choice of benchmarks—provides some assurance that an existing application will run well on a new computer. The challenge lies in deciding what characteristics need to be measured to determine whether an application will run well on a GPU or network of GPUs.

Most GPU applications are numerically intensive, which suggests that all GPU-based metrics should be tied to floating-point performance. Comparisons can then be made between systems and cards with different floating-point capabilities. Bandwidth limitations are an important metric to tie to numerical performance, as global memory, the PCIe bus, and network connectivity are known to bottleneck GPU performance for most applications.

As shown in Equation 10.1 the ratios between floating-point performance and the bandwidths available to keep the floating-point processors busy can be calculated from vendor and hardware information. This ratio makes it easy to see that a hardware configuration that moves data over a four-times DDR InfiniBand connection can cause an order of magnitude decrease in application performance versus the same application running on hardware that moves data across the PCIe bus.

$$Float\ vs.\ bandwidth\ ratio = \frac{flop/s}{bandwidth/s} \qquad (10.1)$$

These observations are not new in HPC. The January 2003 *Report of the National Science Foundation Blue-Ribbon Advisory Panel on Cyberinfrastructure,*[2] known as the Atkins Report, specifies some desirable metrics that are tied to floating-point performance:

- At least 1 byte of memory per flop/s.
- Memory bandwidth (byte/s/flop/s) $\geq$ 1.
- Internal network aggregate link bandwidth (bytes/s/flop/s) $\geq$ 0.2.
- Internal network bi-section bandwidth (bytes/s/flop/s) $\geq$ 0.1.
- System sustained productive disk I/O bandwidth (byte/s/flop/s) $\geq$ 0.001.

Keep in mind that numerical values presented in the Atkins Report are for desirable ratios based on *their* definition of a "representative" workload. Your application may have dramatically different needs. For this reason, it is worthwhile to evaluate your applications to see what ratios currently work and what ratios need to be improved.

A good approach is to use benchmarks to evaluate system performance. This is the thought behind the Top 500 list that is used to rank the fastest supercomputers in the world. The HPC Challenge (HPCC) website[3] provides a more extensive test suite. It will also generate a Kiviat diagram (Kiviat diagrams are similar to the radar plots in Microsoft Excel) to compare systems based on the standard HPCC benchmarks. A well-balanced system looks symmetrical on these plots because it performs well on all tests. High-performance balanced systems visually stand out because they occupy the outermost rings. Out-of-balance systems are distorted, as can be seen in Figure 10.3.

The HPCC website is a good source for benchmarks and comparative data on different computational systems. Be aware that synthetic benchmarks such as those on the HPCC website are very good at stressing certain aspects of machine performance, but they do represent a narrow view into machine performance.

---

[2] http://www.nsf.gov/cise/sci/reports/atkins.pdf.
[3] http://icl.cs.utk.edu/hpcc.

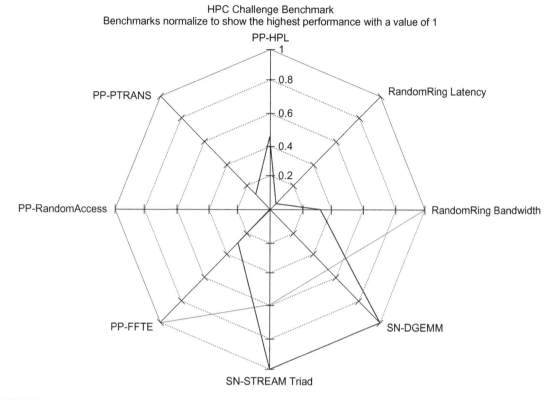

FIGURE 10.3

An example Kiviat diagram.

To provide a more realistic estimate, most organizations utilize benchmark evaluation suites that include some sample production codes to complement synthetic benchmarks—just to see if there is any unexpected performance change, either good or bad. Such benchmarks can also provide valuable insight into how well the processor and system components work together on real-world applications; plus, they can uncover issues that can adversely affect performance such as immature compilers and/or software drivers.

The key point behind balance ratios is that they can help the application programmer or system designer decide whether some aspect of a new hardware system will bottleneck an application. Although floating-point performance is important, other metrics such as memory capacity, storage bandwidth, and storage capacity might be a gating factor. The memory capacity of current GPUs, for example, can preclude the use of some applications or algorithms.

CONSIDERATIONS FOR LARGE MPI RUNS

In designing distributed applications, it is important to consider the scalability of all aspects of the application—not just of the computation!

Many legacy MPI applications were designed at a time when an MPI run that used from 10 to 100 processing cores was considered a "large" run. (Such applications might be good candidates to port to CUDA so that they can run on a single GPU.) A common shortcut taken in these legacy applications is to have the master process read data from a file and distribute it to the clients according to some partitioning scheme. This type of data load cannot scale, as the master node simply cannot transfer all the data for potentially tens of thousands of other processes. Even with modern hardware, the master process will become a bottleneck, which can cause the data load to take longer than the actual calculation.

Scalability of the Initial Data Load

A better approach is to have each process read its own data from a file on a distributed file system. Each process is provided with the filename of a data file that contains the data. They then open the file and perform whatever seek and other I/O operations are needed to access and load the data. All the clients then close the file to free system resources. This simple technique can load hundreds of gigabytes of data into large supercomputers very quickly. The process is illustrated in Figure 10.4.

With this I/O model, much depends on the bandwidth capabilities of the file system that holds the data. Modern parallel distributed file systems can

FIGURE 10.4

A scalable MPI data load for massive data sets.

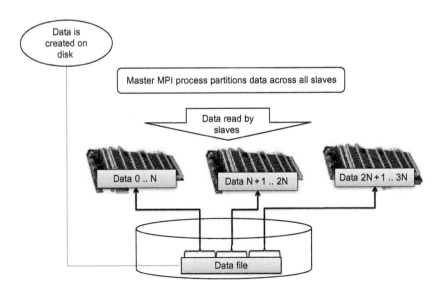

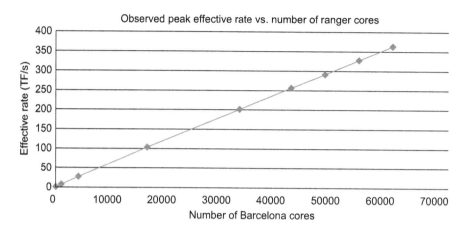

FIGURE 10.5

Example of near-linear scaling to 386 TF/s using 60,000 processing cores.

deliver hundreds of gigabytes per second of storage bandwidth when concurrently accessed by multiple processes. The freely available Lustre file system[4] can deliver hundreds of gigabytes per second of file system bandwidth using this technique and demonstrated scaling to 60,000 MPI processes as shown in Figure 10.5. Commercial file systems such as GPFS (General Parallel File System) by IBM and PanFS by Panasas also scale to hundreds of gigabytes per second and tens of thousands of MPI processes. To achieve high performance, these file systems need to be accessed by a number of concurrent distributed processes. It is not recommended to use this technique with large numbers of MPI clients on older NFS and CIFS file systems.

Using MPI to Perform a Calculation

The general mapping introduced in Chapter 2 has been used in an MPI distributed environment to scale to 500 GPUs on the TACC Longhorn supercomputer. The same mapping has been used to scale to more than 60,000 processing cores on both the CM-200 Connection Machine (Farber, 1992) and the TACC Ranger Supercomputer (Farber & Trease, 2008).

During these runs, the rank 0 process was designated as the master process in a conventional master-slave configuration. The master then:

- Initiated the data load as described previously. Even when using hundreds of gigabytes of data, the data load took only a few seconds using a modern parallel distributed file system.

---

[4] http://lustre.org.

- Performed other initializations.
- Runs the optimization procedure and directs the slave processes.
  - To make the best use of the available resources, the master node also evaluates the objective function along with the slave processes.
  - Most production runs used a variant of Powell's method, as described in *Numerical Recipes* (Press, Teukolsky, & Vetterling, 2007a) or *Conjugant Gradient* (also described in Numerical Recipies).
- On each evaluation of the objective function:
  - Uses **MPI_Bcast()** to broadcast the parameters to all the slave processes.
  - Each slave process (along with the master) calculates the partial sum of the objective function. This does not require any communication and can be optimized to run at full speed on the device as discussed in Chapters 2 and 3.
- Performs its own local calculation of the objective function.
  - Calls **MPI_Reduce()** to retrieve the total sum of all partial results.
  - In general, the **MPI_Reduce()** operation is highly optimized and scales according to $O(log2(\textbf{ntasks}))$, where **ntasks** is the number reported by **MPI_Comm_size()**.
- Supplies the result of the objective function to the optimization method, which causes either:
  - Another evaluation of the objective function.
  - Completion of the optimization process.

The slave processes (those processes with a rank greater than 0):

- Initiate the data load as described previously.
- Remain in an infinite loop until told it is time to exit the application by the master. Inside the loop, each slave:
  - Reads the parameters from the master node.
  - Calculates the partial sum of the objective function.
  - Sends the partial results to the master when requested.

Check Scalability

The scaling behavior of a distributed application is a key performance metric. Applications that exhibit *strong scaling* run faster as the number of processors are added to a fixed problem size. *Linear scaling* is a goal for distributed applications because the runtime of an application scales linearly with the amount of computational available (e.g., a two-times larger system will run the problem in half the time, a four-times larger system will run the problem in one-fourth the time, etc.). *Embarrassingly parallel* problems can exhibit linear runtime behavior because each computation is independent of each other. Applications that require communication to satisfy some dependency can generally achieve at best near-linear scaling. For example, an $O(\log_2(N))$ reduction operation will cause the scaling behavior to slowly diverge from a linear speedup according to processor count. Figure 10.5 illustrates near-linear scaling to 60,000 processing cores using the PCA objective function discussed in Chapter 3.

The 386 teraflop per second *effective rate* for the AMD Barcelona based TACC Ranger supercomputer reported in Figure 10.5 includes all communications overhead. A 500 GPU-based supercomputer run could deliver nearly 500 teraflops of single-precision performance. A colleague refers to these as "honest flops," as they reflect the performance a real production run would deliver.

The effective rate is defined for the PCA mapping is shown in Equation 10.2, "Definition of effective rate for the PCA parallel mapping":

$$Effective\ rate = \frac{TotalOpCount}{T_{broadcast} + T_{objectfunc} + T_{reduce}} \qquad (10.2)$$

where:

- $TotalOpCount$ is the number of floating-point operations performed in a call to an objective function.
- $T_{broadcast}$ is the time required to broadcast the parameters to all the slave processes.
- $T_{objectfunc}$ is the time consumed in calculating the partial results across all the clients. This is generally the time taken by the slowest client.
- T_{reduce} is the time required by the reduction of the partial results.

CLOUD COMPUTING

Cloud computing is an infrastructure paradigm that moves computation to the Web in the form of a web-based service. The idea is simplicity itself: institutions contract with Internet vendors for computational resources instead of providing those resources themselves through the purchase and maintenance of computational clusters and supercomputer hardware. As expected with any computational platform—especially one utilized for high performance and scientific computing—performance limitations within the platform define which computational problems will run well.

Unlike MPI frameworks, cloud computing requires that application be tolerant of both failures and high latency in point-to-point communications. Still, MPI is such a prevalent API that most cloud computing services provide and support it. Be aware that bandwidth and latency issues may cause poor performance when running MPI on a cloud computing infrastructure.

MPI utilizes a fixed number of processes that participate in the distributed application. This number is defined at application startup—generally with **mpiexec**. In MPI, the failure of any one process in a communicator affects all processes in the communicator, even those that are not in direct communication with the failed process. This factor contributes to the lack of fault tolerance in MPI applications.

MapReduce is a fault-tolerant framework for distributed computing that has become very popular and is widely used (Dean & Ghemawat, 2010). In other words, the failure of a client has no significant effect on the server. Instead, the server can continue to service other clients. What makes the MapReduce structure robust is that all communication occurs in a two-party context where one party (e.g., process) can easily recognize that the other party has failed and can decide to stop communicating with it. Moreover, each party can easily keep track of the state held by the other party, which facilitates failover.

A challenge with cloud computing is that many service providers use virtual machines that run on busy internal networks. As a result, communications time can increase. In particular, the time T_{reduce} is very latency-dependent, as can be seen in Equation 10.2. For tightly coupled applications (e.g., applications with frequent communication between processes), it is highly recommended that dedicated clusters be utilized. In particular, reduction operations will be rate-limited by the slowest process in the group. That said, papers like "Multi-GPU MapReduce on GPU Clusters" (Stuart & Owens, 2011) demonstrate that MapReduce is an active area of research.

A CODE EXAMPLE

The objective function from the *nlpcaNM.cu* example from Chapter 3 was adapted to use MPI and this data load technique.

Data Generation

A simple data generator was created that uses the **genData()** method from *nlpcaNM.cu*. This program simply writes a number of examples to a file. Both the filename and number of examples are specified on the command line. The complete source listing is given in Example 10.6, "Source for *genData.cu*":

Example 10.6

```
#include <iostream>
#include <fstream>
#include <stdlib.h>
using namespace std;
```

```
// get a uniform random number between -1 and 1
inline float f_rand() {
  return 2*(rand()/((float)RAND_MAX)) -1.;
}
template <typename Real>
void genData(ofstream &outFile, int nVec, Real xVar)
{
  Real xMax = 1.1; Real xMin = -xMax;
  Real xRange = (xMax - xMin);
  for(int i=0; i < nVec; i++) {
    Real t = xRange * f_rand();
    Real z1 = t + xVar * f_rand();
    Real z2 = t*t*t + xVar * f_rand();
    outFile.write((char*) &z1, sizeof(Real));
    outFile.write((char*) &z2, sizeof(Real));
  }
}

int main(int argc, char *argv[])
{
  if(argc < 3) {
    fprintf(stderr,"Use: filename nVec\n");
    exit(1);
  }
  ofstream outFile (argv[1], ios::out | ios::binary);
  int nVec = atoi(argv[2]);
#ifdef USE_DBL
  genData<double>(outFile, nVec, 0.1);
#else
  genData<float>(outFile, nVec, 0.1);
#endif
  outFile.close();
  return 0;
}
```

The program can be saved in a file and compiled as shown in Example 10.7, "Building *genData.cu*." The C preprocessor variable **USE_DBL** specifies whether the data will be written as 32-bit or 64-bit binary floating-point numbers:

Example 10.7

```
nvcc -D USE_DBL genData.cu -o bin/genData64
nvcc genData.cu -o bin/genData32
```

Data sets can be written via the command line. For example, Example 10.8, "Creating a 32-Bit File with *genData.cu*," writes 10M 32-bit floats to a file *nlpca32.dat*.

Example 10.8

```
bin/genData32 nlpca32.dat 10000000
```

It is very easy to specify the wrong file during runtime. This simple example does not provide version, size, or any other information useful for sanity checking. The Google ProtoBufs project is recommend for a production quality file and streaming data format.[5] Google uses this project for almost all of its internal RPC protocols and file formats.

The *nlpcaNM.cu* example code from Chapter 3 was modified to run in an MPI environment. The changes are fairly minimal but are distributed throughout the code. Only code snippets are provided in the following discussion. The entire code can be downloaded from the book website.[6]

The variable **nGPUperNode** was defined at the beginning of the file. It is assumed that the number of MPI processes per node will equal the number of GPUs in each node (meaning one MPI process is per GPU). The value of **nGPUperNode** allows each MPI process to call **cudaSetDevice()** correctly to use different devices. Other topologies are possible including using one MPI process per node for all GPUs. See Example 10.9, "Modification of the Top of *nlpcaNM*.cu to Use Multiple GPUs per Node":

Example 10.9

```
#include "mpi.h"
const static int nGPUperNode=2;

}
```

The **main()** method of *nlpcaNM.cu* has been modified with the MPI framework shown in Figure 10.1 using the code shown in Example 10.1 (see Example 10.10, "Modified main() method for *nlpcaNM.cu*":

Example 10.10

```
#include <stdio.h>

int main(int argc, char *argv[])
```

---

[5] http://code.google.com/p/protobuf.
[6] http://booksite.mkp.com/9780123884268.

```
{
  int numtasks, rank, ret;
  if(argc < 2) {
    fprintf(stderr,"Use: filename\n");
    exit(1);
  }
  ret = MPI_Init(&argc,&argv);
  if (ret != MPI_SUCCESS) {
    printf ("Error in MPI_Init()!\n");
    MPI_Abort(MPI_COMM_WORLD, ret);
  }

  MPI_Comm_size(MPI_COMM_WORLD,&numtasks);
  MPI_Comm_rank(MPI_COMM_WORLD,&rank);
  printf ("Number of tasks= %d My rank= %d\n", numtasks,rank);

  /******* do some work *******/
#ifdef USE_DBL
  trainTest<double> ( argv[1], rank, numtasks );
#else
  trainTest<float> ( argv[1], rank, numtasks);
#endif

  MPI_Finalize();
  return 0;
}
```

The **setExamples()** method was modified to allocate memory on different GPUs. See Example 10.11, "Modified setExamples Method for *nlpcaNM.cu*":

Example 10.11

```
void setExamples(thrust::host_vector<Real>& _h_data) {
  nExamples = _h_data.size()/exLen;

  // copy data to the device
  int rank;
  MPI_Comm_rank(MPI_COMM_WORLD,&rank);
  cudaSetDevice(rank%nGPUperNode);

  d_data = thrust::device_vector<Real>(nExamples*exLen);
  thrust::copy(_h_data.begin(), _h_data.end(), d_data.begin());
  d_param = thrust::device_vector<Real>(nParam);
}
```

Example 10.12, "Modified trainTest Method for *nlpcaNM.cu*," shows how the data is loaded from disk:

Example 10.12

```cpp
#include <fstream>
template <typename Real>
void trainTest(char* filename, int rank, int numtasks)
{
  ObjFunc<Real> testObj;
  const int nParam = testObj.nParam;
  cout << "nParam " << nParam << endl;

  // read the test data
  ifstream inFile (filename, ios::in | ios::binary);
  // position 0 bytes from end
  inFile.seekg(0, ios::end);
  // determine the file size in bytes
  ios::pos_type size = inFile.tellg();
  // allocate number of Real values for this task
  //   (assumes a multiple of numtasks)
  int nExamplesPerGPU = (size/(sizeof(Real)*testObj.exLen))/numtasks;
  thrust::host_vector<Real> h_data(nExamplesPerGPU*testObj.exLen);
  // seek to the byte location in the file
  inFile.seekg(rank*h_data.size()*sizeof(Real), ios::beg);//
  allocate number of Real values for this task
  inFile.seekg(rank*h_data.size()*sizeof(Real));
  // read bytes from the file into h_data
  inFile.read((char*)&h_data[0], h_data.size()*sizeof(Real));
  // close the file
  inFile.close();

  testObj.setExamples(h_data);
  int nExamples = testObj.get_nExamples();

  if(rank > 0) {
    testObj.objFunc( NULL );
    return;
  }

    ...Nelder-Mead code goes here

  int op=0; // shut down slave processes
  MPI_Bcast(&op, 1, MPI_INT, 0, MPI_COMM_WORLD);
}
```

In this example, binary input stream, **infile** is opened to read the data in the file **filename**. After that:

- The size of the file is determined.

- Each of the **numtasks** processes is assigned an equal amount of the data based on the file size and the number of data per example. The logic is simplified by assuming that the number of examples is a multiple of **numtasks**.
- The host vector **h_data** is allocated.
- A seek operation moves to the appropriate position in the file.
- The data is read into **h_data** and handed off to **setExamples()** to be loaded onto the device.

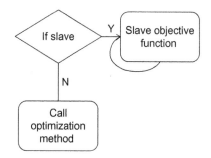

FIGURE 10.6

Logic separating the master from the slave processes.

- As shown in Figure 10.6, the rank of the process is tested:
  - If the rank is greater than zero, this process is a slave. The objective function is called with a NULL parameters argument and the training finishes when that method exits.
  - If the process is a master, the Nelder-Mead optimization code is called.

The objective function implements the logic for both the master and slave processes, as illustrated in Figure 10.7.

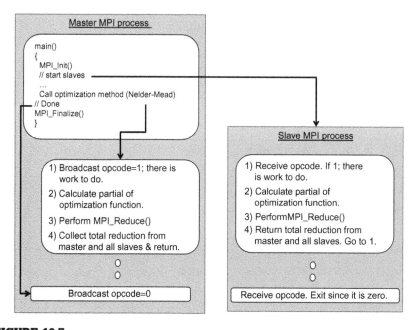

FIGURE 10.7

MPI control flow.

The objective function (Example 10.13) belongs to a slave process when the MPI rank is greater than 0. In this case, the slave state machine:

1. Allocates space in pinned memory for the parameters.
2. It waits for an operation code to be broadcast from the master.
   a. The master tells the slave that all work is done with a zero op code and that it should return.
   b. Otherwise, the slave will move to the next step.
3. The slave waits for the host to broadcast the parameters.
4. After the master broadcasts the parameters, the slave runs the objective function on its data and blocks waiting for the master to ask for the result.
5. After the master requests the reduction result the slave returns to wait for an op code in step 2. This process continues until the master sends a 0 op code.

The objective function (Example 10.13) belongs to the master process when the rank is 0. In this case, the master:

1. Broadcasts a nonzero op code to let all the slaves know there is work to do.
2. Broadcasts the parameters to all the slaves.
3. Runs the objective function on its data.
4. Performs a reduction to sum the partial values from the slave processes.
5. Returns to continue running the optimization method.

Example 10.13

```
Real objFunc(Real *p)
{
  int rank,op;
  Real sum=0.;
  MPI_Comm_rank(MPI_COMM_WORLD,&rank);
  cudaSetDevice(rank%nGPUperNode);

  if(nExamples == 0) {
   cerr << "data not set " << endl; exit(1);
  }

  CalcError getError(thrust::raw_pointer_cast(&d_data[0]),
                     thrust::raw_pointer_cast(&d_param[0]),
                     nInput, exLen);

  if(rank > 0) { // slave objective function
    Real *param;
    cudaHostAlloc(&param, sizeof(Real)*nParam,cudaHostAllocPortable);
    for(;;) { // loop until the master says I am done.
```

```
  MPI_Bcast(&op, 1, MPI_INT, 0, MPI_COMM_WORLD);
  if(op==0) {
    cudaFreeHost(param);
    return(0);
  }
  if(sizeof(Real) == sizeof(float))
    MPI_Bcast(&param[0], nParam, MPI_FLOAT, 0, MPI_COMM_WORLD);
  else
    MPI_Bcast(&param[0], nParam, MPI_DOUBLE, 0, MPI_COMM_WORLD);
  thrust::copy(param, param+nParam, d_param.begin());
  Real mySum = thrust::transform_reduce(
              thrust::counting_iterator<unsigned int>(0),
              thrust::counting_iterator<unsigned int>
              (nExamples),
              getError,
              (Real) 0.,
              thrust::plus<Real>());
  if(sizeof(Real) == sizeof(float))
    MPI_Reduce(&mySum, &sum, 1, MPI_FLOAT, MPI_SUM, 0,
    MPI_COMM_WORLD);
  else
    MPI_Reduce(&mySum,  &sum,  1,  MPI_DOUBLE,  MPI_SUM,  0,
    MPI_COMM_WORLD);
  }
} else { // master process
  double startTime=omp_get_wtime();

  op=1;
  MPI_Bcast(&op, 1, MPI_INT, 0, MPI_COMM_WORLD);
  if(sizeof(Real) == sizeof(float))
    MPI_Bcast(&p[0], nParam, MPI_FLOAT, 0, MPI_COMM_WORLD);
  else
    MPI_Bcast(&p[0], nParam, MPI_DOUBLE, 0, MPI_COMM_WORLD);
  thrust::copy(p, p+nParam, d_param.begin());

  Real mySum = thrust::transform_reduce(
              thrust::counting_iterator<unsigned int>(0),
              thrust::counting_iterator<unsigned int>(nExamples),
              getError,
              (Real) 0.,
              thrust::plus<Real>());

  if(sizeof(Real) == sizeof(float))
    MPI_Reduce(&mySum, &sum, 1, MPI_FLOAT, MPI_SUM, 0,
    MPI_COMM_WORLD);
  else
    MPI_Reduce(&mySum, &sum, 1, MPI_DOUBLE, MPI_SUM, 0,
    MPI_COMM_WORLD);
```

Table 10.3 Table of Results[7]

Number of GPUs	Time per Objective Function	Speedup over one GPU
1	0.0102073	
2	0.00516948	1.98

```
    objFuncCallTime += (omp_get_wtime() - startTime);
    objFuncCallCount++;
  }
  return(sum);
}
```

The application completes after the optimization method returns in the master process. The final line in **testTrain()** broadcasts a zero opcode to all the slaves to tell them to exit. The master process then returns to **main()** to shut down MPI normally.

Table 10.3 shows that running the MPI version of *nlpcaNM.cu* on two GPUs provides a nearly double increase in performance. No network was used as both GPUs were inside the same system. The example code from this chapter ran unchanged to deliver near-linear scalability to 500 GPUs on the Texas Advanced Computing Center (TACC) Longhorn supercomputer cluster. Many thanks to TACC for providing access to this machine.[8]

SUMMARY

MPI and GPUDirect give CUDA programmers the ability to run high-performance applications that far exceed the capabilities of a single GPU or collection of GPUs inside a single system. Scalability and performance within a node are key metrics to evaluate distributed applications. Those applications that exhibit linear or near-linear scalability have the ability to run on the largest current and future machines. For example, the parallel mapping discussed in this chapter, plus Chapters 2 and 3, is now nearly 30 years old. At the time it was designed, a teraflop of computing power was decades beyond the reach of even the largest government research organizations. Today, it runs very effectively on GPU devices, clusters, and even the latest supercomputers. It will be interesting to see how many yottaFlops (10^{24} flops) will be available 30 years from now. Meanwhile, this mapping provides a scalable solution for large data-mining and optimization tasks.

---

[7] More current and extensive results reported on the wiki.
[8] http://gpucomputing.net/CUDAapplicationdesignanddevelopment.

## CHAPTER 11

CUDA for Real Problems

CUDA gives developers the ability to accelerate applications on the GPU by one to three orders of magnitude over conventional processors. Knowing how to think and program in CUDA is the necessary first step in the process of growing and maturing into an adept CUDA programmer. Look to the Internet and technical literature to find projects that provide general solutions and design patterns that can be adapted to your projects. CUDA is fast; reinventing the wheel is slow. The chapters in this book were designed to teach and provide some initial frameworks for future applications. For example, the simple C++ functor framework in Chapter 2 implemented a general parallel mapping for pattern recognition and optimization that runs 85 times faster on a GPU than on a high-end quad-core processor and delivers a 341 times greater increase over single-core performance. Chapter 10 extended this example to use MPI to run on computational clusters containing hundreds of GPUs. The 500 GPU TACC Longhorn cluster is one system that can provide nearly half a petaflop (500,000 gigaflops) of single-precision floating-point performance using this parallel mapping. These examples turn your GPU into an engine to find patterns in complex data that is more powerful than the largest supercomputer that existed prior to 1996.[1] Data visualization is a natural extension of the computational capabilities of GPUs. As shown in Chapter 9, mixing CUDA with OpenGL interoperability means that the data does not even need to move off the GPU. That said, online information and technical literature extends far beyond these examples and the pages of this book. This chapter points the way to other projects for advanced usage and programming.

Do not consider this chapter to be an exhaustive list. Instead, it provides a broad introduction to some of the popular techniques and packages that use

---

[1] The United States Sandia National Laboratory built the first supercomputer that was able to perform more than a trillion floating-point operations in 1996.

CUDA. Most of the methods discussed will provide a link to a downloadable CUDA source package that can be reviewed, built, and used. There are many other excellent resources available on the Internet and in technical literature. A good starting point is the CUDA showcase in the developer zone that contains hundreds of links to CUDA techniques and papers.[2]

At the end of this chapter, the reader will have been introduced to:

- A few techniques to reduce high-dimensional data to low dimensions.
- Force-directed graphs for visualization.
- Multidimensional scaling (MDS).
- Mutual information.
- Monte Carlo methods.
- Molecular modeling.

WORKING WITH HIGH-DIMENSIONAL DATA

We live in the age of data. Automatic systems collect most minute details of transactions and interactions in both physical and social systems. The patterns are there, but where?

With a simple database query or Internet search, it is possible to extract an interesting data set that concatenates a number of different measures (or observations) for each event. The events might be customer purchases or the spectral data of hundreds of stars. Multiple events can be represented as the rows of a matrix in which each row is an event and the columns of each row contain measurements concerning the event. A common question to ask is, "Which rows are similar to each other?" Phrased another way, the question becomes, "Which events, or vectors, are close to each other?"

For many problems, it is possible to calculate the distance between each row in the matrix using a metric such as *Euclidean distance*. Euclidean distance is a measure of distance that one would obtain with a ruler and the Pythagorean formula. Those rows that are close in distance can be considered "similar" to each other and those that are far away are "not similar." There are many other distance measures aside from Euclidean distance, but Euclidean distance is intuitively easy to understand.

The curse of dimensionality discussed in Chapter 3 is why working in a high-dimensional space is not practical for many problems. For example, asking for all rows that are closer than some distance from a given point in high-dimensional space can return either no values (because the sampling is very sparse) or nearly all the data (because the volume of the search region

---

[2] http://developer.nvidia.com/cuda-action-research-apps.

is so large that it encompasses most or all of the known data). In either case, the answer is meaningless.

Decreasing the dimensionality of a search exponentially decreases the volume of the search region. This is one of the reasons why data miners like working in lower-dimensional spaces—it increases the chance of getting a meaningful answer to the question, "Which points in the low-dimensional space are close to each other?" Of course, the projection used to convert the high-dimensional data to the low-dimensional space must preserve the distance relationships between the points.

PCA/NLPCA

As discussed in Chapter 3, autoencoders, Principle Components Analysis (PCA), and Nonlinear Principle Components Analysis (NLPCA) are some of the techniques used to represent high-dimensional data in a lower-dimensional space. The example code in Chapter 3 essentially passed high-dimensional data through an information bottleneck (the bottleneck neurons) in such a way that the high-dimensional data can be reconstructed. Measuring the error between the original and reconstructed high-dimensional data provides a measure of success. A low error implies that the projection to low dimensions preserved the distance relationships between the points in the high-dimensional data.

The example code in Chapter 3 can be adapted to work with your own data sets simply by modifying the **genData()** method. Similarly, the data generator in Chapter 10 can be changed to one that writes your own data to a file. In either case, modifying the *CalcError.h* file will let you define your own PCA or NLPCA architecture. Using one, two, or three bottleneck neurons means that the low-dimensional data can be visualized with most 2D and 3D graphics packages such as gnuPlot, Excel, MATLAB, and many others.

For more information on autoencoders and other neural network based approaches, see the work of Geoffrey Hinton (Hinton & Salakhutdinov, 2006)[3] and many others. The website http://nlpca.org is a good starting point to learn about NLPCA, especially for MATLAB users.

Multidimensional Scaling

An alternative perspective on dimensionality reduction is offered by multidimensional scaling (MDS). MDS is another classical approach that maps a high-dimensional data set to a lower dimensional space, but does so in an attempt to preserve pairwise distances. Numerous variants of the classical method have been developed. An excellent reference is *Multidimensional Scaling* (Cox & Cox, 2008).

---

[3] http://www.cs.toronto.edu/~hinton/.

The Glimmer package implements MDS on the GPU (Ingram, Munzner, & Olano, 2009). Variable speedups depending on data size range from 10–15 times over a conventional processor. The source code can be freely downloaded from the University of British Columbia website.[4]

K-Means Clustering

K-means clustering partitions a number of events into k-clusters in which each event belongs to the cluster with the nearest mean. Data sets with a billion points are common in today's real-world applications. With CUDA GPU acceleration, Hewlett-Packard reports that a data set with a billion data points can be clustered within minutes (Wu, Zhang, & Hsu, 2009). The HP software claims an order of magnitude increased performance over a highly optimized CPU-only version running on eight cores, and about 300 times performance boost over the popular MineBench benchmark (Narayanan et al., 2006) running on a single core. Many other researchers (Hong-tao, Li-li, Dan-tong, Zhan-shan, & He, 2009; Ma & Agrawal, 2009; Shalom, Dash, & Tue, 2008) report large speedups on K-means.

A freely downloadable version of K-means written by Serban Giuroiu is available from GitHub.[5] It is reportedly 50 times faster than a sequential version.

Expectation-Maximization

K-means and MDS are similar to the expectation-maximization (EM) algorithm for mixtures of Gaussians in that they both attempt to find the centers of natural clusters in the data as well as in the iterative refinement approach employed by both algorithms. The EM algorithm is widely used in the fields of signal processing and data mining. A freely downloadable version of the EM method with a reported 170-times increase over a reference CPU implementation is available.[6] NVIDIA published a paper with a similar reported speedup over a naïve implementation (Kumar, Satoor, & Buck, 2009). The EM method can also be implemented as a functor in the optimization framework provided in this book. The CUDA-MEME package discussed later in this chapter is another freely downloadable EM package.

The expectation-maximization algorithm is also used to discover motifs in social network and biological data. GPU-MEME is reported to provide an order of magnitude speedup on a single GPU and two orders of magnitude speedup on a compute cluster (Chen, Schmidt, Weiguo, & Müller-Wittig,

---

[4] http://www.cs.ubc.ca/~sfingram/glimmer/.

[5] https://github.com/serban/kmeans.

[6] http://andrewharp.com/gmmcuda.

2008). CUDA-MEME is a freely downloadable motif discovery software package[7] based on the GPU-MEME paper.

Support Vector Machines

Support vector machines (SVM) are a popular machine learning method to analyze data and recognize patterns. An SVM performs classification by constructing an N-dimensional *hyperplane* (a plane generalized into N dimensions) that optimally separates the data into two categories. They are used for classification and regression analysis, among other tasks. SVM models are closely related to neural networks. In fact, an SVM model using a sigmoid kernel function is equivalent to a two-layer perceptron neural network. Speedups of 150 times on a GPU have been reported in the literature (Catanzaro, Sundaram, & Keutzer, 2008).

SVM can also be implemented as a functor in the optimization framework provided in this book. The cuSVM package can be freely downloaded from the Internet.[8] This same package is accessible from the R statistical language via the **gpuSvnTrain()** method in the gputools package. Speedups between 22 and 172 times the rate of state-of-the-art software are reported by the author (Carpenter, 2011). The CUDA-SVM package from Nanyang Technological University is available on http://sourceforge.net. Another SVM package, multisvm, can be freely downloaded from http://code.google.com.

Bayesian Networks

A Bayesian belief net is a directed graph, together with an associated set of probability tables. The nodes represent variables, which can be discrete or continuous. The arcs in the graph represent causal/influential relationships between variables. The key feature of Bayesian networks is that they can be used to reason about uncertainty. When used in conjunction with statistical techniques, these graphical models have several advantages for data analysis:

- Because the model encodes dependencies among all variables, it can handle missing data.
- A Bayesian network can be used to learn causal relationships, and hence can be used to gain an understanding about a problem domain and to predict the consequences of intervention.
- A Bayesian model has both a causal and probabilistic semantics, which makes it a natural representation to combine prior knowledge (which often comes in causal form) and data.
- Bayesian statistical methods in conjunction with Bayesian networks offer an efficient and principled approach for avoiding the overfitting of data.

---

[7] http://www.nvidia.com/object/meme_on_tesla.html.
[8] http://patternsonascreen.net/cuSVM.html.

Duke University provides a freely available Bayesian software that can also be accessed via MATLAB and the R statistical language.[9] Speedups of 160 times over a conventional multicore processor are reported (Suchard et al., 2010). CUDA allows large data sets to be analyzed with Bayesian techniques (Chen, Schmidt, Weiguo, & Müller-Wittig, 2008).

BEAGLE (Broad-platform Evolutionary Analysis General Likelihood Evaluator) is a high-performance library that can perform the core calculations at the heart of most Bayesian and Maximum Likelihood phylogenetics packages. Phylogenetics is the study of evolutionary relatedness among various groups, species, or populations of organisms that is discovered through molecular sequencing data and morphological data matrices. The authors achieved a 90-times speedup over an optimized CPU version and a 140-times speedup over the general CPU version (Suchard & Rambaut, 2009).[10] This library is used in the Bayesian phylogenetics framework (BEAST).[11]

Mutual information

The concept of mutual information has its origins in information theory and is widely used in many disciplines. For example, mutual information can be used to determine sites in the AIDS virus that are related for structural or functional reasons (Korber, Farber, Wolpert, & Lapedes, 1993). In particular, the paper by Korber et al. demonstrates how *bootstrapping* can be used to determine a confidence that high pair-wise mutual information did not arise by chance. (Bootstrapping in statistics can be implemented by various techniques, including by random sampling with replacement from the original data set.) Mutual information can also be used to improve prediction in machine-learning (Farber, Lapedes, & Sirotkin, 1992). There are numerous texts on this topic (Cover & Thomas, 2006; Stanisław, Carbonell, & Mitchell, 1985) and many sources of information on the Internet.

Pairwise mutual information provides a measure of the amount of information between two random variables. Generally, this measure is expressed in number of bits of information. Mutual information is defined in terms of entropies involving the joint probability distribution, $P(s_i, s'_j)$, of occurrence symbol s at position and s' at position j. It can be expressed as the relation to the log-likelihood ratio of the expected occurrence of pairs (under the

---

[9] http://www.stat.duke.edu/research/software/west/gpu/software.html.

[10] http://beagle-lib.googlecode.com.

[11] http://beast.bio.ed.ac.uk.

assumption of independence) to the observed occurrence. See Equation 11.1, "A definition of mutual information."

$$M(i,j) = \sum_{s_i s_j} P(s_i, s_j') \log P(s_i, s_j') / P(s_i) P(s_j') \qquad (11.1)$$

In medical image analysis, mutual information is used as a similarity measure for multimodal registration. CUDA provides a 50-times speedup, allowing real-time registration of medical images and in robotics (Ines & Hirschmüller, 2008).

There are many freely downloadable implementations on the Internet. CUDA-MI[12] is one; another is the version by Shams at the Australian National University.[13]

FORCE-DIRECTED GRAPHS

Many graph based problems only provide information about the relationships between nodes in a graph. Such problems arise when people send messages to each other, talk on the phone, and travel to various locations. Visualizing mass amounts of such information can be challenging. Excellent surveys on drawing graphs can be found in Di Battista, Eades, Tamassia, and Tollis (1999), and Brandes (2001).

In the absence of other information, force-directed placement algorithms for graph layout based on Hooke's law for springs have been used to create pleasing and informative graph layouts as described by Eades' spring-mass equations (Eades, 1984) and later adapted by Fruchterman and Reingold to emulate particle physics in a simulated annealing algorithm (Fruchterman & Reingold, 1991).

Graph placement and layout remains an active area of research, with Frishman and Ayellet (Frishman & Ayellet, 2008) using GPUs to speed-up incremental graph layout to provide results 17 times faster than a CPU. Godiyal et al. (Godiyal, Hoberock, Garland, & Hart, 2009) use a variation of the Fast Multipole Method (FMM) to estimate the long-distance repulsive forces in force-directed layout. (The FMM method was developed to speed the calculation of long-range forces in the N-body problem.) Multipole computations are efficiently supported with a GPU-based k-d tree (a space-partitioning data structure for organizing points in a k-dimensional space). The authors report their technique achieves impressive speedup over previous CPU and

---

[12] https://sites.google.com/site/liuweiguohome/cuda-mi.
[13] http://users.cecs.anu.edu.au/~ramtin/cuda.htm.

GPU methods, drawing graphs with hundreds of thousands of vertices within a few seconds via CUDA.

MONTE CARLO METHODS

Monte Carlo methods rely on repeated random sampling to compute their results. They are often used in simulating physical and mathematical systems and are especially useful for simulating systems with many coupled degrees of freedom (such as fluids) to model phenomena as well as systems with significant uncertainty in inputs such as the calculation of risk in business. Hubbard notes that Monte Carlo predictions of failures, cost overruns, and schedule overruns are routinely better than human intuition or alternative "soft" methods (Hubbard, 2009).

Monte Carlo methods are widely used in mathematics to evaluate multidimensional definite integrals with complicated boundary conditions. For example, the Metropolis algorithm is a Monte Carlo method for obtaining a sequence of random samples from a probability distribution for which direct sampling is difficult. This sequence can be used to approximate the distribution or to compute an integral to get an expected value.

I had the personal pleasure of knowing Nick Metropolis during my career in the theoretical division at Los Alamos National Laboratory, which demonstrates how knowledge of parallel computing can indirectly enrich your life. He was a wonderful person. The Metropolis algorithm is considered to be among the ten algorithms that have had the greatest influence on the development and practice of science and engineering in the twentieth century (Andrieu, de Freitas, Doucet, & Jordan, 2003; Beichel & Sullivan, 2000). For some applications, Markov chain Monte Carlo (MCMC) simulation is the only known general approach for providing a solution within a reasonable time (Andrieu, de Freitas, Doucet, & Jordan, 2003; Dyer, Frieze, & Kannan, 1991; Jerrum & Sinclair, 1996).

The large number of CUDA projects implementing Monte Carlo methods demonstrates the power of CUDA and interest in this technique. Speedups range from 100 times to over 1,000 times greater on multi-GPU implementations. A good starting reference is "Understanding GPU Programming for Statistical Computation: Studies in Massively Parallel Massive Mixtures" (Suchard, Wang, Chan, Frelinger, Cron, & West, 2010).

A number of Monte Carlo packages are available for free download:

- The MCX (Monte Carlo eXtreme) package quotes 300- to 400-times speedups (Fang & Boas, 2009). The code can be freely downloaded from http://mcx.sourceforge.net.

- GPUSS (GPU Stochastic Simulation for data analysis) is freely available from Oxford University. The authors report a speedup of 500 times on the NVIDIA Community Showcase.[14] This package is accessible from PyCUDA for statistical GPU computing. Please see the Oxford website for an extensive list of publications that use this package.

MOLECULAR MODELING

Molecular modeling has also achieved significant performance benefits using CUDA (Eastman & Pande, 2010; Hampton, Agarwal, Alam, & Crozier, 2010; Roberts, Stone, Sepulveda, Hwu, & Luthey-Schulten, 2009; Rodrigues, Hardy, Stone, Schulten, & Hwu, 2008), including packages such as:

- The NAMD/VMD molecular modeling system (Humphrey, Dalke, & Schulten, 1996; Laxmikant et al., 1999; Stone, Hardy, Ufimtsev, & Schulten, 2010).
- HOOMD-Blue (Anderson, Lorenz, & Travesset, 2008) was written from the ground up for GPUs.
- The OpenMM library for molecular dynamics. The authors report speedups of 100 times over commodity processors.

All of these packages are freely downloadable from the Internet. The paper "GPU-Accelerated Molecular Modeling Coming of Age" (Stone, Hardy, Ufimtsev, & Schulten, 2010) is required reading for those who are interested in molecular modeling. CUDA and GPU computing have also stimulated the development of new approximations for electrostatics that can provide up to three orders of magnitude speedup (Anandakrishnan et al., 2010). Over the past few years, molecular modeling has been a vibrant and growing area of CUDA research.

QUANTUM CHEMISTRY

Quantum chemistry applies quantum mechanics to explain and predict the behavior of chemical processes. Understanding the electronic structure of matter is an important question in materials design and the creation of more efficient batteries, membranes, solar panels, and a multitude of common materials. Many approaches use approximate solutions to the Schrödinger equation for determining the energy levels of molecules and the properties such as conductance, charge distribution, and reactivity. Other quantum chemical results include molecular geometry, the strengths and other characteristics of chemical bonds, optical and other spectra, intermolecular forces, and many other chemical properties and features of chemical behavior.

---

[14] http://developer.nvidia.com/cuda-action-research-apps.

Quantum ESPRESSO is a freely downloadable integrated suite of computer codes for electronic-structure calculations and materials modeling at the nano scale. It is based on density-functional theory, plane waves, and pseudopotentials (both norm-conserving and ultrasoft). A good starting article is "Speeding Up Plane-Wave Electronic-Structure Calculations Using Graphics-Processing Units" (Maintz, Eck, & Dronskowski, 2011). ICHEC has collaborated with the Quantum ESPRESSO project to create a GPU-based version of this code. Current speedups are reported at eight times that of a single-core processor. It is expected that this performance will increase as the GPU project matures.

GPU-enabled quantum chemistry packages such as TeraChem (Ufimtsev & Martinez, 2008, 2009a,b), now called PetaChem, are being deployed at major supercomputing centers such as National Center for Supercomputing Applications (NCSA).

A number of researchers and organizations report excellent speedups on quantum chemistry simulations (Hwu, 2011) including Gaussian and GAMESS (Ufimtsev & Martinez, 2008, 2009). Pseudospectral methods run well on both GPUs and multicore processors. One implementation is BigDFT (BigDFT) (Genovese et al., 2009).

INTERACTIVE WORKFLOWS

GPGPUs provide additional performance benefits for dedicated usage, visualization, and interactive workflows, as they have been designed to be plugged into computers situated next to an instrument or individual's desk. The recent scientific literature demonstrates applications of this technology to a number of instruments and projects. For example, visualization packages such as Visual Molecular Dynamics (VMD) help make molecular modeling more interactive (Stone, Hardy, Ufimtsev, & Schulten, 2010) through the use of haptic feedback (Stone, Kohlmeyer, Vandivort, & Schulten, 2010). Researchers Balanchi and Di Leonardo report a 350-times speedup that allowed them to incorporate real-time hologram generation into an optical micro manipulation workflow (Bianchi & Di Leonardo, 2010).

A PLETHORA OF PROJECTS

The previous examples represent but a few of many research efforts reporting significant benefits from the application of GPGPU technology. Bioinformatics (Schmidt, 2010), systems biology (Dematte & Prandi, 2010), multicellular biological modeling (Christley, Lee, Dai, & Nie, 2010), chemical and protein search (Haque, Pande, & Walters, 2010; Stivala, Stuckey, & Wirth,

2010) are but a few additional broad areas. Use of a good Internet search engine can help identify research projects specific to your interests. Many projects make their software freely available.

As discussed in Chapter 8, several general-purpose libraries to facilitate scientific computation such as NVIDIA's CUBLAS and CUFFT libraries along with the MAGMA (Matrix Algebra on GPU and Multicore Architectures) hybrid CPU/GPU library are also included in the SDK or available for download for free.

SUMMARY

The wealth of CUDA-based applications that have and are being developed makes this chapter incomplete. The intention is to provide links to some (and certainly not all!) important concepts and projects. Most of the referenced projects have software that can be freely downloaded, built, and used. Learning the basics of CUDA can be done quickly. The process of maturation takes much longer and involves reading papers, examining source code, and talking with your peers.

The focus in this chapter has been on projects that can be freely downloaded from the Internet. Numerous for-sale projects are also out there. For example, AMBER is a commercial molecular dynamics application that can run on GPUs.[15] Commercial drug discovery software also runs on GPUs, such as the OpenEye scientific software.[16] Along with learning CUDA, such products show that work can be had for commercial CUDA/GPU development as well as opportunities to start your own technology company.

---

[15] http://ambermd.org/gpus/.

[16] http://eyesopen.com.

## CHAPTER 12

Application Focus on Live Streaming Video

CUDA lets developers write applications that can interact in real time with the user. This chapter modifies the source code from Chapter 9 to process and display live video streams. For those who do not have a webcam, live video can be imported from other machines via a TCP connection, or on-disk movie files can be used. Aside from being just plain fun, real-time video processing with CUDA opens the door to new markets in augmented reality, games, heads-up displays, face, and other generic vision recognition tasks. The example code in this chapter teaches the basics of isolating faces from background clutter, edge detection with a Sobel filter, and morphing live video streams in three dimensions. The teraflop computing capability of CUDA-enabled GPUs now gives everyone who can purchase a webcam and a gaming GPU the ability to write his or her own applications to interact with the computer visually. This includes teenagers, students, professors, and large research organizations around the world.

With the machine-learning techniques discussed in this book, readers have the tools required to move far beyond cookbook implementations of existing vision algorithms. It is possible to think big, as the machine-learning techniques presented in this book scale from a single GPU to the largest supercomputers in the world. However, the real value in machine learning is how it can encapsulate the information from huge (potentially terabyte) data sets into small parameterized methods that can run on the smallest cellphones and tablets.

At the end of this chapter, the reader will have a basic understanding of:

- Managing real-time data with CUDA on Windows and UNIX computers
- Face segmentation
- Sobel edge detection

- Morphing live video image data with 3D effects
- How to create data sets from live streaming data for machine learning

TOPICS IN MACHINE VISION

Machine vision is a well-established field with a large body of published material. What is new is the computational power that GPUs bring to inter-active visual computing. Recall that the first teraflop supercomputer became available to the computer science elite in December 1996. Now even inex-pensive NVIDIA gaming GPUs can be programmed to deliver greater performance.

Commodity webcams and freely available software revolutionize people's ability to experiment with and develop products based on live video streams. Instead of being limited to research laboratories, students can per-form homework assignments using live video feeds from their webcams or based on movie files provided by their teacher. Of course, this can happen between stimulating gaming sessions using the same hardware. It is likely that these same assignments can be performed on a cell phone in the near future, given the rapid pace of development of SoC (System On a Chip) technology such as the Tegra multicore chipsets for cell phones and tablets. For example, cell phones are already being used to track faces (Tresadern, Ionita, & Cootes, 2011).[1]

This chapter provides a framework for study, along with several example kernels that can be used as stepping stones to visual effects, vision recogni-tion, and augmented reality, thus bringing the world of vision research to your personal computer or laptop.

There are many resources on the Web, including a number of freely avail-able computer vision projects, a few of which include:

- **OpenVIDIA:** The OpenVIDIA package provides freely downloadable computer vision algorithms written in OpenGL, Cg, and CUDA-C.[2] The CUDA Vision workbench is a part of OpenVIDIA that provides a Windows-based application containing many common image-processing routines in a framework convenient for interactive experimentation. Additional OpenVIDIA projects include Stereo Vision, Optical Flow, and Feature Tracking algorithms.
- **GPU4Vision:** This is a project founded by the Institute for Computer Graphics and Vision, Graz University of Technology. They provide publically available CUDA-based vision algorithms.

---

[1] A video can be seen at http://personalpages.manchester.ac.uk/staff/philip.tresadern/proj_facerec.htm.
[2] http://openvidia.sourceforge.net.

- **OpenCV:** OpenCV (Open Source Computer Vision) is a library of programming functions for real-time computer vision. The software is free for both academic and commercial use. OpenCV has C++, C, Python, and other interfaces running on Windows, Linux, Android, and Mac OS X. The library boasts more than 2,500 optimized algorithms and is used around the world for applications ranging from interactive art to mine inspection, stitching maps on the Web, and advanced robotics.

3D Effects

The sinusoidal demo kernel from Chapter 9 is easily modified to provide 3D effects on live data. This kernel stores the color information in the **colorVBO** variable. Defining the mesh to be of the same size and shape as the image allows the red, green, and blue color information in each pixel of the image to be assigned to each vertex. Any changes in the height, specified in **vertexVBO**, will distort the image in 3D space. Figure 12.1 shows a grayscale version of how one frame from a live stream is distorted when mapped onto the sinusoidal surface. Images produced by this example code are in full color.

Segmentation of Flesh-colored Regions

Isolating flesh-colored regions in real time from video data plays an important role in a wide range of image-processing applications including game controllers that use a video camera, face detection, face tracking, gesture analysis, sentiment analysis, and many other human computer interaction domains.

Skin color has proven to be a useful and robust cue to use as a first step in human computer processing systems (Kakumanu, Makrogiannis, & Bourbakis, 2007; Vezhnevets, Sazonov, & Andreeva, 2003). Marián Sedláček provides an excellent description of the steps and assumptions used to detect human faces by first isolating skin-colored pixels (Sedláček, 2004).

The red, green, and blue (RGB) colors that represent the color of each pixel that is obtained from a webcam or other video source is not an appropriate representation to identify skin color because the RGB values vary so much when presented with varying lighting conditions and various ethnicities' skin colors. Instead, vision researchers have found that *chromatic colors, normalized RGB,* or "pure" colors for human skin

FIGURE 12.1
An image morphed onto a 3D sinusoidal surface.

FIGURE 12.2

Three faces isolated by skin-colored pixels.

tend to cluster tightly together regardless of skin color or luminance. Normalized pure colors—in which r, g, and b correspond to the red, green, and blue components of each pixel—are defined as "Equation 12.1: The pure red of a pixel and Equation 12.2: The pure green value of a pixel":

$$PureR = \frac{r}{r+g+b} \qquad (12.1)$$

$$PureG = \frac{g}{r+g+b} \qquad (12.2)$$

The normalized blue color is redundant because $PureR + PureG + PureB = 1$.

As Vezhnevets et al. note, "A remarkable property of this representation is that for matte surfaces, while ignoring ambient light, normalized RGB is invariant (under certain assumptions) to changes of surface orientation relative to the light source" (Vezhnevets, Sazonov, & Andreeva, 2003, p. 1). Though Sedláček notes that the region occupied by human skin in the normalized color space is an ellipse, the example code in this chapter utilizes a rectangular region to keep the example code small. Even so, this first step in the image processing pipeline works well, as shown in Figure 12.2. Consult Sedláček to see how additional steps can refine the segmentation process.[3]

Edge Detection

Finding edges is a fundamental problem in image processing, as edges define object boundaries and represent important structural properties in an image. There are many ways to perform edge detection. The Sobel method, or Sobel filter, is a gradient-based method that looks for strong changes in the first derivative of an image.

The Sobel edge detector uses a pair of 3×3 convolution masks, one estimating the gradient in the x-direction and the other in the y-direction. This edge detector maps well to CUDA, as each thread can apply the 3×3 convolution masks to its pixel and adjoining pixels in the image.

Tables 12.1 and 12.2 contain the values for the Sobel masks in each direction.

The approximate magnitude of the gradient, G, can be calculated using:

$$|G| \quad |G_x| \quad | \quad |G_y|$$

Figure 12.3 is a color inverted grayscale image created using a Sobel filter.

---

[3] http://www.cescg.org/CESCG-2004/papers/44_SedlacekMarian.pdf.

Table 12.1 Sobel Convolution Mask for the x-direction (G_x)

−1	0	+1
−2	0	+2
−1	0	+1

Table 12.2 Sobel Convolution Mask for the y-direction (G_y)

+1	+2	+1
0	0	0
−1	−2	−1

FIGURE 12.3
An image demonstrating edge detection with a Sobel filter.

FFmpeg

FFmpeg is a free, open source program that can record, convert, and stream digital audio and video in various formats. It has been described as the multimedia version of a Swiss Army knife because it can convert between most common formats. The name "FFmpeg" comes from the MPEG video standards group combined with "FF" for "fast forward." The source code can be freely downloaded from http://ffmpeg.org and compiled under most operating systems, computing platforms, and microprocessor instruction sets.

The FFmpeg command-line driven application, **ffmpeg,** is used in this chapter, as most readers will be able to download and use a working version for their system. As illustrated in Figure 12.4, **ffmpeg** is used to capture the output from a webcam or other video device and convert it to the rgb24 format, which represents each pixel in each image of the video with a separate red, green, and blue 8-bit value. The **testLive** example program reads the data stream from a TCP socket and writes it to a buffer on the GPU for use with CUDA. Figure 12.4 shows representative images of **testLive** morphing a video

FIGURE 12.4

Video data flow.

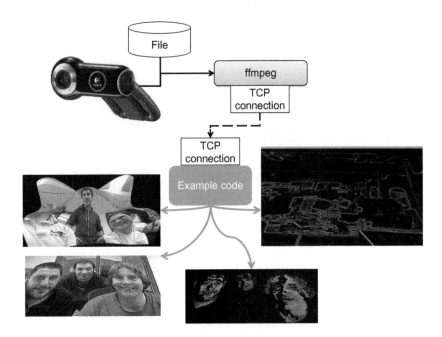

stream in 3D, a flat image displayed in a 3D coordinate system, segregation of faces from the background, and real-time edge detection with a Sobel filter.

The benefit of using the **ffmpeg** application is that no programming is required to convert the video data that can be sent to the GPU. The disadvantage is that the conversion from a compressed format to rgb24 greatly expands the amount of data sent over the TCP socket. For this reason, it is recommended that the conversion to rgb24 happen on the system containing the GPU. A more efficient implementation would use the FFmpeg libraries to directly read the compressed video stream and convert it to rgb24 within the example source code. In this way, the transport of large amounts of rgb24 data over a socket would be avoided.

Those who need to stream data from a remote webcam should:

- Modify the example to read and perform the video conversion inside the application.
- Use a TCP relay program to read the compressed video stream from the remote site and pass it to an instance of **ffmpeg** running on the system that contains the GPU. One option is socat (SOcket CAT), which is a freely downloadable general-purpose relay application that runs on most operating systems.

The following bash scripts demonstrate how to write a 640 × 480 stream of rgb24 images to port 32000 on *localhost*. Localhost is the name of the loopback device used by applications that need to communicate with each other on the same computer. The loopback device acts as an Ethernet interface that does not transmit information over a TCP device. Note that the **ffmpeg** command-line interface is evolving over time, so these scripts might need to be modified at a later date.

- Stream from a Linux webcam (Example 12.1, "Linux Webcam Capture"):

Example 12.1

```
FFMPEG=ffmpeg
DEVICE="-f video4linux2 -i /dev/video0"
PIX="-f rawvideo -pix_fmt rgb24"
SIZE="-s 640x480"

$FFMPEG -an -r 50 $SIZE $DEVICE $PIX tcp:localhost:32000
```

- Stream from Windows webcam (Example 12.2, "Windows Webcam Capture"):

Example 12.2

```
../ffmpeg-git-39dbe9b-win32-static/bin/ffmpeg.exe -r 25 -f vfwcap
-i 0 -f rawvideo -pix_fmt rgb24 -s 640x480 tcp:localhost:32000
```

- Stream from file (Example 12.3, "Stream from File"):

Example 12.3

```
FFMPEG=ffmpeg
s#can be any file name or format: myfile.avi, myfile.3gp, …
FILE="myfile.mpeg"
PIX="-f rawvideo -pix_fmt rgb24"
SIZE="-s 640x480"

$FFMPEG -i $FILE $SIZE $PIX tcp:localhost:32000
```

Streaming from a file will run at the fastest rate that **ffmpeg** can convert the frames, which will likely be much faster than real-time.

TCP SERVER

The following code implements a simple, asynchronous TCP server that:

- Listens on a port specified in the variable **port**
- Accepts a client when one attempts to connect

- Reads **datasize** bytes of data into an array when the client sends data to this server
- Shuts down the connection when the client dies or there is a socket error and waits for another client connection

Any program can provide the rgb24 data, but it is assumed in this example that **ffmpeg** will supply the data.

This server is asynchronous, meaning that it uses the **select()** call to determine whether there is a client waiting to connect or if there is data to be read. If **select()** times out, then control returns to the calling routine, which can perform additional work such as animating images on the screen, changing colors, or other visual effects. This process is discussed in more detail in the rest of this section and is illustrated in Figure 12.5.

The variable **timeout** defines how long **select()** will spend waiting for data to arrive on a socket. The default value is 100 microseconds, which was chosen to balance the amount of CPU time consumed by the application program versus the number of iterations of the graphic pipeline per frame of real-time data.

More information on socket programming can be found on the Internet or in excellent books such as *Advanced Programming in the UNIX Environment* (Stevens, 2005).

FIGURE 12.5

Timeline of asynchronous loads and kernel pipeline.

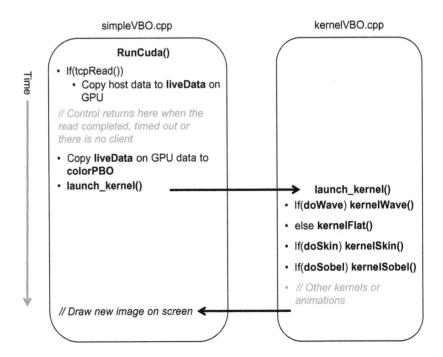

The first part of this file, *tcpserver.cpp*, specifies the necessary include files and variables. The **initTCPserver()** method binds a port that will be used to listen for client connections. It was designed to be added to the **initCuda()** method in *simpleVBO.cu*. See Example 12.4, "Part 1 of *tcpserver.cpp*":

Example 12.4

```
#include <sys/socket.h>
#include <netinet/in.h>
#include <stdio.h>
#include <stdlib.h>
#include <string.h>
#include <unistd.h>
#include <fcntl.h>
#include <limits.h>

int listenfd, connfd=0;
struct sockaddr_in servaddr,cliaddr;
socklen_t clilen;
struct timeval timeout = {0,100};

void initTCPserver(int port)
{
  listenfd=socket(AF_INET,SOCK_STREAM,0);

  bzero(&servaddr,sizeof(servaddr));
  servaddr.sin_family = AF_INET;
  servaddr.sin_addr.s_addr=htonl(INADDR_ANY);
  servaddr.sin_port=htons(32000);
  bind(listenfd,(struct sockaddr *)&servaddr,sizeof(servaddr));
}
```

The **tcpRead()** method asynchronously connects to one client at a time or performs a blocking read of **datasize** bytes of data when available. If no client or client data appears before **select()** times out, then control returns to the calling method. The debugging **fprintf()** statements were kept to help in understanding this code. If desired, the **fprintf()** statements can be uncommented to show how this code works in practice. It is recommended that the timeout should be greatly increased if the "read timeout" statement is uncommented. See Example 12.5, "Part 2 of *tcpserver.cpp*":

Example 12.5

```
int tcpRead(char *data, int datasize)
{
  int n;
  fd_set dataReady;
```

```
if(!connfd) { // there is no client: listen until timeout or accept
  FD_ZERO(&dataReady);
  FD_SET(listenfd,&dataReady);
  if(select(listenfd+1, &dataReady, NULL,NULL, &timeout) == -1) {
    fprintf(stderr,"listen select failed!\n"); exit(1);
  }
  listen(listenfd,1); // listen for one connection at a time

  clilen=sizeof(cliaddr);
  if(FD_ISSET(listenfd, &dataReady)) {
    fprintf(stderr,"accepting a client!\n");
    connfd = accept(listenfd,(struct sockaddr *)&cliaddr,&clilen);
  } else {
    //fprintf(stderr,"no client!\n");
    return(0); // no client so no work
  }
}

if(!connfd) return(0);

// read the data
FD_ZERO(&dataReady);
FD_SET(connfd,&dataReady);
if(select(connfd+1, &dataReady, NULL,NULL, &timeout) == -1) {
  fprintf(stderr,"data select failed!\n"); exit(1);
}

if(FD_ISSET(connfd, &dataReady)) {
  FD_CLR(connfd, &dataReady);
  for(n=0; n < datasize;) {
    int size = ((datasize-n) > SSIZE_MAX)?SSIZE_MAX:(datasize-n);
    int ret = read(connfd, data+n, size);
    if(ret <= 0) break; // error
    n += ret;
  }
  if(n < datasize) {
    fprintf(stderr,"Incomplete read %d bytes %d\n", n, datasize);
    perror("Read failure!");
    close(connfd);
    connfd=0;
    return(0);
  }
  return(1);
} else {
  //fprintf(stderr, "read timeout\n");
}
return(0);
}
```

LIVE STREAM APPLICATION

The live stream application queues CUDA kernels to perform image analysis and animated effects. Which kernels get queued depends on user input. As can be seen in Figure 12.5, new data will be transferred across the PCIe bus to the **liveData** buffer on the GPU only when **tcpRead()** returns a nonzero result, indicating a new frame of data has been read. As discussed previously, **tcpRead()** can return zero as a result of a timeout, in which case no new data needs to be transferred.

Because the kernel pipeline can modify the contents of **colorVBO**, the original video data is copied from **liveData** prior to the start of the pipeline. The copy from **liveData** to **colorVBO** is very fast because it moves data only within the GPU. The **launch_kernel()** method is then called to queue the various kernels depending on the flags set by user keystrokes in the keyboard callback.

The timeout from **tcpRead()** means that the **launch_kernel()** pipeline can be called many times between reads of new images from the live stream. Animated kernels such as **kernelWave()**, which produces the animated wave effect, depend on this asynchronous behavior to create their visual effects. Though not used in this example, the **animTime** variable can be used to control the speed and behavior of the animations.

kernelWave(): An Animated Kernel

The **kernelWave()** method implements the animated sinusoidal 3D surface discussed in Chapter 9. In this kernel (Example 12.6), each pixel in the image is considered as the color of a vertex in a 3D mesh. These vertex colors are held in **colorVBO** for the current frame in the live image. Rendering with triangles generates a smoothly colored surface, regardless of how the image is resized. For demonstration purposes, the surface can also be rendered with lines or dots depending on the user's input via the keyboard.

Example 12.6

```
// live stream kernel (Rob Farber)
// Simple kernel to modify vertex positions in sine wave pattern
__global__ void kernelWave(float4* pos, uchar4 *colorPos,
                           unsigned int width, unsigned int height, float
                           time)
{
    unsigned int x = blockIdx.x*blockDim.x + threadIdx.x;
    unsigned int y = blockIdx.y*blockDim.y + threadIdx.y;

    // calculate uv coordinates
    float u = x / (float) width;
```

```
    float v = y / (float) height;
    u = u*2.0f - 1.0f;
    v = v*2.0f - 1.0f;

    // calculate simple sine wave pattern
    float freq = 4.0f;
    float w = sinf(u*freq + time) * cosf(v*freq + time) * 0.5f;

    // write output vertex
    pos[y*width+x] = make_float4(u, w, v, 1.0f);
}
```

kernelFlat(): Render the Image on a Flat Surface

kernelFlat() simply specifies a flat surface for rendering. This allows viewing of other rendering effects without the distraction of the animated sinusoidal surface. See Example 12.7, "Part 2 of *kernelVBO.cu*":

Example 12.7

```
__global__ void kernelFlat(float4* pos, uchar4 *colorPos,
            unsigned int width, unsigned int height)
{
  unsigned int x = blockIdx.x*blockDim.x + threadIdx.x;
  unsigned int y = blockIdx.y*blockDim.y + threadIdx.y;

  // calculate uv coordinates
  float u = x / (float) width;
  float v = y / (float) height;
  u = u*2.0f - 1.0f;
  v = v*2.0f - 1.0f;

  // write output vertex
  pos[y*width+x] = make_float4(u, 1.f, v, 1.0f);
}
```

kernelSkin(): Keep Only Flesh-colored Regions

This kernel simply calculates the normalized red (**PureR**) and green (**PureG**) values for each pixel in the image. The original RGB colors are preserved if these values fall within the rectangle of flesh-colored tones. Otherwise, they are set to black. See Example 12.8, "Part 3 of *kernelVBO.cu*"

Example 12.8

```
__global__ void kernelSkin(float4* pos, uchar4 *colorPos,
                unsigned int width, unsigned int height,
                int lowPureG, int highPureG,
                int lowPureR, int highPureR)
```

```
{
  unsigned int x = blockIdx.x*blockDim.x + threadIdx.x;
  unsigned int y = blockIdx.y*blockDim.y + threadIdx.y;
  int r = colorPos[y*width+x].x;
  int g = colorPos[y*width+x].y;
  int b = colorPos[y*width+x].z;
  int pureR = 255*( ((float)r)/(r+g+b));
  int pureG = 255*( ((float)g)/(r+g+b));
  if( !( (pureG > lowPureG) && (pureG < highPureG)
      && (pureR > lowPureR) && (pureR < highPureR) ) )
    colorPos[y*width+x] = make_uchar4(0,0,0,0);
}
```

kernelSobel(): A Simple Sobel Edge Detection Filter

The kernel in Example 12.9, "Part 4 of *kernelVBO.cu*," simply applies a Sobel
edge detection filter as discussed at the beginning of this chapter:

Example 12.9

```
__device__ unsigned char gray(const uchar4 &pix)
{
  // convert to 8-bit grayscale
  return( .3f * pix.x + 0.59f * pix.y + 0.11f * pix.z);
}
__global__ void kernelSobel(float4 *pos, uchar4 *colorPos, uchar4
*newPix,
                            unsigned int width, unsigned int height)
{
  unsigned int x = blockIdx.x*blockDim.x + threadIdx.x;
  unsigned int y = blockIdx.y*blockDim.y + threadIdx.y;

  const int sobelv[3][3] = { {-1,-2,-1},{0,0,0},{1,2,1}};
  const int sobelh[3][3] = { {-1,0,1},{-2,0,2},{-1,0,1}};

  int sumh=0, sumv=0;
  if( (x > 1) && x < (width-1) && (y > 1) && y < (height-1)) {
    for(int l= -1; l < 2; l++) {
      for(int k= -1; k < 2; k++) {
        register int g = gray(colorPos[(y+k)*width+x+l]);
        sumh += sobelh[k+1][l+1] * g;
        sumv += sobelv[k+1][l+1] * g;
      }
    }
    unsigned char p = abs(sumh/8)+ abs(sumv/8);
    newPix[y*width+x] = make_uchar4(0,p,p,p);
```

```
  } else {
    newPix[y*width+x] = make_uchar4(0,0,0,0);
  }
}
```

The launch_kernel() Method

As illustrated in Figure 12.5, the **launch_kernel()** method queues kernel calls to perform the various transformation requested by the user. This method was written for clarity and not for flexibility. For example, the use of a static pointer to **newPix** is correct but not necessarily good coding practice. It was kept in this example code to demonstrate how the reader can allocate scratch space for his or her own methods. Once the Sobel filter completes, the scratch data is copied via a fast device-to-device transfer into the **colorVBO**. See Example 12.10, "Part 5 of *kernelVBO.cu*":

Example 12.10

```
extern int PureR[2], PureG[2], doWave, doSkin,doSobel;
// Wrapper for the __global__ call that sets up the kernel call
extern "C" void launch_kernel(float4* pos, uchar4* colorPos,
                              unsigned int mesh_width, unsigned int
                              mesh_height,float time)
{
  // execute the kernel
  dim3 block(8, 8, 1);
  dim3 grid(mesh_width / block.x, mesh_height / block.y, 1);
  if(doWave)
    kernelWave<<< grid, block>>>(pos, colorPos, mesh_width,
    mesh_height, time);
  else
    kernelFlat<<< grid, block>>>(pos, colorPos, mesh_width,
    mesh_height);

  if(doSkin)
    kernelSkin<<< grid, block>>>(pos, colorPos, mesh_width,
    mesh_height,
            PureG[0], PureG[1],
            PureR[0], PureR[1]);
  if(doSobel) {
    static uchar4 *newPix=NULL;
    if(!newPix)
      cudaMalloc(&newPix, sizeof(uchar4)*mesh_width*mesh_height);
```

```
    kernelSobel<<< grid, block>>>(pos, colorPos, newPix,
                        mesh_width, mesh_height);
    cudaMemcpy(colorPos, newPix, sizeof(uchar4)*mesh_width
    *mesh_height,
        cudaMemcpyDeviceToDevice);
  }
}
```

THE simpleVBO.cpp FILE

Only minor changes were made to the *simpleVBO.cpp* file from Chapter 9, but these changes occur in several of the methods. To minimize confusion, the entire file is included at the end of this chapter with the changes highlighted.

These changes include:

- The definition of C-preprocessor variables **MESH_WIDTH** and **MESH_HEIGHT**. These variables should be used at compile time to match the size of the mesh with the image width and height from the **ffmpeg**. By default, the mesh size is set to 640 × 480 pixels, which corresponds to the size specified in the **ffmpeg** command-line scripts at the beginning of this chapter.
- A buffer on the GPU, **liveData**, is created to contain the current frame of video data. By convention, this data is not modified by the GPU between frame loads from the host.
- The **tcpRead()** method is called. As can be seen in the code in the **runCuda()** method later in this chapter, **tcpRead()** has new data that needs to be transferred to the GPU when a nonzero value is returned. The **runCuda()** method then initializes the graphics pipeline by copying the video data to **colorVBO()**.

THE callbacksVBO.cpp FILE

Only minor changes were made to the *callbacks.cpp* file from Chapter 9; a few new variables needed to be defined. Most of the changes occur in the keyboard callback method **keyboard()**. Table 12.3 shows the valid keystrokes.

As mentioned in the discussion on segmentation, a rectangular region is used in the **kernelSkin()** method to identify human skin colors. The actual region occupied by human skin colors is an ellipse in the pure color space. A rectangular region was used because it kept the **kernelSkin()** method small, but with an admitted loss of fidelity. The use of a rectangle does

Table 12.3 Keyboard Commands for testLive

Key	Action
Q	Quit the application
Esc	Quit the application
D	Toggle draw mode
d	Toggle draw mode
S	Slow down rendering by 100 microseconds per frame
s	Speed rendering by 100 microseconds per frame
z	Toggle the 3D sinusoidal animation (on) or make the surface flat (off)
c	Toggle Sobel filtering
x	Toggle segmentation of flesh-colored regions
R	Increase the PureR upper boundary
r	Decrease the PureR upper boundary
E	Increase the PureR lower boundary
e	Decrease the PureR lower boundary
G	Increase the PureG upper boundary
g	Decrease the PureG upper boundary
F	Increase the PureG lower boundary
f	Decrease the PureG lower boundary

allow the user to change the size of the rectangle with a few keystrokes to explore the effect of filtering in the color space and to see the effects of different environments and lighting conditions.

Example 12.11, "*callbacksVBO.cpp*," is the modified version of the Chapter 9 *callbacksVBO.cpp* file:

Example 12.11

```
#include <GL/glew.h>
#include <cutil_inline.h>
#include <cutil_gl_inline.h>
#include <cuda_gl_interop.h>
#include <rendercheck_gl.h>

// The user must create the following routines:
void initCuda(int argc, char** argv);
void runCuda();
void renderCuda(int);

// Callback variables
extern float animTime;
extern int sleepTime, sleepInc;
int drawMode=GL_TRIANGLE_FAN; // the default draw mode
int mouse_old_x, mouse_old_y;
```

```cpp
int mouse_buttons = 0;
float rotate_x = 0.0, rotate_y = 0.0;
float translate_z = -3.0;

// some initial values for face segmentation
int PureG[2]={62,89}, PureR[2]={112,145};
int doWave=1, doSkin=0, doSobel=0;

// GLUT callbacks display, keyboard, mouse
void display()
{
  glClear(GL_COLOR_BUFFER_BIT | GL_DEPTH_BUFFER_BIT);

  // set view matrix
  glMatrixMode(GL_MODELVIEW);
  glLoadIdentity();
  glTranslatef(0.0, 0.0, translate_z);
  glRotatef(rotate_x, 1.0, 0.0, 0.0);
  glRotatef(rotate_y, 0.0, 1.0, 0.0);

  runCuda(); // run CUDA kernel to generate vertex positions

  renderCuda(drawMode); // render the data

  glutSwapBuffers();
  glutPostRedisplay();

  // slow the rendering when the GPU is too fast.
  if(sleepTime) usleep(sleepTime);
  animTime += 0.01;
}

void keyboard(unsigned char key, int x, int y)
{
  switch(key) {
  case('q') : case(27) : // exit
    exit(0);
    break;
  case 'd': case 'D': // Drawmode
    switch(drawMode) {
    case GL_POINTS: drawMode = GL_LINE_STRIP; break;
    case GL_LINE_STRIP: drawMode = GL_TRIANGLE_FAN; break;
    default: drawMode=GL_POINTS;
    } break;
  case 'S': // Slow the simulation down
    sleepTime += sleepInc;
    break;
  case 's': // Speed the simulation up
    sleepTime = (sleepTime > 0)?sleepTime -= sleepInc:0;
    break;
```

```
  case 'z': doWave = (doWave > 0)?0:1; break;
  case 'x': doSkin = (doSkin > 0)?0:1; break;
  case 'c': doSobel = (doSobel > 0)?0:1; break;
  case 'R': PureR[1]++; if(PureR[1] > 255) PureR[1]=255; break;
  case 'r': PureR[1]--; if(PureR[1] <= PureR[0]) PureR[1]++; break;
  case 'E': PureR[0]++; if(PureR[0] >= PureR[1]) PureR[0]-; break;
  case 'e': PureR[0]--; if(PureR[0] <= 0 ) PureR[0]=0; break;
  case 'G': PureG[1]++; if(PureG[1] > 255) PureG[1]=255; break;
  case 'g': PureG[1]--; if(PureG[1] <= PureG[0]) PureG[1]++; break;
  case 'F': PureG[0]++; if(PureG[0] >= PureG[1]) PureG[0]-; break;
  case 'f': PureG[0]--; if(PureG[0] <= 0 ) PureG[0]=0; break;
  }
  fprintf(stderr,"PureG[0] %d PureG[1] %d PureR[0] %d PureR[1] %d\n",
          PureG[0],PureG[1],PureR[0],PureR[1]);
  glutPostRedisplay();
}

void mouse(int button, int state, int x, int y)
{
  if (state == GLUT_DOWN) {
    mouse_buttons |= 1<<button;
  } else if (state == GLUT_UP) {
    mouse_buttons = 0;
  }

  mouse_old_x = x;
  mouse_old_y = y;
  glutPostRedisplay();
}

void motion(int x, int y)
{
  float dx, dy;
  dx = x - mouse_old_x;
  dy = y - mouse_old_y;

  if (mouse_buttons & 1) {
    rotate_x += dy * 0.2;
    rotate_y += dx * 0.2;
  } else if (mouse_buttons & 4) {
    translate_z += dy * 0.01;
  }
rotate_x = (rotate_x < -60.)?-60.:(rotate_x > 60.)?60:rotate_x;
rotate_y = (rotate_y < -60.)?-60.:(rotate_y > 60.)?60:rotate_y;

  mouse_old_x = x;
  mouse_old_y = y;
}
```

BUILDING AND RUNNING THE CODE

The **testLive** application is built in the same fashion as the examples in Chapter 9. Example 12.12, "A Script to Build *testLive*," is the bash build script under Linux:

Example 12.12

```
#/bin/bash
DIR=livestream
SDK_PATH … /cuda/4.0
SDK_LIB0=$SDK_PATH/C/lib
SDK_LIB1= … /4.0/CUDALibraries/common/lib/linux
echo $SDK_PATH
nvcc -arch=sm_20 -O3 -L $SDK_LIB0 -L $SDK_LIB1 -I $SDK_PATH/C/common/
inc simpleGLmain.cpp simpleVBO.cpp $DIR/callbacksVBO.cpp $DIR/
kernelVBO.cu tcpserver.cpp -lglut -lGLEW_x86_64 -lGLU -lcutil_x86_64
-o testLive
```

Running the **testLive** application is straightforward:

1. Start the *testLive* executable in one window. The visualization window will appear on your screen.
2. In a second window, run the script that will send video data to the port 32000 on localhost. Example scripts were provided at the beginning of this chapter for UNIX and for Windows and to convert a video file and send it to the **testLive** example.

THE FUTURE

The three examples in this chapter demonstrate real-time image processing on CUDA. However, they are but a starting point for further experimentation and research.

Machine Learning

A challenge that remains after image segmentation is identification.

Simple but valuable forms of identification can be coded as rules. For example, a game developer can look for two small flesh-colored blobs (hands) that are near a large flesh-colored blob (a face). Height differences between the hands can be used to change the angle of a simulated aircraft to make it bank and turn. Similarly, the distance between the hands can control an action such as zooming into or out of an image.

Many other tasks are not as easy to code as rules or logic in a CUDA kernel. For example, people can easily identify faces in a picture. In these cases, the machine-learning techniques presented in Chapters 2 and 3 can "learn" the algorithm for the developer using the GPU "supercomputer." Examples abound in the literature on the use of machine learning to segment images using skin-colored pixels under general lighting conditions (Kakumanu, Makrogiannis, & Bourbakis, 2007), faces (Mitchell, 1997), and other objects. Hinton notes that machine-learning techniques like transforming autoencoders offer a better alternative than rules-based systems (Hinton, Krizhevesky, & Want, 2011). With a webcam, readers can collect their own images that can be edited and sorted into "yes" and "no" data sets to train a classifier. Both the literature and the Internet contain many detailed studies about how to use such data sets to address many problems in vision recognition.

The Connectome

The Harvard Connectome (http://cbs.fas.harvard.edu) is a project that combines GPGPU computational ability with some excellent robotic technology in an effort that will create 3D wiring diagrams of the brains of various model animals such as the cat and lab mouse. This project exemplifies early recognition of the potential inherent in GPU technology. Data from this project might prove to be the basis for seminal and disruptive scientific research. Instead of guessing, vision researchers and neurologists will finally have a Galilean first-opportunity ability to see, study, and model cortical networks using extraordinarily detailed data created by the Connectome project.

In a 2009 paper, "The Cat Is Out of the Bag: Cortical Simulations with 10^9 Neurons, 10^{13} Synapses," researchers demonstrated that they were able to effectively model cortical networks at an unprecedented scale. In other words, these scientists feel they demonstrated sufficient computational capability to model the entire cat brain:

> The simulations, which incorporate phenomenological spiking neurons, individual learning synapses, axonal delays, and dynamic synaptic channels, exceed the scale of the cat cortex, marking the dawn of a new era in the scale of cortical simulations. (Ananthanarayanan, Esser, Simon, & Modha, 2009, p. 1)

It is clear that massively parallel computational technology will open the door to detailed vision models that will allow neural research to unravel the mystery of how nature processes vision, audio, and potentially memory and thought in the brain. GPUs provide sufficient computational capability that even individuals and small research organizations have the ability to contribute to these efforts, if in no other aspect than to train the people who will make the discoveries.

SUMMARY

CUDA is an enabling technology. As always, the power of the technology resides in the individual who uses it to solve problems. CUDA made it possible to provide working examples in the limited pages of this book to teach a range of techniques starting with the simple program in Chapter 1 that filled a vector in parallel with sequential integers, to massively parallel mappings for machine learning, and finally to the example in this chapter that performs real-time video processing. It is hoped that these examples have taught you how to use the simplicity and power of CUDA to express your thoughts concisely and clearly in software that can run on massively parallel hardware. Coupled with scalability and the teraflop floating-point capability provided by even budget GPUs, CUDA-literate programmers can leverage the power of their minds and GPU technology to do wonderful things in the world.

LISTING FOR simpleVBO.cpp

```cpp
//simpleVBO (Rob Farber)
#include <GL/glew.h>
#include <GL/gl.h>
#include <GL/glext.h>
#include <cutil_inline.h>
#include <cutil_gl_inline.h>
#include <cuda_gl_interop.h>
#include <rendercheck_gl.h>

extern float animTime;

/////////////////////////////////////////////////////////////////////
// VBO specific code
#include <cutil_inline.h>

#ifndef MESH_WIDTH
#define MESH_WIDTH 640
#endif
#ifndef MESH_HEIGHT
#define MESH_HEIGHT 480
#endif
// constants
const unsigned int mesh_width = MESH_WIDTH;
const unsigned int mesh_height = MESH_HEIGHT;
const unsigned int RestartIndex = 0xffffffff;

typedef struct {
  GLuint vbo;
  GLuint typeSize;
```

```
    struct cudaGraphicsResource *cudaResource;
} mappedBuffer_t;

extern "C"
void launch_kernel(float4* pos, uchar4* posColor,
                   unsigned int mesh_width, unsigned int mesh_height,
                   float time);

// vbo variables
mappedBuffer_t vertexVBO = {NULL, sizeof(float4), NULL};
mappedBuffer_t colorVBO = {NULL, sizeof(uchar4), NULL};
GLuint* qIndices=NULL; // index values for primitive restart
int qIndexSize=0;
uchar4 *liveData;

//////////////////////////////////////////////////////////////////
//! Create VBO
//////////////////////////////////////////////////////////////////
void createVBO(mappedBuffer_t* mbuf)
{
  // create buffer object
  glGenBuffers(1, &(mbuf->vbo) );
  glBindBuffer(GL_ARRAY_BUFFER, mbuf->vbo);

  // initialize buffer object
  unsigned int size = mesh_width * mesh_height * mbuf->typeSize;
  glBufferData(GL_ARRAY_BUFFER, size, 0, GL_DYNAMIC_DRAW);

  glBindBuffer(GL_ARRAY_BUFFER, 0);

  cudaGraphicsGLRegisterBuffer( &(mbuf->cudaResource), mbuf->vbo,
                                cudaGraphicsMapFlagsNone );
}

//////////////////////////////////////////////////////////////////
//! Delete VBO
//////////////////////////////////////////////////////////////////
void deleteVBO(mappedBuffer_t* mbuf)
{
  glBindBuffer(1, mbuf->vbo );
  glDeleteBuffers(1, &(mbuf->vbo) );

  cudaGraphicsUnregisterResource( mbuf->cudaResource );
  mbuf->cudaResource = NULL;
  mbuf->vbo = NULL;
}

void cleanupCuda()
{
  if(qIndices) free(qIndices);
  deleteVBO(&vertexVBO);
```

```
   deleteVBO(&colorVBO);
   if(liveData) free(liveData);
}

////////////////////////////
// Add the tcp info needed for the live stream
//////////////////////////////////////////////////////////////////
#define TCP_PORT 32000
typedef struct {
    unsigned char r;
    unsigned char g;
    unsigned char b;
} rgb24_t;

uchar4* argbData;
int argbDataSize;
extern int tcpRead(char*, int);
void initTCPserver(int);

//////////////////////////////////////////////////////////////////
//! Run the Cuda part of the computation
//////////////////////////////////////////////////////////////////
void runCuda()
{
    // map OpenGL buffer object for writing from CUDA
    float4 *dptr;
    uchar4 *cptr;
    uint *iptr;
    size_t start;
    cudaGraphicsMapResources( 1, &vertexVBO.cudaResource, NULL );
    cudaGraphicsResourceGetMappedPointer( ( void ** )&dptr, &start,
                                  vertexVBO.cudaResource );
    cudaGraphicsMapResources( 1, &colorVBO.cudaResource, NULL );
    cudaGraphicsResourceGetMappedPointer( ( void ** )&cptr, &start,
                                  colorVBO.cudaResource );

    rgb24_t data[mesh_width*mesh_height];
    if(tcpRead((char*)data, mesh_width*mesh_height*sizeof(rgb24_t)
    )) {
      // have data
#pragma omp parallel for
      for(int i=0; i < mesh_width*mesh_height; i++) {
        argbData[i].w=0;
        argbData[i].x=data[i].r;
        argbData[i].y=data[i].g;
        argbData[i].z=data[i].b;
      }
      cudaMemcpy(liveData, argbData, argbDataSize, cudaMemcpyHostTo
      Device);
```

```
      }

      //copy the GPU-side buffer to the colorVBO
      cudaMemcpy(cptr, liveData, argbDataSize, cudaMemcpyDeviceTo
      Device);

      // execute the kernel
      launch_kernel(dptr, cptr, mesh_width, mesh_height, animTime);

      // unmap buffer object
      cudaGraphicsUnmapResources( 1, &vertexVBO.cudaResource, NULL );
      cudaGraphicsUnmapResources( 1, &colorVBO.cudaResource, NULL );
}

void initCuda(int argc, char** argv)
{
  // First initialize OpenGL context, so we can properly set the GL
  // for CUDA. NVIDIA notes this is necessary in order to achieve
  // optimal performance with OpenGL/CUDA interop. use command-line
  // specified CUDA device, otherwise use device with highest Gflops/s
  if( cutCheckCmdLineFlag(argc, (const char**)argv, "device") ) {
    cutilGLDeviceInit(argc, argv);
  } else {
    cudaGLSetGLDevice( cutGetMaxGflopsDeviceId() );
  }

  createVBO(&vertexVBO);
  createVBO(&colorVBO);

  // allocate and assign trianglefan indicies
  qIndexSize = 5*(mesh_height-1)*(mesh_width-1);
  qIndices = (GLuint *) malloc(qIndexSize*sizeof(GLint));
  int index=0;
  for(int i=1; i < mesh_height; i++) {
    for(int j=1; j < mesh_width; j++) {
      qIndices[index++] = (i)*mesh_width + j;
      qIndices[index++] = (i)*mesh_width + j-1;
      qIndices[index++] = (i-1)*mesh_width + j-1;
      qIndices[index++] = (i-1)*mesh_width + j;
      qIndices[index++] = RestartIndex;
    }
  }

  cudaMalloc((void**)&liveData,sizeof(uchar4)
  *mesh_width*mesh_height);

  // make certain the VBO gets cleaned up on program exit
  atexit(cleanupCuda);

  // setup TCP context for live stream
  argbDataSize = sizeof(uchar4)*mesh_width*mesh_height;
```

```
  cudaHostAlloc((void**) &argbData, argbDataSize, cudaHostAllocPor
  table );
  initTCPserver(TCP_PORT);

  runCuda();
}

void renderCuda(int drawMode)
{
  glBindBuffer(GL_ARRAY_BUFFER, vertexVBO.vbo);
  glVertexPointer(4, GL_FLOAT, 0, 0);
  glEnableClientState(GL_VERTEX_ARRAY);

  glBindBuffer(GL_ARRAY_BUFFER, colorVBO.vbo);
  glColorPointer(4, GL_UNSIGNED_BYTE, 0, 0);
  glEnableClientState(GL_COLOR_ARRAY);

  switch(drawMode) {
  case GL_LINE_STRIP:
    for(int i=0 ; i < mesh_width*mesh_height; i+= mesh_width)
      glDrawArrays(GL_LINE_STRIP, i, mesh_width);
    break;
  case GL_TRIANGLE_FAN: {
    glPrimitiveRestartIndexNV(RestartIndex);
    glEnableClientState(GL_PRIMITIVE_RESTART_NV);
    glDrawElements(GL_TRIANGLE_FAN, qIndexSize, GL_UNSIGNED_INT,
    qIndices);
    glDisableClientState(GL_PRIMITIVE_RESTART_NV);
  } break;
  default:
    glDrawArrays(GL_POINTS, 0, mesh_width * mesh_height);
    break;
  }

  glDisableClientState(GL_VERTEX_ARRAY);
  glDisableClientState(GL_COLOR_ARRAY);
}
```

Works Cited

Anandakrishnan, R., Scogland, T. R., Fenley, A. T., Gordon, J. C., Feng, W.-c., & Onufriev, A. V. (2010). Accelerating electrostatic surface potential calculation with multi-scale approximation on graphics processing units. *Journal of Molecular Graphics and Modelling, 28*(8), 904–910.

Ananthanarayanan, R., Esser, S. K., Simon, H. D., & Modha, D. S. (2009). The cat is out of the bag: cortical simulations with 10^9 neurons, 10^13 synapses. *Supercomputing 2009.*

Anderson, J. A., Lorenz, C. D., & Travesset, A. (2008). General purpose molecular dynamics simulations fully implemented on graphics processing units. *227*(10), 5342–5359.

Andrieu, C., de Freitas, N., Doucet, A., & Jordan, M. I. (2003). An Introduction to MCMC for Machine Learning. In *Machine Learning, Volume 50* (pp. 5–43). The Netherlands: Kluwer Academic Publishers.

Beichel, I., & Sullivan, F. (2000). The Metropolis algorithm. *Computing in Science & Engineering,* 65–69.

Bell, N., & Garland, M. (2009). Implementing sparse matrix-vector multiplication on throughput-oriented processors Networking, Storage and Analysis. *Proceeding SC '09 Proceedings of the Conference on High Performance Computing.* New York, NY: ACM.

Bianchi, S., & Di Leonardo, R. (2010). Real-time optical micro-manipulation using optimized holograms generated on the GPU. *Computer Physics Communications, 181*(8), 1444–1448.

BigDFT. (n.d.). Retrieved from Institut Nanosciences et Cryogénie: http://inac.cea.fr/L_Sim/BigDFT/.

Botelho, S. S., Lautenschlger, W., de Figueiredo, M. B., Centeno, T. M., & Mata, M. M. (2005). Dimensional Reduction of Large Image Datasets Using Non-linear Principal Components. In M. Gallagher, J. Hogan, & F. Maire (Eds.), *Intelligent Data Engineering and Automated Learning - IDEAL 2005* (Vol. 3578, pp. 31–40). Springer Berlin/Heidelberg.

Botelho, S. S., Lautenschlger, W., de, M. B., Centeno, T. M., & Mata, M. M. (2005). Dimensional Reduction of Large Image Datasets Using Non-linear Principal Components. In M. Gallagher, J. Hogan, & F. Maire (Eds.), *Intelligent Data Engineering and Automated Learning - IDEAL 2005* (Vol. 3578, pp. 31–40). Springer Berlin/Heidelberg.

Brandes, U. (2001). Drawing Graphs. In M. Kaufmann, & D. Wagner, *Drawing on physical analogies* (pp. 71–86). Springer-Verlag.

Cao, W., Yao, L., Li, Z., Wang, Y., & Wang, Z. (2010). Implementing Sparse Matrix-Vector multiplication using CUDA based on a hybrid sparse matrix format. *Computer Application and System Modeling (ICCASM)* (pp. V11-161–V11-165). Taiyuan: IEEE.

Carpenter, A. (2011). *http://patternsonascreen.net/cuSVM.html.* Retrieved July 2011, from http://patternsonascreen.net/cuSVM.html: http://patternsonascreen.net/cuSVM.html.

Catanzaro, B., Sundaram, N., & Keutzer, K. (2008). Fast support vector machine training and classification on graphics processors. *Proceedings of the 25th international conference on Machine learning.* New York: ACM.

Che, S., Boyer, M., Meng, J., Tarjan, D., Sheaffer, J., Lee, S., et al. (2009). Rodinia: A Benchmark Suite for Heterogeneous Computing. *Proceedings of the IEEE International Symposium on Workload Characterization (IISWC)* (pp. 44–54). IEEE.

Che, S., Sheaffer, J., Boyer, M., Szafaryn, L. G., Szafaryn, L., Wang, L., et al. (2010). A Characterization of the Rodinia Benchmark Suite with Comparison to Contemporary. *IEEE International Symposium on Workload.* IEEE.

Chen, C., Schmidt, B., Weiguo, L., & Müller-Wittig, W. (2008). GPU-MEME: Using Graphics Hardware to Accelerate Motif Finding in DNA Sequences. In M. Chetty, A. Ngom, & S. Ahmad, *Pattern Recognition in Bioinformatics* (pp. 448–459). Heidelberg: Springer Berlin.

Christley, S., Lee, B., Dai, X., & Nie, Q. (2010). Integrative multicellular biological modeling: a case study of 3D epidermal development using GPU algorithms. *BMC Systems Biology, 4*(1), 107–.

Coddington, P. (1997). Random Number Generators for Parallel Computers. *The NHSE Review.*

Coon, B. W., Mills, P. C., Oberman, S. F., & Siu, M. Y. (2008). *Patent No. 7434032.* United States of America.

Corley, C. D., Farber, R. M., & Reynolds, W. N. (2011). Thought Leaders During Crises in Massive Social Networks. *Statistical Analysis and Data Mining,* to be published.

Cormen, T. H., Leiserson, C. E., & Rivest, R. L. (2001). {*Introduction to algorithms.*} (2nd ed.). The MIT Press.

Cormen, T. H., Leiserson, C. E., & Rivest, R. L. (2001). *Introduction to algorithms* (2nd ed.). Cambridge, MA: The MIT Press.

Cover, T. M., & Thomas, J. A. (2006). *Elements of information theory.* John Wiley and Sons.

Cox, M. A., & Cox, T. F. (2008). *Multidimensional Scaling.* Springer Handbooks of Computational Statistics.

Craighead, M. (2002). *NV_primitive_restart.* Retrieved June 2011, from opengl.org: http://www.opengl.org/registry/specs/NV/primitive_restart.txt.

Dean, J., & Ghemawat, S. (2010). MapReduce: a flexible data processing tool. *ACM.*

Dehne, F., & Yogaratnam, K. (2010, Feb). *http://arxiv.org/abs/1002.4482.* Retrieved June 2011, from Cornell University: http://arxiv.org/abs/1002.4482.

Dematte, L., & Prandi, D. (2010). GPU computing for systems biology. *Brief Bioinform, 11*(3), 323–333.

Di Battista, G., Eades, P., Tamassia, R., & Tollis, I. G. (1999). *Graph Drawing: Algorithms for the Visualization of Graphs.* Englewood Cliffs, NJ: Prentice Hall.

Diamantras, K. I., & Kung, S. Y. (1996). *Principal Component Neural Networks.* John Wiley and Sons.

Diamos, G. (2009). *The Design and Implementation of Ocelot's Dynamic Binary Translator from PTX to Multi-Core x86.* CERCS Tech Report.

Duda, R. O., & Hart, P. E. (1973). *Pattern Classification and Scene Analysis.* New Yourk: Wiley.

Dyer, M., Frieze, A., & Kannan, R. (1991). A random polynomial-time algorithm for approximating the volume. *Journal of the ACM,* 1–17.

Eades, P. (1984). A heuristic for graph drawing. *Congressus Nutnerantiunt,* 149–160.

Eastman, P., & Pande, V. S. (2010). Efficient nonbonded interactions for molecular dynamics on a graphics processing unit. *J. Comput. Chem., 31*(6), 1268–1272.

Ediger, D., Jiang, K., Riedy, J., Bader, D. A., Corley, C., Farber, R., et al. (2010). Massive Social Network Analysis: Mining Twitter for Social Good. *39th International Conference on Parallel Processing* (pp. 583–593). IEEE.

El Zein, A. H., & Rendell, A. P. (2011). Generating optimal CUDA sparse matrix–vector product implementations for evolving GPU hardware. *Concurrency and Computation: Practice and Experience.*

Fang, Q., & Boas, D. A. (2009). Monte Carlo simulation of photon migration in 3D turbid media accelerated by graphics processing units. *Optics Express*, 20178–20190.

Farber, R. (2007, February). HPC balance and common sense. *Scientific Computing*, p. 12+.

Farber, R. (2008, November 1). *Extending High-level languages with CUDA*. Retrieved June 2011, from Doctor Dobb's Journal: http://drdobbs.com/high-performance-computing/211800683.

Farber, R. (2009, July/August). Numerical Precision: How much is enough? *Scientific Computing*, p. 14+.

Farber, R. (2010, November). Redefining What is Possible. *Scientific Computing*.

Farber, R. M. (1992). Efficiently Modeling Neural Networks on Massively Parallel Computers. *Proceedings of the Third International Workshop on Neural Networks and Fuzzy Logic* (pp. 3–11). Houston: NASA.

Farber, R. M., Lapedes, A. S., Rico-Martinez, R., & Kevrekidis, I. G. (1993). Identification of continuous-time dynamical systems: Neural network based algorithms and parallel implementation. *Society for Industrial and Applied Mathematics (SIAM) conference on parallel processing for scientific computing*. Norfolk, VA.

Farber, R. M., Lapedes, A. S., Rico-Martinez, R., & Kevrekidis, I. G. (1993). Identification of continuous-time dynamical systems: Neural network based algorithms and parallel implementation. *Society for Industrial and Applied Mathematics (SIAM) conference on parallel processing for scientific computing*. Norfolk, VA: American Mathematical Society.

Farber, R., & Trease, H. (2008). ssively Parallel Near-Linear Scalability Algorithms with Application to Unstructured Video Analysis. *TACC TeraGrid08 Conference*. Las Vegas.

Farber, R., Lapedes, A., & Sirotkin, K. (1992). Determination of Eukaryotic Protein Coding Regions Using Neural Networks and Information Theory. *J. Mol. Biology*, 471–479.

Farooqui, N., Kerr, A., Diamos, G., Yalamanchili, S., & Schwan, K. (2011). A Framework for Dynamically Instrumenting GPU. *GPGPU-4 Proceedings of the Fourth Workshop on General Purpose Processing on Graphics Processing Units*. New York, NY: ACM.

Fatica, M. (2009). Accelerating linpack with CUDA on heterogenous clusters. *Proceedings of 2nd Workshop on General Purpose Processing on Graphics Processing Units*. ACM.

Frishman, Y., & Ayellet, T. (2008). Online Dynamic Graph Drawing. *IEEE Transactions on Visualization and Computer Graphics*.

Fruchterman, T. M., & Reingold, E. M. (1991). Graph Drawing by Force-directed Placement. *Journal Software—Practice & Experience*, 1129–1164.

Genovese, L., Ospici, M., Deutsch, T., Méhaut, J.-F., Neelov, A., & Goedecker, S. (2009). Density Functional Theory calculation on many-cores hybrid CPU-GPU architectures.

Godiyal, A., Hoberock, J., Garland, M., & Hart, J. C. (2009). Rapid Multipole Graph Drawing on the GPU. In I. G. Tollis, & M. Patrignani, *Graph Drawing* (pp. 90–101). Berlin, Heidelberg: Springer-Verlag.

Gropp, W., Lusk, E. L., & Skjellum, A. (1999). *Using MPI*. The MIT Press.

Haixiang, S., Schmidt, B., Weiguo, L., & Müller-Wittig, W. (2010). A Parallel Algorithm for Error Correction in High-Throughput Short-Read Data on CUDA-Enabled Graphics Hardware. *Journal of Computational Biology*, 17(4), 603–615.

Hampton, S., Agarwal, P. K., Alam, S. R., & Crozier, P. S. (2010). Towards microsecond biological molecular dynamics simulations on hybrid processors., (pp. 98–107).

Haque, I. S., Pande, V. S., & Walters, W. P. (2010). SIML: A Fast SIMD Algorithm for Calculating LINGO Chemical Similarities on GPUs and CPUs. *Journal of Chemical Information and Modeling*, 50(4), 560–564.

Harish, P., & Narayanan, P. J. (2007). Accelerating large graph algorithms on the GPU using CUDA. *Proceeding HiPC'07 Proceedings of the 14th international conference on High performance computing.* Berlin: Springer-Verlag.

Harvey, M. J., & De Fabritiis, G. (2010). Swan: A tool for porting CUDA programs to OpenCL. *Computer Physics Communications,* 1093–1099.

Hertz, J. A., Krogh, A. S., & Palmer, R. G. (1991). *Introduction to the Theory of Neural Computation.* Redwood City, CA: Addison-Wesley.

Hinton, G. E. (2011). *Geoffrey E. Hinton.* Retrieved 2011, from University of Toronto: http://www.cs.toronto.edu/~hinton/.

Hinton, G. E., & Salakhutdinov, R. R. (2006, July 28). Reducing the Dimensionality of Data with Neural Networks. *SCIENCE,* pp. 504–507.

Hinton, G. E., Krizhevesky, A., & Want, S. D. (2011). Transforming Auto-encoders. *ICANN,* (pp. 44–51). Espoo, Finland.

Hong-tao, B., Li-li, H., Dan-tong, O., Zhan-shan, L., & He, L. (2009). K-Means on Commodity GPUs with CUDA. *World Congress on Computer Science and Information Engineering,* (pp. 651–655).

Hopcroft, J. E., & Ullman, J. D. (2006). *Introduction to Automata Theory, Languages, and Computation.* Reading, MA: Addison-Wesley.

Hopfield, J. J., & Tank, D. W. (1985). "Neural" Computation of Decisions in Optimization Problems. *Biological Cybernetics,* 141–152.

Hsieh, W. W. (2001). Nonlinear principal component analysis by neural networks. *Tellus,* 599–615.

Hsieh, W. W. (2004). Nonlinear multivariate and time series analysis by neural network methods. *Rev. Geophys.,* 1–25.

Hubbard, D. (2009). *The Failure of Risk Management: Why It's Broken and How to Fix It.* Wiley.

Humphrey, W., Dalke, A., & Schulten, K. (1996). VMD - Visual Molecular Dynamics. *14,* 33–38.

Hwu, W.-m. W. (2011). *GPU Computing Gems.* Morgan Kaufmann.

Hwu, W.-m. W. (Ed.). (2011). *GPU Computing Gems Emerald Edition.* Morgan Kaufmann.

Hwu, W.-m. W. (2011). *GPU Computing Gems Emerald Edition.* Morgan Kaufmann.

Ines, E., & Hirschmüller, H. (2008). Mutual Information Based Semi-Global Stereo Matching on the GPU. In G. Bebis, R. Boyle, B. Parvin, D. Koracin, P. Remagnino, F. Porikli, et al., *Advances in Visual Computing* (pp. 228–239). Heidelberg: Springer Berlin.

Ingram, S., Munzner, T., & Olano, M. (2009). Glimmer: Multilevel MDS on the GPU. *IEEE Transactions on Visualization and Computer Graphics,* 249–261.

Jerrum, M., & Sinclair, A. (1996). The Markov chain Monte Carlo method: an approach to approximate counting. In D. Hochbaum, *Approximation algorithms for NP-hard problems* (pp. 482–519). PWS Publishing.

Kakumanu, P., Makrogiannis, S., & Bourbakis, N. (2007). A survey of skin-color modeling and detection methods. *Pattern Recognition,* 1106–1122.

Kirk, d., & Hwu, W.-m. W. (2010). *Programming Massively Parallel Processors: A Hands-on Approach.* Morgan Kaufmann.

Kolda, T. G., Lewis, R. M., & Torczon, V. (2007). Optimization by direct search: new perspectives on some classical and modern methods. *SIAM J. Sci. Comput,* 2507–2530.

Korber, B. T., Farber, R. M., Wolpert, D. H., & Lapedes, A. S. (1993). Covariation of mutations in the V3 loop of human immunodeficiency virus type 1 envelope protein: an information theoretic analysis. *PNAS,* 7176–7180.

Kramer, M. A. (1991). Nonlinear Principle Component Analysis Using Autoassociative Neural Netowrks. *AIChE Journal,* 233–243.

Kumar, N., Satoor, S., & Buck, I. (2009). Fast Parallel Expectation Maximization for Gaussian Mixture Models on GPUs Using CUDA. *High Performance Computing and Communications, 2009. HPCC '09. 11th IEEE International Conference on* (pp. 103–109). Seoul: IEEE.

Lapedes, A. S., & Farber, R. (1987). How Neural Networks Work. *Proceeding of IEEE Denver Conference on Neural Netorks.* Denver: IEEE.

Lapedes, A., & Farber, R. (1987). Nonlinear signal processing using neural networks: Prediction and system modelling. *Nonlinear signal processing using neural networks: Prediction and system modelling.* San Diego.

Laxmikant, K., Skeel, R., Bhandarkar, M., Brunner, R., Gursoy, A., Krawetz, N., et al. (1999). NAMD2: Greater scalability for parallel molecular dynamics. *151*, 283–312.

Little, J. (1961). proof for the queuing formula: L = w. *Operations research*, 383–387.

Ma, W., & Agrawal, G. (n.d.). A translation system for enabling data mining applications on GPUs. *Proceeding ICS '09 Proceedings of the 23rd international conference on Supercomputing.* New York, NY: ACM.

MAGMA. (n.d.). (The University of Tennessee) Retrieved from Innovative Computing Laboratory: http://icl.cs.utk.edu/magma.

Maintz, S., Eck, B., & Dronskowski, R. (2011). Speeding up plane-wave electronic-structure calculations using graphics-processing units. *Computer Physic Communications*, 1421–1427.

Malony, A. D., Biersdorff, S., Shende, S., Jagode, H., Tomov, S., Jukeland, G., et al. (2011). Parallel Performance Measurement of Heterogeneous Parallel Systems with GPUs. *ICPP2011.*

Malony, A. D., Biersdorff, S., Spear, W., & Mayanglamba, S. (2010). An experimental approach to performance measurement of heterogeneous parallel applications using CUDA. *Proceedings of the 24th ACM International Conference on Supercomputing*, 127–136.

McKinnon, & McKinnon, K. I. (1999). Convergence of the Nelder–Mead simplex method to a non-stationary point. *SIAM J Optimization*, 148–158.

Micikevicius, P. (2010). 3D Finite Difference Computation on GPUs using CUDA. *Proceeding GPGPU-2 Proceedings of 2nd Workshop on General Purpose Processing on Graphics Processing Units.* New York, NY: ACM.

Micikevicius, P. (2010). *Analysis-Driven Optimization (GTC 2010).* Retrieved 2011, from 2010 NVIDIA GTC: http://www.nvidia.com/content/GTC-2010/pdfs/2012_GTC2010.pdf.

Minsky, M., & Papert, S. (1969). *Perceptrons: An Introduction to Computational Geometry.* Cambridge, MA: The MIT Press.

Mitchell, T. (1997). *Machine Learning.* McGraw Hill.

Monahan, A. H. (2000). Nonlinear Principal Component Analysis by Neural Networks: Theory and Application to the Lorenz System. *Journal of Climate*, 821–835.

Narayanan, R., Ozisikyilmaz, B., Zambreno, J., Jayaprakash, P., Memik, G., & Choudhary, A. (2006). MineBench: A Benchmark Suite for Data Mining Workloads. *Proceedings of the International Symposium on Workload Characterization (IISWC)* (pp. 182–188). San Jose: IEEE.

Nath, R., Stanimire, T., & Dongerra, J. (2010, July 20). *An Improved MAGMA GEmm for Fermi.* Retrieved April 2011, from http://icl.cs.utk.edu: http://icl.cs.utk.edu/projectsfiles/magma/pubs/fermi_gemm.pdf.

Nelder, J. A., & Mead, R. (1965). A Simplex Method for Function Minimization. *The Computer Journal*, 308–313.

Oja, E. (1982). Simplified neuron model as a principal component analyzer. *Journal of Mathematical Biology*, 267–273.

Papakonstantinou, A., Gururaj, K., Stratton, J. A., Chen, D., Cong, J., & Hwu, W.-m. W. (2009). FCUDA: Enabling Efficient Compilation of CUDA Kernels onto FPGAs. *Proceedings of the Symposium on Application Specific Processors.* Proc. IEEE Symp. Application.

Petrini, F., Kerbyson, D. J., & Pakin, S. (2003). The Case of the Missing Supercomputer Performance. *SC03*. ACM.

Petrini, F., Kerbyson, D. J., & Pakin, S. (2003). The Case of the Missing Supercomputer Performance: Achieving. *Proceedings of Supercomputing 2003*. Phoneix.

Press, W. H., Teukolsky, S. A., & Vetterling, W. T. (2007). *Numerical Recipes 3rd Edition: The Art of Scientific Computing*. Cambridge University Press.

Roberts, E., Stone, J. E., Sepulveda, L., Hwu, W.-M. W., & Luthey-Schulten, Z. (2009). Long time-scale simulations of in vivo diffusion using GPU hardware., (pp. 1–8).

Rodrigues, C. I., Hardy, D. J., Stone, J. E., Schulten, K., & Hwu, W.-M. W. (2008). GPU acceleration of cutoff pair potentials for molecular modeling applications. (pp. 273–282). ACM.

Rummelhardt, D. E., Hinton, G. E., & Williams, R. J. (1986). Learning representations by back-propagating errors. *Nature, 323*, 533–536.

Rummelhart, D. E., McClelland, J. L., & The PDP Research Group. (1987). *Parallel Distributed Processing*. The MIT Press.

Saunders, M., Simon, H., & Yip, E. (1988). Two Conjugate Gradient-Type Methods of Unsymmetric Linear Equations. *SIAM J. Num. Anal.*, 927–940.

Schmidt, B. (Ed.). (2010). *Bioinformatics: High Performance Parallel Computer Architectures*. Francis and Taylor.

Schölkopf, B., & Klaus-Robert Müller, A. (1998). Nonlinear Component Analysis as a Kernel Eigenvalue Problem. *Neural Computation*, 1299–1319.

Scholz, M. (2007). Analysing Periodic Phenomena by Circular PCA. *Lecture Notes in Computer Science, 4414/2007*, 38–47.

Scholz, M. (2011). *Nonlinear PCA*. Retrieved 2011, from nlpca: nlpca.org.

Sedláček, M. (2004). Evaluation of RGB and HSV Models in Human Faces Detection. Central European Seminar on Computer Graphics, Budmerice. *CompSysTech'2004*, (pp. 125–131).

Sejnowski, T. J., & Rosenberg, C. R. (1987). Parallel networks that learn to pronounce English text. *Complex Systems*, 145–168.

Shalom, S. A., Dash, M., & Tue, M. (2008). Efficient K-means Clustering Using Accelerated Graphics Processors. In I.-Y. Song, J. Eder, & T. Nguyen, *Data Warehousing and Knowledge Discovery* (pp. 166–175). Heidelberg: Springer Berlin.

Shi, Z., & Zhang, B. (2011, June). *http://bioinfo.vanderbilt.edu/gpu-fan/*. Retrieved June 2011, from Vanderbilt.edu: http://bioinfo.vanderbilt.edu/gpu-fan/.

Stanislaw, M. R., Carbonell, J. G., & Mitchell, T. M. (1985). *Machine learning: an artificial intelligence approach*. Morgan Kaufmann.

Stevens, R. W. (2005). *Advanced Programming in the UNIX Environment*. Addison-Wesley Professional.

Stivala, A., Stuckey, P., & Wirth, A. (2010). Fast and accurate protein substructure searching with simulated annealing and GPUs. *BMC bioinformatics, 11*(1), 446–.

Stone, J. E., Hardy, D. J., Ufimtsev, I. S., & Schulten, K. (2010). GPU-accelerated molecular modeling coming of age. *Journal of Molecular Graphics and Modelling, 29*(2), 116–125.

Stone, J. E., Ufimtsev, I. S., Schulten, K., & Hardy, D. J. (2010). GPU-accelerated molecular modeling coming of age. *Journal of Molecular Graphics and Modelling*, 116–125.

Stone, J., Kohlmeyer, A., Vandivort, K., & Schulten, K. (2010). Immersive Molecular Visualization and Interactive Modeling with Commodity Hardware. In G. Bebis, R. Boyle, B. Parvin, D. Koracin, R. Chung, R. Hammound, et al. (Eds.), *Advances in Visual Computing* (Vol. 6454, pp. 382–393). Springer Berlin/Heidelberg.

Stratton, J. A., Stone, S. S., & Hwu, W.-m. W. (2008). MCUDA: An Efficient Implementation of CUDA Kernels for Multi-Core CPUs. *The 21st International Workshop on Languages and Compilers for Parallel Computing* (pp. 16–30). Springer LNCS 2008.

Stuart, J. A., & Owens, J. D. (2011). Multi-GPU MapReduce on GPU Clusters. *Proceedings of the 25th IEEE International Parallel and Distributed Processing Symposium*. Anchorage, AK: IEEE.

Suchard, M. A., Wanq, Q., Chan, C., Frelinger, J., Cron, A., & West, M. (2010, Jun 1). Understanding GPU Programming for Statistical Computation: Studies in Massively Parallel Massive Mixtures. *J Comput Graph Stat., 19*(2), 419–438.

Suchard, M., & Rambaut, A. (2009). Many-Core Algorithms for Statistical Phylogenetics. *Bioinformatics*, 1370–1376.

Suchard, M., Wang, Q., Chan, C., Frelinger, J., Cron, A., & West, M. (2010). Understanding GPU Programming for Statistical Computation:. *Journal of Computational & Graphical Statistics*, 419–438.

The Max Planck Institute. (2004). *Fractal Landscape and Texture Generation*. Retrieved June 2011, from mpi-inf.mpg.de: http://www.mpi-inf.mpg.de/departments/irg3/ws0405/cg/rcomp/29/x173.html.

Thearling, K. (1995). Massively Parallel Architectures and Algorithms for Time Series Analysis. In L. Nadel, & D. Stein, *1993 Lectures in Complex Systems*. Addison-Wesley.

Townsend, R., Sankaralingam, K., & Sinclair, M. D. (2011). Leveraging the untapped computation power of GPUs: fast spectral synthesis using texture interpolation. In W.-m. W. Hwu, *GPU Computing Gems* (p. 886). Morgan Kaufmann.

Tresadern, P., Ionita, M. C., & Cootes, T. (2011). Real-Time Facial Feature Tracking on a Mobile Device. *International Journal of Computer Vision*.

Ufimtsev, I. S., & Martinez, T. J. (2008). Quantum Chemistry on Graphical Processing Units. 1. Strategies for Two-Electron Integral Evaluation. *Journal of Chemical Theory and Computation, 4*(2), 222–231.

Ufimtsev, I. S., & Martinez, T. J. (2009). Quantum Chemistry on Graphical Processing Units. 2. Direct Self-Consistent-Field Implementation. *Journal of Chemical Theory and Computation, 5*(4), 1004–1015.

Ufimtsev, I. S., & Martinez, T. J. (2009). Quantum Chemistry on Graphical Processing Units. 3. Analytical Energy Gradients, Geometry Optimization, and First Principles Molecular Dynamics. *Journal of Chemical Theory and Computation, 5*(10), 2619–2628.

Vezhnevets, V., Sazonov, V., & Andreeva, A. (2003). A Survey on Pixel-Based Skin Color Detection Techniques. *GRAPHICON03*, (pp. 85–92).

Volkov, V. (2010). Programming inverse memory hierarchy: case of stencils on GPUs. *GPU Workshop for Scientific Computing, International Conference*.

Volkov, V. (2010, September 22). *Volkov 10-GTC*. Retrieved April 21, 2011, from cs.berkeley .edu: http://www.cs.berkeley.edu/~volkov/volkov10-GTC.pdf.

Volkov, V. (2010, June 30). *volkov 10-PMAA*. Retrieved April 2011, from http://eech.berkeley .edu: http://www.eecs.berkeley.edu/~volkov/volkov10-PMAA.pdf.

Vuduc, R. (2010, August 2). *Teragrid Conference 2010*. Retrieved April 2011, from Analysis and Tuning Case Study: http://www.hpcgarage.org/tg10–gpu-tutorial/.

Wong, H., Papadopoulou, M.-M., Sadooghi-Alvandi, M., & Moshovos, A. (2010). Demystifying GPU Microarchitecture through microbenchmarking. *2010 IEEE International Symposium on Performance Analysis of Systems & Software (ISPASS)* (pp. 235–246). IEEE.

Wu, R., Zhang, B., & Hsu, M. (2009). Clustering billions of data points using GPUs. *Proceedings of the combined workshops on UnConventional high performance computing workshop plus memory access workshop*. ACM.

Index

Printed and bound by CPI Group (UK) Ltd, Croydon, CR0 4YY

03/10/2024

01040315-0002